Lecture Notes of the Institute for Computer Sciences, Social Informatics and Telecommunications Engineering 331

More information about this series at http://www.springer.com/series/8197

Wuyungerile Li · Dalai Tang (Eds.)

Mobile Wireless Middleware, Operating Systems and Applications

9th EAI International Conference, MOBILWARE 2020
Hohhot, China, July 11, 2020
Proceedings

 Springer

Editors
Wuyungerile Li (ID)
Inner Mongolia University
Hohhot, China

Dalai Tang
Inner Mongolia University
Hohhot, China

ISSN 1867-8211 ISSN 1867-822X (electronic)
Lecture Notes of the Institute for Computer Sciences, Social Informatics
and Telecommunications Engineering
ISBN 978-3-030-62204-6 ISBN 978-3-030-62205-3 (eBook)
https://doi.org/10.1007/978-3-030-62205-3

This Springer imprint is published by the registered company Springer Nature Switzerland AG
The registered company address is: Gewerbestrasse 11, 6330 Cham, Switzerland

Preface

We are delighted to introduce the proceedings of the 9th edition of the 2020 European Alliance for Innovation (EAI) International Conference on MOBILe Wireless MiddleWARE, Operating Systems, and Applications (MobilWare 2020). This conference has brought together researchers, developers, and practitioners from around the world who are leveraging mobile wireless technology to develop more operating systems and applications. The theme of MobilWare 2020 was "Mobile Computing, Operating Systems, and Applications." Due to the safety concerns and travel restrictions caused by COVID-19, EAI MOBILWARE 2020 took place online in a live stream. Participants were still able to enjoy unique interactive benefits.

The technical program of MobilWare 2020 consisted of 21 full papers, including 21 invited papers in oral presentation sessions at the main conference tracks. The conference tracks were: Track 1 – MobilWare 2020; Track 2 – Big Data, Data Mining and Artificial Intelligence Workshop; and Track 3 – Blockchain and Internet of Things workshop. Aside from the high-quality technical paper presentations, the technical program also featured three keynote speeches and two technical workshops. The three keynote speeches were Prof. Celimuge Wu from The University of Electro-Communications, Japan; Prof. Winston K. G. Seah from Victoria University of Wellington, New Zealand; and Dr. Zheli Liu from Nankai University, China. The two workshops organized were the Big Data, Data Mining and Artificial Intelligence Workshop and the Blockchain and Internet of Things Workshop. The Big Data, Data Mining and Artificial Intelligence Workshop aimed to address Big Data challenges in scientific and engineering through Big Data, Data Mining, and Artificial Intelligence methodologies and approaches. The Blockchain and Internet of Things Workshop aimed to gain insights into state-of-the-art advances and innovations in theories, systems, infrastructure, tools, testbeds, technologies, and applications, etc. Coordination with the steering chairs, Imrich Chlamtac, Carl K. Chang, Paolo Bellavista, and Thomas Magedanz, was essential for the success of the conference. We sincerely appreciate their constant support and guidance. It was also a great pleasure to work with such an excellent Organizing Committee team and we thank them for their hard work in organizing and supporting the conference. In particular, the Technical Program Committee, led by Dr. Dalai Tang, Dr. Mu Zhou, and Dr. Bo Cui, who completed the peer-review process of technical papers and made a high-quality technical program. We are also grateful to conference manager, Martin Karbovanec, for his support and all the authors who submitted their papers to the MobilWare 2020 conference and workshops.

We strongly believe that the MobilWare conference provides a good forum for researchers, developers, and practitioners to discuss all science and technology aspects that are relevant to mobile wireless. We also expect that the future MobilWare conferences will be as successful and stimulating, indicated by the contributions presented in this volume.

September 2020

Wuyungerile Li
Bing Jia
Baoqi Huang

Organization

Steering Committee

Chair

Imrich Chlamtac   University of Trento, Italy

Members

Carl K. Chang   Iowa State University, USA
Paolo Bellavista   University of Bologna, Italy
Thomas Magedanz   FOKUS Fraunhofer Institute, Germany

Organizing Committee

General Chair

Baoqi Huang   Inner Mongolia University, China

General Co-chairs

Junxing Zhang   Inner Mongolia University, China
Xiaolin Zhang   Inner Mongolia University of Science and Technology,
                           China

TPC Chair and Co-chair

Wuyungerile Li   Inner Mongolia University, China
Xiao Chen   Jilin Agricultural University, China

Web Chair

Xuebin Ma   Inner Mongolia University, China

Publicity and Media Chair

Genxiong Zhang   Inner Mongolia Electronic Information Vocational
                           Technical College, China

Workshops Chairs

Zhixiao Wang   University of Göttingen, Germany
Dalai Tang   Inner Mongolia University of Finance and Economics,
                           China

Sponsorship and Exhibit Chair

Gang Xu   Inner Mongolia University, China

Publications Chair

Bing Jia   Inner Mongolia University, China

Panels Chair

Mu Zhou   Chongqing University of Posts
                                and Telecommunications, China

Tutorials Chair

Bo Cui   Inner Mongolia University, China

Demos Chair

Yiming Wu   Hangzhou Dianzi University, China

Posters and PhD Track Chair

Zhibin Zhang   Inner Mongolia University, China

Local Chair

Xiangyu Bai   Inner Mongolia University, China

Conference Manager

Barbora Cintava   EAI

Technical Program Committee

Dalai Tang   Inner Mongolia University of Finance and Economics,
                                China
Mu Zhou   Chongqing University of Posts
                                and Telecommunications, China
Bo Cui   Inner Mongolia University, China
Hang Zhang   University of Göttingen, Germany
Gang Xu   Inner Mongolia University, China
Yiming Wu   Hangzhou Dianzi University, China
Long Zhao   Beihang University, China
Xu Qiaozhi   Inner Mongolia University, China
Yu Gu   Hefei University of Technology, China
Xuebin Ma   Inner Mongolia University, China
Winston Seah   Victoria University of Wellington, New Zealand
Wuyungerile Li   Inner Mongolia University, China
Bing Jia   Inner Mongolia University, China
Genxiong Zhang   Inner Mongolia University, China
Dedong Gao   Zhejiang University, China
Zhixiao Wang   Xi'an University of Technology, China

Contents

Big Data, Data Mining and Artificial Intelligence

Blockchain and Internet of Things

MobilWare 2020

Soft Tissue Deformation Estimation Model Based on Spatial-Temporal Kriging for Needle Insertion Procedure

Linze Wang, Juntao Zhang, Mengxiao Zhao, and Dedong Gao$^{(\boxtimes)}$

School of Mechanical Engineering, Qinghai University, Xining 810016, China
gaodd@zju.edu.cn

Abstract. The percutaneous surgery needs to know the soft tissue deformation in real time, but the existing prediction model cannot solve the problem. As a statistical interpolation method, kriging can effectively characterize the transformation of discrete point information into continuous facial information, so it can alleviate this problem. The tissue displacement of each identifying point in chronological order is obtained through the image processing of the experiment, and the spatial-temporal variogram function is selected to adapt the properties of soft tissue deformation in the needle insertion process. The permanent of spatial-temporal kriging is obtained based on the variogram function model of space and time, and the average error is 0.5 mm. The correlation of time and space is considered in spatial-temporal kriging, so the accuracy is higher. The kriging model compared with the data of another group of experiments, the average deviation is 0.2 mm. The feasibility and practicability of the model are verified.

Keywords: Soft tissue · Kriging · Spatial-temporal · Variogram

1 Introduction

Needle puncture surgery is a common treatment in medicine. Puncturing into the soft tissue reach the target to achieve diagnosis, treatment, sampling, stimulation and other purposes. Most of these puncture points are concentrated in organs, the common clinical application of tissue biopsy, local anesthesia, blood routine examination and others [1, 2]. In this process, the main causes of puncture error are: imaging equipment resolution limit, image coordinate deviation, target positioning error, human error, as well as the tissue deformation and needle deflection brought about by the target motion error [3–5]. In order to improve the accuracy of puncture and reduce the error, it is necessary to master the biological characteristics of soft tissue. The establishment of a soft tissue prediction model for real-time interaction between soft tissue and needle is of great significance for improving puncture accuracy and reducing puncture error [6].

Okamura et al. [7] put forward the empirical puncture force model, the puncture force is divided into three parts at first: stiffness forces, friction force and cutting. Stiffness forces is produced before the puncture of the membrane, and the friction force and

W. Li and D. Tang (Eds.): MOBILWARE 2020, LNICST 331, pp. 3–18, 2020.
https://doi.org/10.1007/978-3-030-62205-3_1

cutting are caused by the puncture of the membrane. The stiffness forces is fitting to a quadratic polynomial model, the friction force is represented by a modified Karnopp model, and the cutting power is a constant value. Podder et al. [8] considered the influencing factors of puncture force for the first time, and deduced a statistical model to estimate the maximum puncture force. The puncture force data were obtained by living experiments, and the statistical model of estimating maximum puncture force was verified based on individual parameters (such as body mass index, Gleason Fraction, pre-treatment, prostate volume) and specific treatment methods (such as puncture needle model, maximum puncture speed). Asadian [9] is based on the puncture force model proposed by Okamura, a modified LuGre model is used to simulate the acupuncture force, and the hysteresis characteristics of friction in the puncture process are analyzed and verified, and the dynamic process of friction is described in a complete description. Hing et al. [10] through linear elastic finite element analysis to develop the operating system to predict soft tissue deformation and puncture force. Misra [11] studied the mechanism of tissue fracture, the linear or nonlinear elasticity of tissue, and the effect of puncture needle deflection angle on the axial force and transverse force of needle. Using the contact and soft melt belt model, the finite element analysis is used to infer that the deflection angle of the smaller needle and the elasticity of the larger tissue will increase the stress of the needle tip. DiMaio and Sakcydean [12] explored the relationship between puncture force and tissue deformation for the first time. The axial force distribution of the needle is divided into two parts: the friction force between the needle and the tissue evenly distributed along the axial axis, and the peak power at the tip of the needle. Experiments show that the friction force of unit length increases with the increase of injection speed, and the peak at the tip of the needle is hardly changed with the speed of injection. Carra [13] studied the puncture force model of multi-layer tissue, in which the Hunt-Crossley model was used in the stiffness force of the membrane, and the use of the Dah friction model was adopted, and the cutting was a specific constant value corresponding to a particular tissue. In the whole puncture process, the puncture force is expressed by superposition principle and segmented function. Maurin [14] compared the puncture force between artificial and robotic operation during the biopsy of porcine living liver, and analyzed two types of puncture: one is direct puncture (other anatomical layers are removed), and the other is percutaneous puncture. Experiments show that the contribution of other anatomical layers to puncture force in percutaneous puncture is larger, and the puncture force of robot operation is relatively small. For the first time, Mahvash [15] analyzed the mechanical properties of acupuncture soft tissue by means of fracture mechanics, and the puncture membrane was described as the strain energy at the tip of the needle that exceeded the fracture toughness, prompting the crack to expand suddenly, and thus punctured the membrane. It is proved that increasing the feed speed of needle can reduce the peak of puncture force and tissue deformation. Sun Yinshan [16] of Harbin Institute of Technology and others put forward the generalized needle force model, which decomposes the stiffness forces into two parts using the Maurin model and the Simone model respectively. And put forward the robot assisted needle strategy: First, the needle into the liver moment, the robot automatically stops the needle, until the soft tissue back to relaxation, and then to halve the speed of the puncture; second, after the needle into the liver, if the puncture force exceeds a specific threshold, the robot immediately stops the needle. Xuan Xinxiang [17] of Aeronautics and Astronautics and others based on the puncture force model proposed by Okamura, the modified Karnopp model was applied to the study of the mechanical properties of needle into corneal tissue. Gao Dedong [18], Tsinghua University, and others proposed a quasi-static finite element method for the analysis of soft tissue deformation, and a two-dimensional quasi-static finite element model of soft tissue deformation was created by using overlapping element method in ANSYS.

Researchers have carried out a lot of experimental research on acupuncture soft tissue, using experiments to observe the corresponding experimental phenomena (such as needle and tissue deformation, failure mechanism, etc.) and verify the accuracy of calculation or simulation results. Experimental platforms are often assisted by puncture robots, biological soft tissues (or imitation of soft tissues), imaging equipment, and control equipment. Okamura and Simone [19] using bovine liver as the experimental object, the deformation of liver tissue was measured by CT, and the stiffness of tissue, the resistance of the back membrane, the friction force and shear forces were measured, and the effect of needle deflection angle and needle diameter on puncture force was verified. Maurin et al. [14] took pig kidneys and liver as the research object, studied the change law of acupuncture into living tissue, and compared the difference between manual and robot. Considering the laboratory experimental conditions, it is not possible to scan the real biological tissue by CT and MRI, so many scholars use alternative materials with good transparent optical properties as the research object, and measure the deformation of the tissue and needle through high-speed cameras. DiMaio and Salcudean [20] used PVC material as the experimental object, implanted the regular calibration point in the gel, and then used high-speed camera to measure and analyze the tissue deformation. Jiang Shan et al. [21] have prepared transparent PVA materials with similarities in microstructure, mechanical properties and biological tissues, and have been used in puncture experimental research.

This paper is to study the deformation model of flexible needle puncture soft tissue. Based on the soft tissue puncture experiment, the identification object was set in the corresponding soft tissue (pork in this experiment), and the position coordinates of the flexible needle in the puncture soft tissue were recorded by B-ultrasound. Based on the image acquisition experiment, the image processing of flexible needle into soft tissue images was carried out to obtain the deformation of flexible needle and soft tissue in the process of injection. Combined with kriging model and soft tissue deformation are analyzed. In the previous soft tissue model, it was not good to solve the contradiction between accuracy and real-time, and often sacrificed another attribute for one attribute. In order to improve the contradiction between the two, this paper proposes a soft tissue prediction method based on spatiotemporal kriging method, which can effectively simplify the computation amount and improve the real-time performance of the model under certain precision. It can greatly simplify the calculation and improve the accuracy of the model under ensuring certain precision. In order to reduce the puncture error and improve the accuracy of the puncture to provide a reference.

2 Spatial-Temporal Kriging Model

2.1 Kriging Preliminaries

The idea of the kriging model was originally proposed by South African engineer Krige in his 1951 master's thesis and used this method to find a gold mine for the first time [22]. Then, in 1963, the method was systematized by the French mathematician Matheron, which formed a complete theory and model and named the method kriging [23], and was widely used in the field of ground statistical analysis. In the 1981, Professor Sacks et al. [24] once again promoted the kriging model, from the geological, hydrological, meteorological and other natural science fields to aerospace, automotive engineering and other fields of engineering science.

2.2 Spatial-Temporal Kriging Model

Commonly used kriging models include, ordinary Kriging (OK), simple Kriging (SK), and so on. They are widely used as an excellent interpolation algorithm in all walks of life, but they are spatial kriging models only can be depicted in a certain space at a specific time of the situation does not describe the process of continuous changes in space transactions. The puncture process of the puncture needle is a continuous process, and the doctor needs to know at all times what part of the needle is in the patient and the deformation of the soft tissue around the needle. The commonly used kriging model can no longer accurately describe the puncture process. And spatiotemporal Kriging not only takes into account the influence of space factors, but also adds the time factor, so that it can describe a continuous process, it can describe the deformation of soft tissue in the puncture process.

This paper extends on the basis of ordinary kriging and adds time parameters on the basis of ordinary Kriging.

$$Z^*(s_0, t_0) = \sum_{i=1}^{n} \lambda_i Z(s_i, t_i) \tag{1}$$

In the formula, $Z^*(s_0, t_0)$ is the estimate of space-time point, (s_0, t_0) and λ_i is the weighted coefficient of the adjacent observation value $Z(s_i, t_i)$. The kriging interpolation is based on the variogram function as the basic premise, in formula (1), the weighted coefficient λ_i is determined by the spatiotemporal variogram function. The calculation formula for the introduction of Lagrange coefficient μ to get parameter λ_i is:

$$\sum_{i=1}^{n} \lambda_i \gamma[(s_i, t_i) - (s_j, t_j)] + \mu = \gamma[(s_j, t_j) - (s_0, t_0)], \ j = 1, \ldots, n$$

$$\sum_{i=1}^{n} \lambda_i = 1$$

The weighted coefficient λ_i and Lagrange coefficient μ can be obtained from the above two-style.

2.3 Stationary Hypothesis

Hypothesis $Z(s, t)$ is a space-time stochastic process defined on $R^k \times T$, where R^k represents a k-dimensiona space, T represents time, an arbitrary sample point (s_i, t_i), $i = 1, \ldots, n$ position in space-time field, and h_s is a spatial distance between sample points and h_t is a time distance. If $Z(s, t)$ of the expectations are constant m, and the covariance function $Cov[Z(s, t), Z(s+h_s, t+h_t)]$ depends only on h_s and h_t independent of the specific position (s, t), then $Z(s, t)$ satisfies the second order stationary hypothesis, if the variance $Var[Z(s, t) - Z(s + h_s, t + h_t)]$ is limited and depends only on h_s and h_t, then $Z(s, t)$ satisfies the intrinsic hypothesis.

Therefore, when $Z(s, t)$ satisfies the second order stationary hypothesis or the intrinsic hypothesis, its covariance function can define

$$C(h_s, h_t) = Cov[Z(s + h_s, t + h_t) - Z(s, t)] \tag{2}$$

The variogram function is:

$$\gamma(h_s, h_t) = \frac{1}{2}E[Z(s + h_s, t + h_t) - Z(s, t)]^2 = \sigma^2 - C(s, t) \tag{3}$$

σ^2 is the variance of $Z(s, t)$.

2.4 Variogram

Variogram function is the most important step in constructing kriging model, and its function selection directly affects the interpolation accuracy of the model. The selection of the theoretical model of variogram function is mainly based on the relationship between distance and variation value, as well as the professional theory or experience to determine the appropriate theoretical model, but also can use scatter plot to speculate the appropriate theoretical model [25]. The area variables that are two points apart in space are recorded as $z(s_i + h_s, t_i + h_t)$ and $z(s_i.t_i)$ respectively, the spatial spacing is h_s, and the variogram function of $N(h_s, h_t)$ of the time interval h_t is [26]:

$$\gamma^*(h_s, h_t) = \frac{1}{2N(h_s, h_t)} \sum_{i=1}^{N(h_s, h_t)} [z(s_i + h_s, t_i + h_t) - z(s_i, t_i)]^2 \tag{4}$$

At present, the basic variogram function model is spherical model, exponential model, Gaussian model, power function model, pure nugget gold model and so on, and many new variation function models can be obtained by linear combination or multiplication of existing models [27, 28].

The parameters such as nugget, partial sill, sill and range of variogram function represent the spatial variation and correlation degree, and the strength of spatial correlation can be reflected by the partial sill/sill, if the greater the value, the stronger the spatial correlation. According to the theory of variogram function, the values of the two points in the same position should be equal, and with the increase of the distance (h), the numerical difference between the two points increases, until the sill value is tended, and the interval distance between the sampling points is range.

Due to the sampling error and spatial variation, two points are very close but there is also a nugget with a variogram function value of not zero. The discontinuity of the variogram function at the origin is called the Nugget Effect, and the data values of the adjacent two samples tend to vary greatly, the properties of the material change greatly in a very short distance. The nugget/sill is called the substrate effect, which is used to represent the variation characteristics between samples, and can also reflect the correlation, if the larger the value indicates more variation between samples caused by random factors. When the ratio of the nugget to the sill is ≤25%, the variable autocorrelation degree is strong, and if the ratio is between 25% and 75%, it is a medium autocorrelation level, and if the ratio is ≥75%, it is a weak autocorrelation level.

The soft tissue is mostly homogeneous material, so the nugget effect is weak, the nugget is very small so that the substrate effect is also very small, has a strong spatial correlation. Needle puncture surgery requires continuous, uniform and stable puncture process, in order to ensure the success of the puncture and reduce the patient's pain, so the time is also continuous and there is no variation, the nugget effect is weak and has a strong time correlation. The kriging interpolation method is based on the correlation of random variables in time and space.

3 Experimental Materials and Methods

3.1 Materials and Equipment

The choice of biological soft tissue material is a long about 25 cm, wide about 10 cm, thick about 5 cm of a shape of the regular pig leg meat. The meat in this area is evenly thick and easy to process into shape rules to facilitate the insertion of identifiers. Pork leg meat has typical soft tissue mechanical characteristics of anisotropy, and its mechanical properties in the direction of fiber and vertical fiber are different. Its mechanical properties can be obtained by SHPB experiment [29], in the case of strain rate of 0.02/S, the direction of the fiber is 121.00 ± 28.76 kPa, the ultimate strength is 63.73 ± 18.53 kPa, the damage strain is 0.934 ± 0.189; vertical fiber direction modulus is 47.60 ± 19.30 kPa, limit strength is 22.94 ± 3.63 kPa, damage strain is 1.077 ± 0.111 [30]. The identifier uses an iron nail with a diameter of about 2.3 mm and is arranged at a 1.5 cm distance interval.

The meat container is a custom U-type acrylic fixture, transparent colorless material easy to observe the placement of the meat, U-shaped adjustable shape can firmly fix the position of the meat. The needle is implemented by a three-axis puncture system, which can complete the movement of the XY plane and the rotation around the x axis, used to puncture the soft tissue of the needle and can adjust the posture and the position of the needle. The collection of pictures is completed by a medical B-ultrasound machine, the highest resolution of the B-ultrasound machine is 1 mm and provides two different probes of lower frequency convex and linear array, for experimental accuracy and image processing considerations, the test uses linear array probe to collect images.

The meat with the identifier is placed on the special fixture, and the puncture system is used to carry out the puncture experiment, and the B-ultrasound image is collected by the ultrasonic probe frame on the meat. Because of the limitation of the scanning width of the linear array ultrasonic probe, the internal situation of the whole organization cannot be observed at once, so the B-ultrasound image collected must be integrated in turn. The stitched image is generally JPG format, which is not convenient for direct image processing. The general use of PS to convert its format to BMP format in image processing. Using Matlab to binarization it, improve the contrast of the image to reduce the difficulty of subsequent processing, corrosion removal of small, discrete, large area of noise in the image, expansion is that identifier image to amplify the recovery, noise reduction to remove the large noise spots, the marker marks the centroid of the remaining image and sends its coordinates to the specified location, and finally converts the coordinate units on the image from pixels to millimeters. The position of the identifier in the soft tissue can be obtained. The displacement of the identifier in the puncture process can be obtained by comparing the coordinate position of the image with different puncture depth.

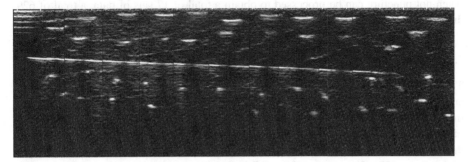

Fig. 1. B-ultrasonic image of needle into soft tissue.

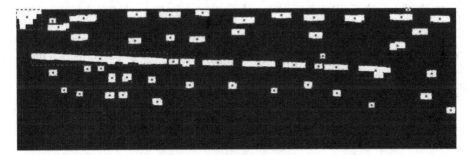

Fig. 2. Position of identifiers.

Figure 1 is a B-ultrasound image when the needle puncture is completed, the needle trajectory can be clearly seen, and because it is a flexible needle, deflection occurs in the soft tissue. The white spot area in the figure is the identifier in the tissue, because the B-ultrasound is ultrasonic reflection imaging, so in the distance from the B-ultrasound probe near the upper part, the image is clearer and because the distance is too close to a certain of lateral elongation. But because the centroid of the image is finally extracted from the image processing process, the lateral image elongation does not affect the position of the centroid. So the distortion in the B-ultrasound image has less effect on the coordinates of the identified points. The image after Matlab processing is shown in Fig. 2, the middle slender image is connected to the trajectory of the needle, and the small white square around the needle is the identifiers after treatment. The black dots in the figure are the centroid of each image and the coordinates of the identifiers in the soft tissue. The position of the identifier in the soft tissue to be obtained through a series of steps in images processing. Due to various reasons such as device resolution limit and parameter setting in image processing, the identifier is not fully identified in the image processing at last. The displacement of 37 markers can be obtained by comparing it with the B-ultrasound image when the puncture is not carried out. Using the puncture needle progress as the time data, each puncture into the 1 cm to collect a B-ultrasound image. The final needle into the soft tissue about 16 cm, coupled with the image collected when not puncture can be processed to obtain a total of 17 sets of data, a total of 629 displacement data.

3.2 Spatial-Temporal Variogram Model

The spatial-temporal variogram function is extended by the spatial variogram function, and the time domain data has been added on the basis of the spatial domain. There are many differences between spatial domain and time domain. There exist many differences of parameters' properties in the spatial domain and time domain, such as the unit and the amount of data. Therefore, this paper uses the space-time model to fit the changes of soft tissue [27]. The structure is as follows:

$$C_{st}(h_s, h_t) = k_1 C_s(h_s)C_t(h_t) + k_2 C_s(h_s) + k_3 C_t(h_t) \tag{5}$$

$$\gamma_{st}(h_s, h_t) = (k_1 C_t(0) + k_2)\gamma_s(h_s) + (k_1 C_s(0) + k_3)\gamma_t(h_t) - k_1\gamma_s(h_s)\gamma_t(h_t) \tag{6}$$

In the formula, C_{st} is spatiotemporal covariance, C_s is spatial covariance, C_t is time covariance, γ_{st} is spatiotemporal variogram function, γ_s is spatial variogram function, γ_t is time variogram function, $C_{st}(0, 0)$, $C_s(0)$, $C_t(0)$ are corresponding sill values respectively.

From the (5) formula,

$$C_{st}(0, 0) = k_1 C_s(0)C_t(0) + k_2 C_s(0) + k_3 C_t(0) \tag{7}$$

According to the derivation of reference [31], k_1, k_2 and k_3 can be solved by the following formula,

$$\begin{cases} k_1 = \dfrac{C_s(0) + C_t(0) - C_{st}(0, 0)}{C_s(0)C_t(0)} \\ k_2 = \dfrac{C_{st}(0, 0) - C_t(0)}{C_s(0)} \\ k_3 = \dfrac{C_{st}(0, 0) - C_s(0)}{C_t(0)} \end{cases} \tag{8}$$

The fitting data is the spatial data of 37 identifiers after image processing, and 17 groups of time data, and the variogram of the space domain is calculated by the curve fitting and the variogram of the time domain and fitted by the curve. As shown in Figs. 3 and 4.

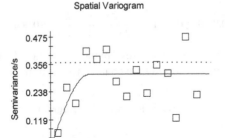

Fig. 3. Variogram of space.

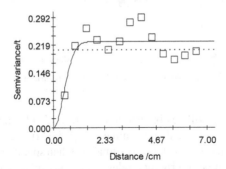

Fig. 4. Variogram of time.

The discrete block is the sample semi-variance, the curve is the corresponding fitting variogram function model, the relative spatial variogram function and the time variogramfunction are respectively,

$$\gamma(h_s) = 0.0001 + 0.3121(\frac{3}{2} \cdot \frac{h_s}{23.7} - \frac{1}{2} \cdot \frac{h_s^3}{23.7^3}) \tag{9}$$

$$\gamma(h_t) = 0.0001 + 0.2281(1 - e^{-\frac{h_t^2}{0.67^2}}) \tag{10}$$

Simultaneous formula (7) and formula (8), solvable $k_1 = 11.4448, k_2 = -1.6117$, $k_3 = -2.5731$, and formula (9) and formula (10) together with the formula (6) can get the spatiotemporal variogram function

$$\gamma_{st}(h_s, h_t) = (0.0001 + 0.3121(\frac{3}{2} \cdot \frac{h_s}{23.7} - \frac{1}{2} \cdot \frac{h_s^3}{23.7^3})) + 0.9999(0.0001 + 0.2281(1 - e^{-\frac{h_t^2}{0.67^2}}))$$

$$-11.4448(0.0001 + 0.3121(\frac{3}{2} \cdot \frac{h_s}{23.7} - \frac{1}{2} \cdot \frac{h_s^3}{23.7^3}))(0.0001 + 0.2281(1 - e^{-\frac{h_t^2}{0.67^2}}))$$

As shown in Fig. 5, the model fuses spatial variogram functions and temporal variogram functions, while preserving the characteristics of their trend changes.

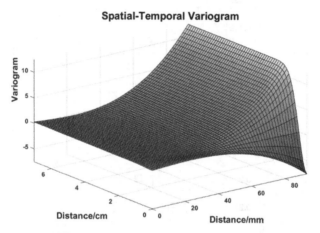

Fig. 5. Spatial-temporal variogram model.

The variation function will be obtained into the formula (1), the corresponding spatiotemporal kriging model is calculated. Unlike the spatial kriging model, adjacent sample points in space and time are involved in estimation when spatiotemporal interpolation. Therefore, the spatial-temporal kriging model is more granular and has continuity.

4   Results and Discussion

The spatiotemporal interpolation of the previously collected puncture data is carried out by using the variogram model described above, and the interpolation results are verified by cross-verification method. The interpolation results are in agreement with the actual situation, and the Fig. 6 is a prediction diagram of soft tissue deformation in different depths of puncture, in which the warmer the color represents the larger the displacement, and the colder the color represents the smaller the displacement. As can be seen from Fig. 6 that when the puncture needle first enters the soft tissue, the needle tip displacement is huge and the influence range is huge. This is because the needle tip has just stabbed into the soft tissue, the soft tissue is still glued to the needle tip area, resulting in the needle tip site displacement range beyond the normal impact range, in the figure shows that the displacement into a wave forward reduction. When stabbed into 6 cm, the needle tip affects the range to restore to the normal range of influence. It is about an elliptical area of 2 cm in length and 1 cm in width, and the displacement starts from the center of the needle and gradually decreases from the middle to the sides. When puncture acupuncture into 12 cm, it can be obvious that the puncture needle has a downward offset phenomenon. The puncture needle is a beveled flexible puncture needle caused by the influence of the cutting force of the needle tip. In the last picture, the puncture needle was inserted into the 16 cm, almost completely inserted into the soft tissue, the needle body began to deflect downward, the impact range of the needle was extended to the sides by about 1.5 cm from the center of the needle. This is in line with the actual situation.

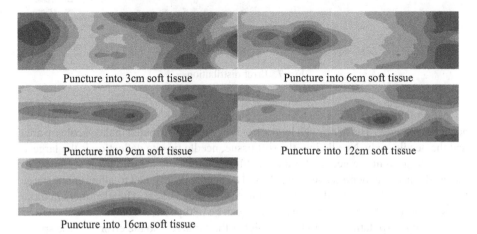

Puncture into 3cm soft tissue   Puncture into 6cm soft tissue

Puncture into 9cm soft tissue   Puncture into 12cm soft tissue

Puncture into 16cm soft tissue

Fig. 6. Soft tissue deformation at different depths.

Cross-validation uses all data to estimate trends and autocorrelation models. It removes one data location at a time, and then predicts the associated data value. Compares the predicted value of the ellipsis position with the actual value,then repeat this procedure for the second point, and so on. Cross-validation compares the measured and predicted values for all points. After cross-validation is complete, if there are large errors in some data locations, those locations may be shelved as exceptions, and the trend model and autocorrelation model need to be redrafted. Cross-validation includes mean, root-mean-square, mean standardized, root-mean-square standardized, average standard error five evaluation indicators, in which the mean and root-mean-square are closer to zero, the better the average standard error and the mean standardized are as small as possible, the more the root-mean-square standardized is closer to 1 the better. Because the spatial interpolation scale range of this paper is very small, the average standard error and the root-mean-square error of each point are the main precision evaluation indexes, combined with the mean, the mean standardized error, the root-mean-square standardized error and so on. As you see from Table 1, the difference accuracy of spatiotemporal kriging is maintained at a high level. As the average standard error of the main measure, the value has a high precision level below 0.1.

Table 1. Analysis of interpolation accuracy.

Type	Depth	Mean	Root-Mean-Square	Mean Standardized	Root-Mean-Square Standardized	Average Standard Error
Spatiotemporal model	16 cm	0.0121	0.3387	0.0913	1.0658	0.4177
Space model	16 cm	−0.0152	0.4496	0.0691	1.3439	0.4529

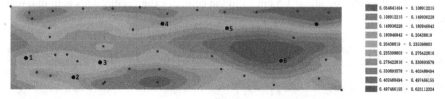

Fig. 7. Error distribution.

Most of the errors in Fig. 7 are below 0.5 mm, the error is small, and the interpolation accuracy is higher. The areas with large error are mainly distributed in the needle tip area and the needle body. Needle into the soft tissue, needle tip site deflection is the largest, in order to prevent the needle, hit the identifier to affect the measurement accuracy, so the needle tip area identifier setting is less. The needle is designed to allow enough area to allow the needle to pass through and thus less of the markers. The identifiers in these areas are sparse, the spatial information that can be interpolated is scarce, and the closer the kriging interpolation method is, the higher the accuracy, so the error of these sparse regions is larger.

The spatiotemporal Kriging model is compared with the simple space kriging model. Spatial kriging interpolation uses the data when puncture into 16 cm, regardless of the time factor, the comparison results are shown in Table 1. It is found that in the five criteria for measuring interpolation accuracy, the accuracy of the remaining four spatiotemporal models is higher than that of the spatial model, except for the mean standardized. This indicates that the spatial-temporal kriging model has higher accuracy and its interpolation results are closer to the actual value. Selecting 6 identification points for error comparison, the results are shown in Table 2, no matter where the space-time model accuracy is better than the spatial model accuracy, the error is reduced by an average of 20%. Identification points 1–5 are selected in areas where the Identification points are dense), spatial information is more abundant, so the accuracy of the improvement is not improved, about 10%–20%. And the identification point 6 is empty around, with very few identification points. At this time, the interpolation results of the spatial model have a large error, and the space-time model is adopted, considering the lack of spatial information supplemented by the information of the adjacent point of view, the interpolation accuracy has been significantly improved, and the far exceeding the average value has been increased by 34%.

Table 2. Comparison the accuracy of spatial-temporal kriging and spatial kriging.

Number	Spatial-temporal kriging	Spatial kriging	Improvement of accuracy (%)
1	0.2194	0.2832	22.5501
2	0.1672	0.1906	12.2954
3	0.2104	0.2624	19.8415
4	0.1556	0.1967	20.9028
5	0.2201	0.2541	13.3873
6	0.4769	0.7242	34.1481

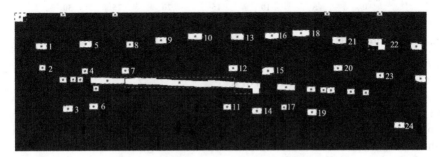

Fig. 8. The Identifier coordinates of the test.

In order to verify the feasibility of the model, another set of test data is selected for verification. Select the experimental data for the puncture 16 cm data, after image processing and other steps, the final results as shown in Fig. 8. From the Fig. 8, it can be seen that the middle bending part is still the needle, around the spread of the white square as the identifier, and 24 points are selected as the verification point. These points are distributed on both sides of the needle body and are covered with the entire image. The 2,4,7,12,15 and other points are close to the needle body, and the 1,5,8,9 points is far away from the needle body and runs through the image, while the 3,6,11 and other points are distributed under the needle body. The selected points are distributed across parts of the image and are far closer to the distance of the needle body. The above results analysis can verify that the spatiotemporal Kriging model has predictive power for each location.

The data predicted by the spatiotemporal kriging model are compared with the data of the verification test itself and plotted into a scatter plot, as shown in Fig. 9. The maximum deviation occurs at the 12th verification point is 0.64 mm, the minimum deviation is 0.01 mm at the 1th verification point, and the average deviation is 0.2 mm. It is proved that the interaction model of needle and soft tissue constructed by spatiotemporal kriging interpolation method is fully satisfied with the requirement of millimeter grade accuracy of needle puncture operation, and the accuracy is higher to meet the needs of operation.

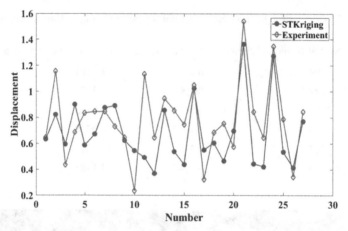

Fig. 9. Comparison the identification displacement of spatial-temporal kriging model and test.

5 Conclusions and Future Work

The needles puncture soft tissue is a continuous process. The displacement of soft tissue in the puncture process is not only strongly correlated in space, but also closely related to the depth (time). In the estimation, therefore, considering the measurement value near the point in time can effectively improve the interpolation accuracy, and the process of needles puncture can be restored as much as possible. The suitable variogram model is an important foundation of high precision kriging interpolation, and the this paper using kriging model product by spatiotemporal variogram model which combines spatial and time model, so that it retains the changing trends of each other. Experimental results show that the model has high accuracy, which is better than the simple spatial kriging interpolation, both in the description of the puncture process and the accuracy of the model, and also realizes the prediction in the future [31]. However, the time factor added to the model, the amount of data in the experiment is greatly increased, which also increases the calculation and the difficulty of the variogram function, so it is very important for the spatiotemporal model to choose the sampling frequency and data processing method.

Kriging model compares with the traditional soft tissue model, such as mass-spring model and finite element model, the advantage of spatiotemporal kriging model is that it can greatly simplify the calculation under the condition of ensuring high precision, so the real-time performance is greatly increased. The spatiotemporal variogram model used in this paper extends the time parameters on the basis of ordinary kriging interpolation, but in the actual process, many factors can affect the deformation of soft tissue, such as different soft tissues have different parameters. In the subsequent research, more factors of soft tissue, such as elastic modulus, will be considered to optimize the variogram function and improve the spatiotemporal kriging accuracy.

References

1. Rizun, P.R., Mcbeth, P.B., Louw, D.F.: Robot- assisted neu- rosurgery. Surg. Innov. **11**, 99–106 (2004)
2. Zivanovic, A., Davies, B.L.: A robotic system for blood sampling. IEEE Trans. Inf. Technol. Biomed. **4**(1), 8–14 (2000)
3. Carr, J.J., Hemler, P.F., Halford, P.W., Freimanis, R.I., Choplin, R.H., Chen, M.Y.: Stereotactic localization of breast lesions: how it works and methods to improve accuracy. Radiographics: a review publication of the Radiological Society of North America **21**(2), 463–473 (2001)
4. Hussain, H.K., Kingston, J.E., Domizio, P., Norton, A.J., Reznek, R.H.: Imaging-guided core biopsy for the diagnosis of malignant tumors in pediatric patients. Am. J. Roentgenol. **176**(1), 43–47 (2001)
5. Roberson, P.L., Narayana, V., McShan, D.L., Winfield, R.J., McLaughlin, P.W.: Source placement error for permanent implant of the prostate. Med. Phys. **24**(2), 251–257 (1997)
6. Gao, D.: Tissue deformation mechanism and dynamic path planning for flexible needle into soft tissue. Zhejiang University (2017)
7. Okamura, A.M., Simone, C., O'Leary, M.D.: Force modeling for needle insertion into soft tissue. IEEE Trans. Bio-Med. Eng. **51**(10), 1707–1716 (2004)
8. Podder, T.K., Sherman, J., Clark, D.P.: Evaluation of robotic needle insertion in conjunction with in vivo manual insertion in the operating room. In: IEEE International Workshop on Robot & Human Interactive Communication (2005)
9. Asadian, A., Kermani, M.R., Patel, R.V.: A compact dynamic force model for needle-tissue interaction. In: International Conference of the IEEE Engineering in Medicine & Biology (2010)
10. Hing, J.T., Brooks, A.D., Desa,i J.P.: Reality-Based Estimation of Needle and Soft-Tissue Interaction for Accurate Haptic Feedback in Prostate Brachytherapy Simulation. In: Thrun, S., Brooks, R., Durrant-Whyte, H., (eds) Robotics Research. Springer Tracts in Advanced Robotics, vol 28. Springer, Berlin, Heidelberg (2007) https://doi.org/10.1007/978-3-540-481 13-3_4
11. Misra, S., Reed, K.B., Schafer, B.W., Ramesh, K.T., Okamura, A.M.: Mechanics of flexible needles robotically steered through soft tissue. Int. J. Robot. Res. **29**, 1640–1660 (2010)
12. Dimaio, S.P., Salcudean, S.E.: Needle insertion modelling and simulation. In: IEEE International Conference on Robotics & Automation (2002)
13. Carra, A., Avila-Vilchis, J.C.: Needle insertion modeling through several tissue layers. In: International Asia Conference on Informatics in Control (2010)
14. Maurin, B., et al.: In: Vivo Study of Forces During Needle Insertions (2015)
15. Mahvash, M.: Haptic rendering of cutting. a fracture mechanics approach, Hapticse, Electron. J. Haptics Res. **2**, 1–12 (2011)
16. Yinshan, S., Dongmei, W., Zhijiang, D., Lining, S.: Modeling of needle insertion force in porcine livers for studying needle insertion strategies of robot-assisted percutaneous surgery. Chinese High Technol. Lett. **21**, 948–953 (2011)
17. Xuan, X., Yang, Y., Wang, Z., Deng, S., Liu, X.: Mechanical model of suture acupuncture into corneal tissue. Chinese High Technol. Lett. **19**, 951–956 (2009)
18. Dedong, G., Yipeng, G., Haojun, Z.: A finite element approach for simulating soft tissue deformation during needle insertion. J. Comput. Aided Des. Comput. Graph. **21**, 1601–1605 (2009)
19. O'leary, M.D., Simone, C., Washio, T.: Robotic needle insertion: effects of friction and needle geometry. In: IEEE International Conference on Robotics & Automation (2003)
20. Dimaio, S.P., Salcudean, S.E.: Needle steering and motion planning in soft tissue. IEEE Trans. Biomed. Eng. **52**, 965–974 (2005)

21. Jiang, S., Liu, S., Feng, W.: PVA hydrogel properties for biomedical application. J Mech Behave Biomed. Mater. **4**(7), 1228–1233 (2011)
22. Krige, D.G.: A statistical approach to some basic mine valuation problems on the witwatersrand. J. Mech. Behav. Biomed. Mater. **4**, 18 (1953)
23. Matheron, G.: Principles of geostatistics. Econ. Geol. **58**, 1246–1266 (1963)
24. Santner, T.J., Williams, B.J., Notz, W.I.: Design and analysis of computer experiments. Asta Adv. Stat. Anal. **4**, 409–423 (1989)
25. Clark, D.S.: Adjudication to administration: a statistical analysis of federal district courts in the twentieth century. S. Cal. L. Rev. **55**, 65 (1981)
26. Webster, R.: Quantitative spatial analysis of soil in the field. Adv. Soil Sci. **3**, 537–542 (1985)
27. Cesare, L.D., Myers, D.E., Posa, D.: Estimating and modeling space–time correlation structures. Stat. Probab. Lett. **51**, 9–14 (2001)
28. Ma, C.: Families of spatio-temporal stationary covariance modes. J. Stat. Plan. Inference **116**, 489–501 (2003)
29. Wang, B., Zheng, Y., Hu, S.: Dynamic tensile properties of porcine hind leg muscles. Expl. Shocks **30**, 449–455 (2010)
30. Wang, B.: Research on dynamic mechanical properties of soft muscle tissue. University of Science and Technology of China (2010)
31. Cesare, D.L., Myers, E.D., Posa, D.: Product-sum covariance for space -time modeling, An environmental application. Environmetrics **12**, 11–23 (2001)

Research on the Application of Personalized Course Recommendation of Learn to Rank Based on Knowledge Graph

Hao Wu[✉] and FanJun Meng

Inner Mongolia Normal University, Hohhot 010020, Inner Mongolia, China
292866851@qq.com, ciecmfj@imnu.edu.com

Abstract. Aiming at the problem that the computer technology level of most non computer major students in Colleges and universities is not even, which can not be effectively aimed at teaching, Use the evaluation data of students for each course chapter to integrate the Knowledge Graph, Build a hybrid model of sequencing learning, student user migration and basic characteristics, Finally, the top-N recommended courses are sorted. In general, the recommendation algorithm is only applied to the recommendation service of e-commerce platform, The personalized recommendation algorithm proposed in this paper is mainly used to serve students to improve the quality of course teaching.

Keywords: Learning to rank · Knowledge Graph · Personalized recommendation algorithm · Interest conversion · Node2vec

1 Introduction

The basic course of university computer is an important subject in the study of University and College, almost every major of college students in the first semester of college will be required to take computer basic public courses, its main function is to offer a course for some non-computer major students who don't know how to operate computers, the basic operation methods, application skills and methods of computer are introduced, the ability of logical thinking, computer operation, software use and calculation thinking of non-computer major undergraduates has been cultivated, the course of college computer foundation is widely accepted, covering most non-computer majors, so it has very practical application significance. But now students of different majors have different understanding of computer software and hardware, for example, the freshmen majoring in communication, electronics and electrical are very skilled in the use of computer technology and common software, some students can reach the level of simple programming, however, students majoring in sports, music, art and so on have a poor understanding of computer technology, some students are still unfamiliar with the use of keyboard and mouse, different family environment and background also affect students' computer technology level. Therefore, the following problems exist in the teaching of *University Computer Foundation* and the opening of the course chapters:

W. Li and D. Tang (Eds.): MOBILWARE 2020, LNICST 331, pp. 19–30, 2020.
https://doi.org/10.1007/978-3-030-62205-3_2

1. The normal arrangement of course chapters and the traditional course recommendation can not meet the requirements of students with different computer operation levels.

2. Traditional course recommendation can't meet the needs of students' multiple course chapters, such as collaborative filtering algorithm, content-based recommendation algorithm and hybrid recommendation algorithm

So how to ensure that students who have a good foundation of computer operation or who have been exposed to computer technology or who don't know computer really get the course chapters that are really suitable for them, it will not only affect students' acquisition of knowledge, it will also affect the teaching effect of teachers, So as to affect the teaching of *University Computer Foundation.*

Around the above issues, in this paper, we propose a personalized course recommendation algorithm based on ordered learning of Knowledge Graph. In paper [1], a personalized recommendation algorithm based on ranking learning of knowledge map is proposed, this paper constructs Knowledge Graph through the content of *University Computer Foundation,* embedding into low dimensional space after deep learning, then through the similarity calculation of course knowledge points, construction of ordered learning feature model, student user interest transfer model, finally, the model is built by mixing with the basic feature model, Top-N recommendation through ranking learning. The proposed algorithm has achieved good results, it can play a positive role in recommending different curriculum chapters to students with different needs.

2 Related Research Theory

2.1 Knowledge Graph Embedded in N-Dimensional Spatial Network Representation

Since 2012, Google proposes the concept of Knowledge Graph, it has been widely used and studied in various fields, it has become the basic technology module of various intelligent services, it is often mentioned with ontology technology and can integrate entity context information. To address the timeliness of cold start and recommended course chapters, now the technology of knowledge map is developing continuously, it has developed and accumulated many open ontology databases, there is a significant improvement in improving the performance of the algorithm.

Perozzi B et al. Introduced deep learning technology into the network for the first time, the deepwalk algorithm, which makes it represent the field of learning, treats each node as a word in natural language processing (NLP), move randomly in the network, extract the generated mobile route, take the moving path as a sentence, the result obtained is used as the input of word2vec algorithm, the result obtained is used as the input of word2vec algorithm. In this way, the nodes in its network are inserted into an n-dimensional space, as shown in Fig. 1, with the distributed representation method, we can find the relationship connection between entities more intuitively, Grover A and others changed the generation method of random moving sequence node2vec by further expanding the deepwalk algorithm, a random moving method with bias is proposed, as shown in Fig. 2, in this method, two parameters, p and q, can be used to search the neighbor nodes with Depth First Movement (Depth-First Search) and Breadth First Movement (Breadth-First Search) simultaneously.

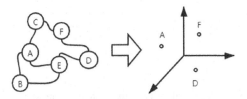

Fig. 1. Embedding knowledge map into n-dimensional space

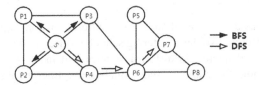

Fig. 2. Breadth and depth first movement from nodes

Breadth First Movement emphasizes more on adjacent nodes and shows the isomorphism between them, The Depth First Movement shows the homogeneity between nodes on a further level, the conditional probability of its movement:

$$P(d_i = x | d_{i-1} = c) = \begin{cases} \frac{\pi_{CX}}{T}, & if\ (c, x) \in E \\ 0, & otherwise \end{cases} \tag{1}$$

The probability that π_{CX} is not normalized in the formula, T is the normalization constant, in the most general case, The weight ω_{cx} between nodes c and x can be used as a non-normalized probability $\pi_{CX} = \omega_{cx}$. t is the last node, c is the current node, x is the next possible node under the second order random movement, the relationship between the non-normalized probability and the weight is: $\pi_{CX} = \alpha_p(t, x) \times \omega_{cx}$, The $\alpha_{pq}(t, x)$ coefficient is as follows:

$$\alpha_{pq}(t, x) = \begin{cases} \frac{1}{p}, & if\ l_{tx} = 0. \\ 1, & if\ l_{tx} = 1. \\ \frac{1}{q}, & if\ l_{tx} = 2. \end{cases} \tag{2}$$

Where l_{tx} is the nearest distance between node t and x, p is the return parameter, q is in-out parameter. Node2vec embedded method has high computational efficiency and adaptability, get the characteristics of nodes in the network, and it can take into account the macro and local information in the network, as shown in Fig. 3, node2vec algorithm.

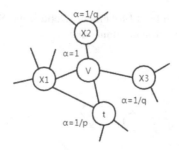

Fig. 3. Node2vec algorithm student interest transfer model

3 Student Interest Transfer Model

Due to the continuous alternation of students in different majors and academic years, the computer technology of students entering school at different times will change, the degree of attention and interest in different courses will increase or decrease, traditional recommendation algorithms include collaborative filtering algorithm, semantic based recommendation algorithm, knowledge-based recommendation algorithm, etc. these algorithms can not be extended and can not reflect the dynamic changes of students' behaviors and changing data. Therefore, the problem of students' interest transfer cannot be solved effectively. However, the recommendation algorithm combined with students' migration model can effectively improve the personalized recommendation effect of students.

The difference of students' interest in different chapters of different University Computer Foundation courses by adding different weights to different nodes in the Knowledge Graph model.students' interest transfer model can dynamically update the connection weight between nodes in the Knowledge Graph by the number and time of students' behaviors towards the system, in order to reflect the students' interest transfer. The more similar the student's behavior in the system is to the current time, the more times the same behavior occurs, the more weight is allocated between the nodes, the more interested or concerned students are in this node. In contrast, the less weight between nodes.

The formula between student S_i and C_j is:

$$\omega_{ij} = \sum\nolimits_{x=1}^{n} \left(\frac{\omega}{1 + e^{(t-t_x)-t_0}} + \omega \right) \tag{3}$$

In formula (3), the current time is t, the number of times the same behavior is expressed as n, t_x refers to the behavior time of students' feedback on the course chapters, The time factor of students' interest transfer is expressed as t0, ω is the weight threshold, it means students change over time, that is to say, the recommendation ability it brings is constantly weakening, Gradually tends to constant ω, so we can modify the Knowledge Graph dynamically according to the students' interest transfer model. Compared with the traditional recommendation algorithm, the recommendation algorithm based on Learn to Rank can more effectively reflect the different preferences of users and improve the accuracy of recommendation.

3.1 Recommendation System and Personalized Recommendation Algorithm of Learn to Rank

In this paper, we mainly study an algorithm based on Knowledge Graph for ordering learning personalized recommendation courses, The basic idea is: First, a basic Knowledge Graph has been established, then the algorithm is represented by node2vec network based on deep learning, then, the entities contained in the Knowledge Graph are embedded in a lower dimensional space. Second, calculate the similarity between user courses, in order to build the input training model of sorting learning, then the importance of different features adjusted by the objective function is taken as a reference, make it reach the best result, centralized integration of feature weights generated by basic recommendation model, merging into a student interest transfer model, model fusion with basic recommendation, Build a mixed model to be the basic recommendation model of interest transfer, Finally, the algorithm of sorting learning on the constructed model, got the top-N recommendation list. The algorithm proposed in this paper can take into account the long-term and short-term preferences of students for courses and the transfer of students' interests and other reasons, it can also take into account the weight proportion between heterogeneous features of Knowledge Graph.

As shown in Fig. 4, follow this simple flow chart, Can effectively improve the personalized recommendation effect, it scan effectively improve the personalized recommendation effect.

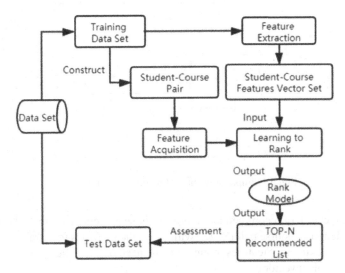

Fig. 4. Simple flow chart of Learn to Rank (LTR)

3.2   Recommendation Algorithm Based on Learn to Rank

At present, the results of Pessiot J et al. Research are only based on users' ratings of individual projects, the result of recommendation can not reflect the user's preference effectively and accurately. For collaborative filtering algorithm, etc., there are students with sparse scores, cold start and so on, aiming at the problems of traditional recommendation algorithm, the relevant personnel consider adding the Learn to Rank technology to the recommendation process of the recommendation algorithm. The method of Learn to Rank is used to transform the calculation of recommendation scores among students' users into a two classification problem of multi feature vectors, which can better solve the problem of multiparameter estimation caused by multi-dimensional features. Simple flow chart of recommended model, as shown in Fig. 5.

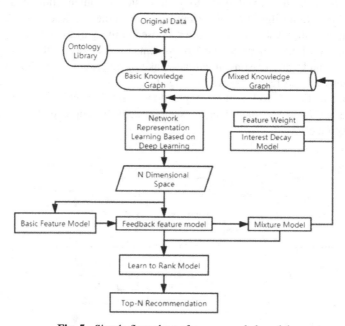

Fig. 5. Simple flow chart of recommended model

In the framework of recommendation process of sequencing learning, The first is to mark the student user course pair (S_i, C_j) with $y_{S_iC_j}$, the second is to extract its features, the second is to extract its features, obtain the eigenvector $\vec{x}_{S_iC_j}$, then we construct and get the set X of eigenvectors:

$$X = \left\{ \vec{x}_{S_1C_1}, \vec{x}_{S_1C_2}, \vec{x}_{S_1C_3}, \vec{x}_{S_1C_4}, \cdots, \vec{x}_{S_iC_j} \right\} \subseteq R^n \tag{4}$$

That is, the corresponding set of tags Y:

$$Y = \left\{ \vec{y}_{S_1C_1}, \vec{y}_{S_1C_2}, \vec{y}_{S_1C_3}, \vec{y}_{S_1C_4}, \cdots, \vec{y}_{S_iC_j} \right\} \tag{5}$$

Where n represents the dimension of $\vec{x}_{S_1C_1}$, the final requirement of using ranking learning is to obtain a decision function $f:R_n \rightarrow Y$ in an optimal way, let the prediction set Y' made by f for all the training instance sets (x, y) better correspond to the real mark Y, finally get the proportion set Z of weight:

$$Z = \left\{ \eta_1, \eta_2, \eta_3, \cdots \eta_{|feature|} \right\} \tag{6}$$

Using machine learning method to solve the problem of sorting in sorting learning, it is based on the idea of classification problem and regression problem solving in machine learning, the goal of using sort learning is to learn a sort function from the training data, it can be used in text retrieval to measure the importance and relevance of text and sort the text. The advantages of using ordered learning are: The recommendation algorithm based on sorting learning can more effectively reflect the different preferences of users and improve the accuracy of recommendation. And it can summarize a large number of complex features and automatic parameter updating, a large number of available methods can be used to avoid over fitting problems. According to the investigation, The existing classical sorting learning algorithms are: LambdaMart, RankingSVM, RankBoost, AdaRank, RankNet and so on.

3.3 Feature Extraction of Knowledge Graph with Weight Depth Movement

Traditional collaborative filtering recommendation algorithm or other algorithms mainly use adjacency matrix to store and operate data, using this method to represent data will bring about calculation efficiency problems, for example, an adjacency matrix A uses the storage space of $|Y| \times |Y|$, when $|Y|$ increases to the million level, it often encounters problems in calculation and processing, and 0 accounts for most of the adjacency matrix, resulting in data sparsity, because of the sparsity of the data, a lot of difficulties arise in the application of fast and effective statistical learning methods.

Using Knowledge Graph can combine semantic fusion with context fusion and fuse heterogeneous feature information, then, the weight of each edge shows the relationship between each node. This paper proposes a course recommendation algorithm based on ordered learning of Knowledge Graph and makes deep movement on the Knowledge Graph, it can take into account the homogeneity between nodes and the isomorphism between nodes, it can also better integrate heterogeneous information and consider the interest transfer of learning users.

This research mainly studies the course of University Computer Foundation, among them, curriculum entity mainly includes teachers, curriculum, types of knowledge points and other major features, a series of heterogeneous characteristics listed can simply summarize the course, using the features of the course chapters, it can get a basic Knowledge Graph, as shown in Fig. 6.

In the research, Node2vec algorithm is used to learn the characteristics of Knowledge Graph network, map the corresponding entity to the space of N dimension, through the space of n-dimensional vector, the closer the distance is at the geometric level, the more relevant the solid is, the algorithm in this paper uses vector cosine similarity to measure the correlation between entities e_i and e_j, Expressed as $Cos(e_i, e_j)$:

$$Cos(e_i, e_j) = cos(e_i, e_j) = \frac{\vec{e}_i \cdot \vec{e}_j}{\|\vec{e}_i\| \times \|\vec{e}_i\|} = \frac{\sum_{t=1}^{n} e_{it} e_{jt}}{\sqrt{\sum_{t=1}^{n} e_{it}^2} \sqrt{\sum_{t=1}^{n} e_{jt}^2}} \tag{7}$$

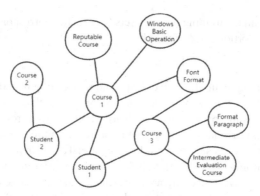

Fig. 6. Integration of context and heterogeneous information to build the knowledge graph of curriculum chapters

Then deal with the training set, Mark the student user course (S_i, C_j) with yij, on the established basic Knowledge Graph, Calculate the similarity of student user courses (S_i, C_j) in a single course, calculate the similarity of student user courses (S_i, C_j) in a single course, through context feature, then the eigenvector $\vec{x}_{S_i C_j}$ is constructed:

$$\vec{x}_{S_i C_j} = \left\{ Cos(S_i, C_j)_1, Cos(S_i, C_j)_2, \cdots, Cos(S_i, C_j)_{|feature|} \right\} \qquad (8)$$

Set up training set $(y_{ij}, S_i, \vec{x}_{S_i C_j})$ as input of sorting learning algorithm model, according to the optimization function, a decision function f: $R_n \to Y$ is obtained, then, according to the decision function, we get the list of top-N recommendations, and the weight proportion set $Z = \left\{ \eta_1, \eta_2, \eta_3, \cdots \eta_{|feature|} \right\}$ of the multi-dimensional feature pair is generated, set up feedback model by Z.

In addition, the weight in the Knowledge Graph can show students' preference for the course chapters, correlation between features and Curriculum, in paper [2], in the recommended algorithm, the relationship between user and item is expressed by scoring more than 4 in the data set, set the weight of the edge between to 1, then no relationship is set to 0, that is, the corresponding edges are regarded as 0,1 values, therefore, the recommendation algorithm in paper [2] does not care about the relevance and importance of different features to the recommendation results, the influence of user's preference factors is also not considered, the preference and interest of users will change over time is not considered.

In conclusion, this paper improves this algorithm, this paper uses a mixed recommendation model which combines student user interest transfer, foundation and feedback model.

3.4 Mix Recommendation Model Combining Interest Transfer and Long-Term and Short-Term Preference

Long term consideration, students' preferences and interests are relatively stable, because personalized recommendation based on a large number of historical data of student users can reflect the basic preferences of student users, a mixed Knowledge Graph model based on student user interest migration model and feedback model, using this model, we can measure the dynamic change of course content, the short-term dynamic change of students' interest and other time effective factors.

According to the ranking learning personalized recommendation model based on the basic Knowledge Graph in the previous section, we can get the weight set $Z = \{\eta_1, \eta_2, \eta_3, \cdots \eta_{|feature|}\}$ of multi-dimensional features for recommendation results, then, the factor set Z which affects the weight is combined with the student user migration model to build a mixed Knowledge Graph, a dynamic updating method of weight between entities of the mixed Knowledge Graph based on RWij:

$$RW_{ij} = \begin{cases} \lambda \times rating \times w_{ij} \times \eta_k, \text{ if } r_{ij} = k; \\ \eta_{other}, \text{ if } r_{ij} = others; \end{cases} \tag{9}$$

In method RW_{ij}, RW_{ij} is expressed as the weight of the edge between entity I and entity J after dynamic update, ωij is the degree of interest processed by the student user interest transfer model, k is the evaluation relationship between student user i and Course Chapter j, rating value refers to the students' evaluation of the course chapters, λ is the normalization factor, let $\lambda \times rating$ normalize at the initial weight 1, avoid the influence of exaggerated evaluation in random movement.

Pair the student user course chapters in the training set (S_i, C_j), based on the mixed Knowledge Graph which combines the interest transfer of all students and the characteristics of the course chapters,

node2vec deep moving is adopted, obtain the characteristics of similarity $Cos(S_i, C_j)$, mix. In combination with formula (7) in the previous section, construct mixed feature model:

$$\vec{x}_{S_iC_j} = \left\{ Cos(S_i, C_j)_1, Cos(S_i, C_j)_2, \cdots, Cos(S_i, C_j)_{|feature|}, Cos(S_i, C_j)_{mix} \right\} \tag{10}$$

Set up a set $(y_{ij}, S_i, \vec{x}_{S_iC_j})$ as the input of learning ordering model, finally, the top-N recommendation list is generated. the algorithm in this study can effectively combine multi-dimensional features, it can also take into account the long-term and short-term preferences of student users, can improve the effect of personalized recommended courses.

3.5 Basic Description of Algorithm

The simple basic description of the algorithm is as follows, as shown in Table 1.

Table 1. The steps of personalized course recommendation based on Knowledge Graph

Algorithm: Personalized Course recommendation of ordered learning based on Knowledge Graph
Input: Data Set S, Ontology library
Output: Top-N Recommendation List
1:Combining data set s with context information of ontology library, Set up basic Knowledge Graph. 2:Using Node2vec model to extract network features of Knowledge Graph. 3:Training with sorting learning model,get the feature based model,Get decision function $f:R_n \rightarrow Y$. 4:Using decision function $f:R_n \rightarrow Y$ to generate feedback, combined with student user interest transfer model, and get the mixed Knowledge Graph. 5:Repeat step 2, extracting the step 4 mixed Knowledge Graph feature model. 6:Combine the feature models from step 3 and step 5 to form a mixed feature model. 7:Repeat step 3 to get the top-N recommendation list.

4 Conclusion

This paper is based on the brief introduction of the background of the Knowledge Graph of the course chapters of University Computer Foundation in Colleges and universities, this paper proposes and introduces the main workflow of a sort learning personalized course recommendation algorithm based on Knowledge Graph, according to the preferences of students' users and the deviation of students' interests over time, the corresponding countermeasures are put forward in the algorithm flow, It has practical significance for the recommendation of University Computer Foundation's course chapters and even for the recommendation methods of other college courses.

Acknowledgement. This research was financially supported by National Natural Science Foundation of China (Research on Construction of Big Data-driven Multi-dimensional Blended Teaching Model in Mongolian-Chinese Bilingual SPOC Environment Gant No. 61841703), Natural Science Foundation of Inner Mongolia of China (Research on Identification Algorithm of Genomic Structure Variation Based on Deep Neural Network in Cloud Computing Environment Grant No. 019BS06001), Natural Science Foundation of Inner Mongolia of China (Research on Application of Big Data Analysis Technology in Mongolian-Chinese Bilingual SPOC Environment Multidimensional Mixed Teaching Model Grant No. 2019MS06014), Inner Mongolia Normal University Research start-up project (Grant No. 2017YJRC020).

References

1. Yang, J., Hu, B., Wang, X., Wu, Y., Zhao, G.: A personalized recommendation algorithm forsorting learning of knowledge graph. Microcomputer System **39**(11), 2419–2423 (2018)
2. Palumbo, E., Rizzo, G.,Troncy, R.: Entity2rec:learning user-item relatedness from knowledge graphs for Top-N item recommendation[C]. In: Eleventh ACM Conference on Recommender Systems, pp. 32–36. ACM (2017)

3. Zhang, X., Yujie, S.: Discussion and suggestions on the teaching reform of University Computer Foundation in the new era [J]. Computer Prod. Circul. pp. 170 (2019)

4. He, R., et al.: Hybrid Teaching Research on University Computer Foundation Based on micro course and rain class. Comput. Knowl. Technol. **15**(03), 170–171 (2019)

5. Huang, H., Yu, J., Xizo, L., Xi, Y.: Overview of knowledge graph research. Comput. Syst. Appl. **28**(06), 1–12 (2019)

6. Perozzi, B., Al-Rfou, R., Skiena, S.: DeepWalk: online learning of social representations[C]. In: ACM SIGKDD International Conference on Knowledge Discovery and Data Mining, pp. 701–710. ACM (2014)

7. Mikolov, T., Sutskever, I., Chen, K., et al.: Distributed representations of words and phrases and their compositionality[C]. In: Advances in Neural Information Processing Systems, pp. 3111–3119 (2013)

8. Grover, A., Leskovec, J.: Node2vec: scalable feature learning for networks[C]. In: Proceedings of the 22nd ACM SIGKDD International Conference on Knowledge Discovery and Data Mining, pp. 855–864. ACM (2016)

9. Pessiot, J.F.,Truong, T.V., Usunier, N., et al.: Learning to rank for collaborative filtering[C]. In: ICEIS 2007-Proceedings of the Ninth International Conference on Enterprise Information Systems, Vol. Aidss, pp. 145–151. Funchal, Madeira, Portugal, DBLP (2007)

10. Huang, Z., Zhang, J., Tian, C., Sun, S., Yang, Y.: A review of the research on recommendation algorithm based on sorting learning. J. Software **27**(3), 691–713 (2016)

11. Lin, Y., Liu, Z., Sun, M., et al.: Learning entity and relation embeddings for knowledge graph completion[C]. In: Twenty-Ninth AAAI Conference on Artificial Intelligence, pp. 2181–2187. AAAI Press, (2015)

12. Ren, L.: Research on the application of collaborative filtering algorithm in college curriculum recommendation. Fujian Comput. **35**(08), 21–26 (2019)

13. He, P.: Research on top-N recommendation algorithm based on sorting learning [D]. Beijing University of technology (2016)

14. Lu, H., Shi, Z., Liu, Z.: Collaborative filtering recommendation algorithm integrating user interest and scoring difference. Computer engineering and application. pp. 1–8 (2020).http://kns.cnki.net/kcms/detail/11.2127.tp.20191115.1136.004.html

15. Zhou, W., Zhang, W., Yang, B., Liu, Y., Zhang, L., Zhang, Y.: Research on Personalized Recommendation Algorithm for microblog. Computer program: 1–7 (2020) http://kns.cnki.net/kcms/detail/31.1289.tp.20191108.1440.004.html

16. Li, B.: Design and implementation of news recommendation system based on project characteristics and sequencing learning [D]. Beijing University of Posts and telecommunications (2019)

17. Wu, H.: Research and application of recommendation algorithm based on hybrid filtering [D]. Nanjing University of Posts and telecommunications (2018)

18. Liu, Y.: Research on Personalized Learning Resource Recommendation Based on knowledge graph [D]. Henan Normal University (2018)

19. Gu, Y., Wu, Z., Guan, Z., Zhai, P.: Overview of learning analysis research based on education big data [J]. China Educ. Inf. pp. 1–6 (2018)

20. Yu, L.: On the reform of computer basic teaching in Higher Vocational Education in the new era. Intelligence, p. 52 (2017)

21. Pei, Z.: Teaching reform and innovation of computer basic education in the new era. Asia Pacific Educ. p. 65 (2016)

22. Wenjun, W., Weifeng, L.: Large scale open online education in the era of big data. Comput. Educ. **44**(20), 9–10 (2013)

23. Ma, L., Feng, F., Huang, S.: Design of MOOC intelligent autonomous learning system based on big data analysis. Mod. Electron. Technol. **40**(20), 64–66 (2017)

24. Yang, J., Qiao, P., Li, Y., Wang, N.: A review of machine learning classification problems and algorithms. Stat. Dec. Mak. **35**(06), 36–40 (2019)
25. He, Q., Li, N., Luo, W., Shi, Z.: Overview of machine learning algorithms under big data. Patt. Recogn. Artif. Intell. **27**(04), 327–336 (2014)
26. Chen, K., Zhu, Y.: Machine learning and related algorithms [J]. Stat. Inf. Forum, pp. 105–112 (2007)
27. Shaoqing, W., Xinxin, L., Fuzhen, S., Chun. F.: Review of personalized news recommendation technology. Computer Sci. Expl. pp. 1–14 (2020)
28. Jinyin, H., et al.: Personalized learning recommendation based on online learning behavior analysis. Comput. Sci. **45**, 422–426 (2018)
29. Zhang, Y., Zhang, J., Zou, Y., Xu, D., Wang, L.: Research and construction of Park personalized recommendation system based on collaborative filtering recommendation algorithm. Mod. Inf. Technol. **2**(4), 82–84 (2018)
30. Yin, Y., Du, C.: Thinking about the teaching mode of computer basic courses in medical colleges. Comput. Knowl. Technol. **6**(23), 6557–6558 (2010)

Research on Community-Based Opportunistic Network Routing Protocol

Zhanwei Liu[✉], Wenbo Yuan, Na Su, and Hui Wang

School of Electronics and Automation, Inner Mongolia Electronic Information
Vocational Technical College, Hohhot 010070, Inner Mongolia, China
lzw981@qq.com

Abstract. The opportunity network is realized through the internode movement to achieve inter-network communication. There is not a complete communication path between the source node and the destination node in the network. This paper studies the opportunity network routing protocol based on the community. First, comparing the advantages and disadvantages of GN and K-means two community partition algorithm, Select the algorithm with high accuracy, high data transmission rate, and delay of the small GN algorithm. Then the GN algorithm is applied to the and Spray and Wait routing protocol. Regardless of the size of the network, the node density, The protocol is scalable and can maintain good performance.

Keywords: Opportunity network · GN · K - means · Spray and Wait routing protocol

1 Introduction

In recent years, wireless communication technology has developed at an unprecedented speed, but traditional multi-hop wireless networks, such as Wireless Sensor Network [1], MANET [2], and Wireless Mesh Network [3], do not interrupt the wireless network connection and split Cellular mobile communication network technology has strong network coverage, but it is obviously insufficient in data service support; wireless local area network has developed rapidly in recent years, but its coverage is very limited, thus promoting Opportunistic Networks [4,5] the birth and development. Opportunistic networks are a new type of network that can transmit information when the wireless link is down and there is no end-to-end path. It is regarded as an important direction for the development of mobile AdHoc networks, which is of great significance to ubiquitous computing.

Early routing algorithms in opportunistic networks include flood-based Epidemic Routing [6], direct transmission routing algorithms, Spray and Wait [7], Spray and Focus [8], and Prophet [9] algorithms, but the bandwidth occupied by Epidemic Routing Larger, it will waste network resources, and the direct transmission algorithm is a single copy routing algorithm. Although the network

© ICST Institute for Computer Sciences, Social Informatics and Telecommunications Engineering 2020
Published by Springer Nature Switzerland AG 2020. All Rights Reserved
W. Li and D. Tang (Eds.): MOBILWARE 2020, LNICST 331, pp. 31–43, 2020.
https://doi.org/10.1007/978-3-030-62205-3_3

overhead is small, the transmission success rate is low and the average delay is large. The Spray and Wait routing algorithm include two phases: spray and wait. In the spraying phase, each time it connects with other nodes, it will allocate 1/2 message copy to the other party. After the number of message copies is 1, it enters the waiting phase. In the waiting phase, the node holds the message until it meets the destination node. Spray and Focus routing algorithm is an improved algorithm of Spray and Wait, which changes the waiting phase into the focusing phase. In the focusing phase, the node selects the appropriate forwarding node based on the utility value. The Prophet algorithm [10] combines two types of forwarding methods, infection forwarding, and encounter prediction. Based on the forwarding probability of the meeting node to the destination node, it is determined whether to forward messages to the meeting node. Therefore, it can limit the number of copies in the network and improve the transmission success rate.

Peng et al. [11] proposed a quota routing algorithm DPER based on delivery probability prediction. This algorithm predicts the delivery probability of other nodes based on the local information of the node and determines the allocated message copy quota based on the delivery probability. Pan Hui et al. [12] proposed a routing algorithm Bubble Rap based on social attributes. This routing algorithm judges the forwarding node based on the destination community and the ranking obtained from the node centrality. When the message is outside the destination community, the forwarding node is judged according to the global ranking; when the message is inside the destination community, it is judged according to the local ranking.

Community division is to divide the nodes in the network into multiple communities according to the strength of the relationship between the nodes. The community division algorithms in opportunistic networks are mostly based on the community division algorithms of complex networks. The more classic algorithms include the GN algorithm [13] and the K-means algorithm [14] and so on.

2   Comparative Analysis of Community Division Algorithms

2.1   Community Division Algorithm

GN Algorithm

The GN algorithm was proposed by Girvan and Newman in 2002, and it is a representative splitting method. The edge intermediary is defined as the number of shortest paths through any two nodes of the edge in the network. Continuously deleting the edge with the largest intermediary from the network will divide the entire network into more closely related communities.

In the community structure detection algorithm, the denseness of the reasonable division of the internal connection of the community should be higher than the expected level of the random connection network, and the Q function is used to quantitatively describe the modularity of the community division. Suppose the complex network has been divided into n communities, then first define an $n \times n$ dimensional symmetric matrix e, where element e_{ij} represents the proportion of the edges connecting nodes in community i and community j to all sides, and $Tre = \sum_i e_{ii}$ of this matrix represent all the ratio of the edges that connect the nodes in the community to the total number of edges [15][16][17], define the total value $a_i = \sum_i e_{ij}$ of the column (or row) to represent the ratio of all edges connected to nodes in community i to the total number. According to the definition of e_{ij} and a_i, the Q function can be expressed as:

$$Q = \sum_i \left(e_{ii} - a_i^2\right) = Tre - \|e^2\|$$

Where $"\|e^2\|"$ is the modulo of the matrix, that is, the sum of the elements in e^2.

If the number of edges between nodes within the community is not as many as those obtained by random connection, the value of the Q function is negative. When the value of the Q function approaches 1, it indicates that the division of the community structure is reasonable. In practical applications, the value of Q is generally between 0.3 and 0.7.

The basic flow of the GN algorithm is as follows:

(1) Calculate the edge median of each edge in the network;

(2) Find the edge with the largest number of edges and remove it from the network;

(3) Recalculate the edge intermediaries of the remaining edges in the network;

(4) Repeat steps (2) and (3) until each node is a separate community;

Take the data source of karate club as an example, run the GN algorithm, and get the results shown in Fig. 1:

```
The original network was:
1  2  3  4  5  6  7  8  9  10  11  12  13  14  15  16  17  18  19  20  21  22  23  24  25  26  27  28  29  30  31  32  33  34

Program analysis shows that the original network is likely to split into 2 communities:
community1: 3  9  10  15  16  19  21  23  24  25  26  27  28  29  30  31  32  33  34
community2: 1  2  4  5  6  7  8  11  12  13  14  17  18  20  22

The key edges leading to the split and the process of splitting are:

Based on the original networkRemove the edge (edge with the largest intermediary):
v(1,32), v(1,3), v(1,9), v(14,34), v(20,34), v(3,33), v(2,31), v(2,3), v(3,4), v(3,8), v(3,14),
Will be split into 2 groups, the situation after the split is:
community1: 3  9  10  15  16  19  21  23  24  25  26  27  28  29  30  31  32  33  34
community2: 1  2  4  5  6  7  8  11  12  13  14  17  18  20  22
Process finished with exit code 0
```

Fig. 1. Results from running in the Eclipse environment

Divided results into two communities:
Society 1 {3, 9, 10, 15, 16, 19, 21, 23, 24, 25, 26, 27, 28, 29, 30, 31, 32, 33, 34}
Society 2 {1, 2, 4, 5, 6, 7, 8, 11, 11, 12, 13, 14, 17, 18, 20, 22}

Draw the results of community division with NetDraw software, as shown in Fig. 2:

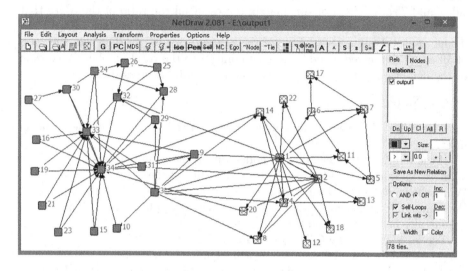

Fig. 2. The results of community division drawn by NetDraw software

Take Fig. 3 as an example to illustrate the execution flow of the GN algorithm:

1. Use the shortest path algorithm to find the shortest path from vertex 1 to vertex 8 in Fig. 3(a) (red part in the figure)

2. Repeat step 1 to detect the shortest path between all vertices of the network, and calculate the edge intermediaries of all edges, as shown in Fig. 3(b).

3. Count the maximum number of edges and delete it to get the community structure shown in Fig. 3(c).

4. Run the GN algorithm to get the results shown in Fig. 4:

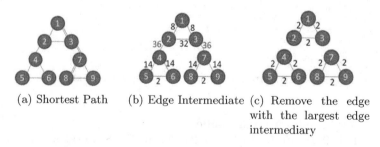

(a) Shortest Path   (b) Edge Intermediate   (c) Remove   the   edge with the largest edge intermediary

Fig. 3. Execution process of GN algorithm (Color figure online)

```
"C:\Program Files\Java\jdk-12.0.1\bin\java.exe" "-javaagent:G:\IntelliJ IDEA\install\IntelliJ ]
The original network was:
1 2 3 4 5 6 7 8 9
Program analysis shows that the original network is likely to split into 3 communities
community1: 4 5 6
community2: 7 8 9
community3: 1 2 3
The key edges leading to the split and the process of splitting are:

Based on the original networkremove the edge (edge with the largest intermediary): v(2,4),
Will be split into 2 groups, the situation after the split is:
community1: 4 5 6
community2: 1 2 3 7 8 9

and remove the edge (edge with the largest intermediary): v(3,7),
Will be split into 3 groups, the situation after the split is:
community1: 4 5 6
community2: 7 8 9
community3: 1 2 3
Process finished with exit code 0
```

Fig. 4. Running results of GN algorithm

From the experimental results, the first example uses a karate club data source. The result of community division using the GN algorithm is exactly the same as the result of community division. The second example uses an ordinary graph as the data source and GN The community division results obtained by the algorithm are the same as the actual ones, so the community division accuracy of the GN algorithm is high.

K-Means Algorithm

K-means algorithm is a typical algorithm in common clustering algorithms. First, the value of the parameter k needs to be determined, and then the set of n objects is divided into k clusters by the distance of the distance, so that the clustering result is that the distance within the cluster is close. The similarity is high, and the distance between clusters is long, the similarity is low. The similarity of a cluster is a measure of the mean of the objects in the cluster and can be regarded as the center of mass or center of gravity of the cluster.

1. Three points of K-means algorithm for clustering

(1) Select a certain distance as the similarity measure between data samples

When using the K-means clustering algorithm, the Euclidean distance is often used to calculate the distance between data samples. Besides, you can also choose Manhattan distance as the similarity measure of the algorithm according to actual needs. That is to say, given a data set $X = \{Xml, m = 1, 2, \cdots, total\}$, the samples in X use d description attributes $A_1, A_2, \cdots, A_d$, and d attribute descriptions are all continuous attributes. Given data samples $X_i = (X_{i1}, X_{i2}, \cdots, X_{id})$ and $X_j = (X_{jl}, X_{j2}, \cdots, X_{jd})$, where $X_{i1}, X_{i2}, \cdots, X_{id}$ and $X_{jl}, X_{j2}, \cdots, X_{jd}$ are the similarities between samples X_i and X_j respectively, usually expressed by the distance $d(X_i, X_j)$ between them. The smaller the distance is, the more similar the samples X_i and X_j are, and the smaller the difference is; the larger the distance is, the less similar the samples X_i and X_j are, and the greater the difference is. Euclidean distance is calculated by Eq. (1):

$$d(X_i, X_j) = \sqrt{\sum_{k=1}^{d} (X_{ik}, X_{jk})^2} \tag{1}$$

(2) Choose a criterion function to evaluate clustering performance

The squared error and criterion function are methods used by the K-means clustering algorithm to evaluate clustering performance. Detailed description: Given a data set X, it is assumed that X contains k clustering subsets $X_1, X_2, \cdots, X_k$; it only includes descriptive attributes and does not include category attributes. The number of samples in each subset is $n_1, n_2, \cdots, n_k$; the average representative points (also called cluster centers) of each clustering subset is $m_l, m_2, \cdots, m_k$.

Then the squared error is expressed as Eq. (2):

$$E = \sum_{i=1}^{k} \sum_{p \in X_i} \|p - m_i\| \tag{2}$$

2. K-means algorithm description

(1) Selection method of initialization cluster center.

a. Rely on the experience to judge and analyze the data samples, and then select C suitable initial cluster centers from the sample set;

b. Select the 1st-C sample data of the entire sample set as the initial cluster center;

c. The entire sample set is then group C, and the average value of all sample data in each group is calculated, which is the C initial cluster centers;

(2) The initial clustering is based on the distance between the sample data and each cluster center, and the samples are assigned to the nearest class. The specific process is to first take a sample and assign it to the class represented by its nearest cluster center according to the nearest principle, and then classify all samples into the appropriate class according to this method and recalculate the cluster. Class center, that is, the sample mean, update the cluster center, and perform iterative operations.

(3) The error square is used to judge whether the clustering is reasonable, and the classification is modified if it is not reasonable. Judge and modify repeatedly until the algorithm termination condition is reached.

3. K-means algorithm example

Suppose the data object set S is shown in Table 1. As a two-dimensional sample for cluster analysis, the required number of clusters is $k = 2$.

Table 1. Data object collection

Point	X coordinate	Y coordinate
O_1	2	0
O_2	3	2
O_3	3	0
O_4	0	6
O_5	1	7

(1) Select $O_1(2,0)$, $O_2(3,2)$ as the initial cluster center, that is, $M_1 = O_1 = (2,0)$, $M_2 = O_2 = (3,2)$.

(2) For the remaining data objects, the data is assigned to the nearest cluster according to the distance between the data and the center of each cluster.

To O_3 :

$d(M_1, O_3) = \sqrt{(3-2)^2 + (0-0)^2} = 1$

$d(M_2, O_3) = \sqrt{(3-3)^2 + (0-2)^2} = 2$

$d(M_1, O_3) < d(M_2, O_3), Coming\ from\ O_3\ to\ C_1$

In the same way we can get $d(M_2, O_4) < d(M_1, O_4)$, that is, O_4 is assigned to C_2; $d(M_2, O_5) < d(M_1, O_5)$, that is, O_5 is assigned to C_2, and new clusters $C_1 = \{O_1, O_3\}$, and $C_2 = \{O_2, O_4, O_5\}$ are obtained after the update.

Calculate the square error criterion with a single variance of:

$E_1 = [(3-2)^2 + (0-0)^2] = 1$

$E_2 = [(0-3)^2 + (6-2)^2] + [(1-3)^2 + (7-2)^2] = 49$

The overall mean-variance is: $E = E_1 + E_2 = 50$.

(3) Calculate the center of a new cluster.

$M_l = ((2+3)/2, (0+0)/2) = (2.5, 0)$

$M_2 = ((3+0+1)/3, (2+6+7)/3) = (1.33, 5)$

(4) Repeat 2, 3 to get O_1, then O_2, O_3 assigned to C_l, O_4 and O_5 assigned to C_2.

(5) Update to get new clusters $C_1 = \{O_1, O_2, O_3\}$ and $C_2 = \{O_4, O_5\}$. The center is $M_1(2.67, 0.67)$ and $M_2(0.5, 6.5)$, the single variance is $E_1 = 3.33$ and $E_2 = 1$, and the overall average error is $E = 4.33$.

It can be seen from the above that after the first iteration, the overall average error is reduced from 50 to 4.33, and the cluster center is unchanged, so the iteration process is stopped and the algorithm ends.

4. K-means algorithm execution steps

a. Determine k initial cluster centers;

b. Assign the remaining nodes to the nearest cluster according to the minimum distance principle;

c. Calculate the mean of each cluster and use it as the new cluster center;

d. Repeat steps b and c until the cluster center no longer changes;

e. The end, get k clusters;

5. The experimental process uses a set of 3D data sources and community division results, as shown in Table 2:

Table 2. Data object collection and community division results

Point	X coordinate	Y coordinate	Z coordinate	Affiliate
O_1	100	10	20	0
O_2	15	50	30	0
O_3	74	88	20	0
O_4	91	66	88	0
O_5	36	88	36	0
O_6	23	13	10	1
O_7	22	17	18	2
O_8	56	57	55	1
O_9	52	59	100	1
O_{10}	80	78	60	3
O_{11}	73	19	20	1
O_{12}	53	28	10	1
O_{13}	65	72	30	3
O_{14}	67	31	50	1
O_{15}	48	92	90	4
O_{16}	0	28	10	1
O_{17}	74	95	70	4
O_{18}	16	73	10	2
O_{19}	85	15	20	3
O_{20}	62	0	50	1
O_{21}	58	36	50	1
O_{22}	19	8	20	1
O_{23}	59	45	80	1
O_{24}	25	52	30	1
O_{25}	45	48	50	1
O_{26}	46	57	30	1
O_{27}	22	54	22	1
O_{28}	88	34	50	3
O_{29}	53	77	90	4
O_{30}	11	71	40	2
O_{31}	30	56	40	1
O_{32}	0	51	8	1
O_{33}	24	63	40	1
O_{34}	92	32	90	3
O_{35}	87	83	30	3
O_{36}	46	26	40	1
O_{37}	98	93	100	3
O_{38}	34	71	20	4
O_{39}	94	12	20	3
O_{40}	33	38	30	1
O_{41}	26	28	44	1
O_{42}	90	53	40	3
O_{43}	79	39	20	3
O_{44}	59	26	19	1
O_{45}	55	52	48	1
O_{46}	10	91	33	2
O_{47}	21	59	77	1
O_{48}	57	62	22	3
O_{49}	68	16	55	1

According to Table 2, the data division results shown in Fig. 5 can be obtained:

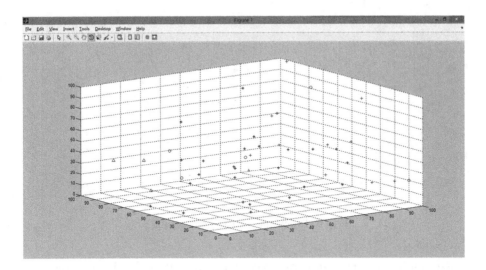

Fig. 5. K-means division of 3D data

The processing results are shown in Fig. 6:

According to Fig. 6, we can see that the K-means algorithm is less accurate than the GN algorithm, so the GN algorithm is selected.

2.2 Comparative Analysis of GN Algorithm and K-Means Algorithm

Analysis of GN Algorithm

The community division effect of the GN algorithm is more accurate than other algorithms, and it is suitable for medium-scale networks with the number of nodes n less than 10,000.

The disadvantage of the GN algorithm is that the time complexity is relatively large, so the analysis effect on large-scale complex networks is not ideal, and it takes a long time. The time complexity is $O(n^3)$, and n is the number of nodes. To solve this problem, people have proposed many improved algorithms based on the GN algorithm, such as a Newman Fast Algorithm based on the GN algorithm, which actually is a condensed algorithm based on the idea of greedy algorithm, which can analyze a complex network of 1 million nodes.

Analysis of K-Means Algorithm

K-means algorithm is simple and fast. It can efficiently process large-scale data sets and is suitable for continuous data sets. When the result cluster is dense, the cluster is distinct from the cluster, and the clustering is better when the data distribution is convex or spherical.

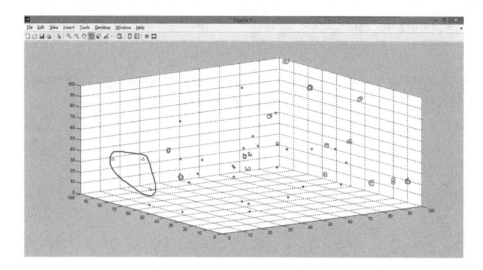

Fig. 6. Processing of K-means results

K-means clustering is an iterative clustering algorithm. During the iterative process, the members in the cluster are continuously moved until the ideal cluster set is obtained. The time complexity is $O(t \times k \times n)$ and t is the number of iterations. The final clustering result of the K-means clustering algorithm largely depends on the initial center point, which is randomly selected. The traditional K-means algorithm may converge to a local optimum instead of a global optimum. Some methods to improve K-means performance have been proposed, but most of them require additional input, such as a threshold for the number of data points in the data set. The performance of the K-means clustering algorithm depends on the initial position of the clustering center, that is, the random initial value selection may lead to different clustering results, and even there are no solutions, and the algorithm performs "noise points" and "solitary points" The data is very sensitive, a small amount of this type of data will have a very large impact on the average.

Solution: Set different initial values and compare the calculation results until the result stabilizes, but this is time consuming and wastes resources.

Although the K-means algorithm is simple and fast, the experimental results are too dependent on the choice of initial values, so K-means is not used as a routing protocol. Although the time complexity of the GN algorithm is relatively large, the accuracy is relatively high. For the accuracy of the experiment, the GN algorithm is selected as the routing protocol.

2.3   Community-Based Routing Protocols

Spray and Wait (SW) algorithm [18] is a routing algorithm based on the community in this experiment. It is a multi-copy routing scheme proposed by Spyropoulos et al. The SW algorithm is divided into two phases. In the S phase, each message will generate a corresponding copy and sent to multiple different forwarding points, so that some data packets in the source node will be diffused to neighboring nodes; in the W phase, if there is no When the destination node is found, multiple nodes holding the copy of the message switch to the direct sending state and forward the message to the destination node.

The Spray and Wait algorithm has two modes, Binary mode, and non-Binary mode. In Binary mode, the algorithm mechanism is that when the source node encounters a new relay node, it sends half of the data packets to the new relay node, leaving half of the data packets on its own; the source node and the relay node repeat the above process until When there is only one data packet in all nodes, the node transfers to the Wait phase and adopts direct transmission to the destination node. The Spray and Wait algorithm has an L parameter, which describes the number of packets.

The Spray and Wait algorithm is based on a flooding strategy, combining the fastness of infectious routing, the simplicity, and simplicity of direct transmission, and is committed to effectively balancing delay and energy consumption. The transmission rate is high, the transmission delay is small, and it is close to the optimal; It has good scalability and can maintain good performance regardless of the size of the network and the change in node density [18, 19].

3 Experimental Analysis of Spray and Wait Routing Protocol

As shown in Fig. 7, there are five communities, namely:

$C1 = \{S, 1, 2, 3\}$, $C2 = \{4, 5\}$, $C3 = \{12, 13\}$, $C4 = \{7, 8, 10, 11\}$, $C5 = \{D, 14, 15, 16\}$

The process of sending a message from the source node S in the community C1 to the destination node D in the community C5 is as follows:

(1) If node S and node D are in the same community, the message is directly forwarded in the community; otherwise, step (2) is performed;

(2) Node S and Node D are not in the same community, and then send the message to the neighboring communities C3 and C4;

(3) If the destination node D has been encountered, perform the forwarding in step (1), otherwise, continue to forward;

(4) Until the destination node D receives the message;

During the entire process of message forwarding above, during the Spray phase, a copy of each message in the community will be generated and sent to the nodes of the neighboring community, so that the data packets in the source node will be diffused to the surrounding communities. The destination node is not found during the message forwarding process, and the forwarding is continued until the destination node receives the data.

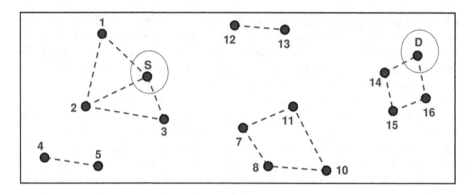

Fig. 7. Spray and wait routing

4 Conclusion

This paper proposes a community-based opportunistic network routing protocol. The research is mainly divided into two parts. The first part is based on the existing opportunistic network routing protocol to propose the community-based opportunistic network routing protocol. First, compare the advantages and disadvantages of the two community division algorithms of GN and K-means, decide to use a more accurate GN algorithm for community division, and then perform message routing on the divided communities. This paper uses the Spray and Wait routing protocol, which is fast, simple, and has a high transmission rate.

Acknowledgment. The authors wish to thank Inner Mongolia Higher Education Research Project under Grant NJZY17472.

References

1. Akyildiz, I.F., Su, W., Sankarasubramaniam, Y., Cayirci, E.: A survey on sensor networks. IEEE Commun. Mag. **40**(8), 102–114 (2002)
2. Loo, J., Mauri, J., Ortiz, J.: Mobile ad hoc networks. Current Status and Future Trends, Mobile Ad Hoc Networks (2012)
3. Akyildiz, I.F., Wang, X.: A survey on wireless mesh networks. IEEE Commun. Mag. **43**(9), S23–S30 (2005)
4. Stavroulaki, V., et al.: Opportunistic networks. IEEE Veh. Technol. Mag. **6**(3), 52–59 (2006)
5. Yong-Ping, X., Li-Min, S., Jian-Wei, N., Yan, L., et al.: Opportunistic networks. J. Softw. **20**(1), 124–137 (2009)
6. Heinzelman, W.R., Chandrakasan, A., Balakrishnan, H.: Energy-efficient communication protocol for wireless microsensor networks. In: Proceedings of the 33rd Annual Hawaii International Conference on System Sciences, p. 10. IEEE (2000)
7. Vahdat, A., Becker, D., et al.: Epidemic routing for partially connected ad hoc networks (2000)

8. Spyropoulos, T., Psounis, K., Raghavendra, C.S.: Spray and wait: an efficient routing scheme for intermittently connected mobile networks. In: Proceedings of the 2005 ACM SIGCOMM Workshop on Delay-tolerant Networking, pp. 252–259 (2005)
9. Spyropoulos, T., Psounis, K., Raghavendra, C.S.: Spray and focus: efficient mobility-assisted routing for heterogeneous and correlated mobility. In: Fifth Annual IEEE International Conference on Pervasive Computing and Communications Workshops (PerComW 2007), pp. 79–85. IEEE (2007)
10. Lindgren, A., Doria, A., Lindblom, J., Ek, M.: Networking in the land of northern lights: two years of experiences from dtn system deployments. In: Proceedings of the 2008 ACM Workshop on Wireless Networks and Systems for Developing Regions, pp. 1–8 (2008)
11. Min, P., Pei-Lin, H., Kai-Ping, X., Han-Cheng, L.: Delivery probability prediction based efficient routing in DTN. Chin. J. Comput. **34**(01), 176–183 (2011)
12. Hui, P., Crowcroft, J., Yoneki, E.: Bubble rap: social-based forwarding in delay-tolerant networks. IEEE Trans. Mob. Comput. **10**(11), 1576–1589 (2010)
13. Newman, M.E.: Assortative mixing in networks. Phys. Rev. Lett. **89**(20), 208701 (2002)
14. Chou, X.: The Improvement and Application of K-Means Algorithm. Ph.D. thesis, Beijing University of Posts and Telecommunications (2012)
15. Yu, Z., Yu-dong, L., Zhao, J.: Vector similarity measurement method. Tech. Acoustics **28**(4), 532–536 (2009)
16. Sun, J.G., Liu, J., Zhao, L.Y.: Clustering algorithms research. J. Softw. **19**(1), 48–61 (2008)
17. Fu-ding, X., Da-wei, Z., et al.: Density set algorithm search for communities in complex networks. J. Univ. Electr. Sci. Technol. China **40**(4), 483–490 (2011)
18. Peleg, S., Friedlander, B.: The discrete polynomial-phase transform. IEEE Trans. Signal Process. **43**(8), 1901–1914 (1995)
19. Xianda, Z., Bao: Non-Stationary Signal Analysis and Processing. National Defense Industry Press, Beijing (1998)

A Comprehensive Cellular Learning Automata Based Routing Algorithm in Opportunistic Networks

Feng Zhang[(✉)]

School of Computer and Information Technology, Shanxi University, Shanxi 030006, China
zhangfeng@sxu.edu.cn

Abstract. A distinctive cellular learning automata based routing algorithm is proposed which exploits the ambient nodes feature to polish up the performance of opportunistic networks. The factors of each phase in the routing procedure of store-carry-forward are taken into account. Messages would be dropped on the basis of the dropping probability when congestion occurs during the store phase. Energy consumption would be balanced according to the threshold set by the node itself which is used to accept messages in the carry phase. Connection duration between nodes has been estimated to reduce the energy waste caused by fragment messages transmission during the forwarding process. To evaluate the validity of our proposed algorithm, we conduct comprehensive simulation experiments on the ONE platform. The results show that the proposed routing algorithm achieves higher delivery ratio and less overhead ratio. In addition, it gains a balance of energy consumption and an enhancement of the whole network performances.

Keywords: Opportunistic networks · Routing algorithm · Energy efficient · Cellular learning automata · Ambient intelligence

1 Introduction

With the rise of smart mobile devices, the mobile Internet has achieved great success in recent years. This brings huge data volumes that can be generated and propagated. Although the cellular network has been improved rapidly, there are still some limitations in specific scenarios such as sparsely populated areas, large gatherings and disasters. In these circumstances, the communication infrastructure of cellular network might not be economically beneficial or increasingly costly or almost to be infeasible [1, 2].

These restricts boost the blossom of the opportunistic networks, which are a special type of mobile ad-hoc networks (MANETs). When nodes in the opportunistic networks are moving within wireless transmission range, they can directly communicate with each other via the equipped short-range wireless technology such as Wi-Fi or Bluetooth. This

This work is partly supported by the Natural Science Foundation of Shanxi Province under Grant 201901D111035.

W. Li and D. Tang (Eds.): MOBILWARE 2020, LNICST 331, pp. 44–56, 2020.
https://doi.org/10.1007/978-3-030-62205-3_4

is very essential when the infrastructure collapses during natural or man-made disasters. Opportunistic networks are usually composed of spatially distributed human carried mobile devices with short range wireless communication modules. There may never be an end-to-end transmission path available between a source and a destination node in opportunistic networks [3]. The traditional routing protocols in MANETs would not work well due to the sparse restrict resource and the mobility of nodes in opportunistic networks. Compared with the traditional infrastructure-based cellular networks, opportunistic networks adopt a new routing paradigm which is store-carry-forward. Once this pattern is defined, the architect can focus on more specific details of the routing algorithm. In this way, intermediate nodes typically relay messages through random contacts [4]. Nodes usually store messages first and then carry them as they move around in the networks. If an appropriate opportunity arises, messages will be forwarded or replicated to the destination or other relay nodes. Due to the limited buffer capacity of nodes, the unfair load distribution and the unrestricted volumes of traffic will lead to capacity saturation in a buffer, resulting in congestion, and the severely degraded network performance accordingly [5]. On the other hand, as the devices people carried are always powered by batteries and it is very difficult to charge the batteries during the movement. So the energy consumption is a fatal element influencing the network lifetime in opportunistic networks. Nodes that have run out or severely low on battery power will not be able to participate in messages relay in the future [6].

Generally, the resources of nodes in the opportunistic network are limited, and they act as relay stations for other nodes when routing messages. To increase delivery ratio of messages, replication-based policies are applied to allow multiple messages to exist. But this may increases a risk of congestion and excessive energy consumption [7, 8]. Therefore, how to make the best use of finite resource of local and ambient nodes to achieve good routing performance including message delivery ratio, overhead ratio and energy utilization is a great challenge topic and study hotspot in opportunistic networks. All the factors should be devised carefully throughout the whole store-carry-forward procedure. In this paper, a comprehensive routing algorithm based on the cellular learning automata is proposed. In this scheme, nodes in opportunistic networks are considered as cellular, and each element is updated by the automata assigned to the node. Nodes update their own internal state on discrete cycles periodically according to the same regulation. Then efficient routing algorithm including congestion control and energy balance are addressed based on the local state and ambient state of nodes.

The remainder of this paper is organized as follows. Section 2 gives an overview of some existing related work and the concept of cellular learning automata. Section 3 presents the proposed comprehensive routing algorithm. Simulation results and analysis are shown and discussed in Sect. 4. At last, we conclude this paper in Sect. 5.

2 Related Work

In this section, we firstly introduce the concept and mathematical model of DICLA which is the fundamental model used in this paper. Then we address the key area of routing protocols in the opportunistic networks. Some recently researches in opportunistic networks are followed.

2.1 Dynamic Irregular Cellular Learning Automata

CLA (Cellular Learning Automata) is a useful mathematical model for many discrete problems and phenomena, and the characteristics of CA and LA [9] are combined together. The abstract environment of LA is replaced by the cells around LA, and the rule of CA is evolved according to the reinforcement signal. The states of cells mean different actions. On the basis of CLA, the Irregular Cellular Learning Automata (ICLA) and Dynamic Irregular Cellular Learning Automata (DICLA) are developed [10, 11]. An ICLA is a CLA which the restriction of rectangular grid structure in traditional CLA is removed. A DICLA is an ICLA with the variable structure according to the given principle. In other words, the adjacency matrix of the underlying graph of the ICLA can be changed over time in DICLA. This dynamic feature and universality are necessary for the applications that cannot be totally modeled with rectangular grids such as Mobile Ad hoc Networks and Wireless Sensor Networks, Opportunistic Networks, web mining, grid computing and data aggregation [12].

2.2 Routing Issue

Routing messages in opportunistic networks present challenges (such as constantly moving and intermittent connectivity). This is because that the absence of the steady and stable connections between source and destination which are exist in other traditional network. Also the limited resource of nodes such as energy and storage are other factors that must be carefully considered. Routing schemes must implement techniques that are efficient and ingenious to increase the performance benefit of opportunistic networks.

To address temporary connection, random moving and limited resource challenges, the distinctive routing strategies are determined and separate the routing phase into three steps, store, carry and forward. Routing strategy in opportunistic networks always involves appropriate forwarding scheme, efficient buffer management and balanced energy utilization. Multiple copies forwarding scheme is the most common and widely used strategy [13, 14]. The representative algorithm is the Epidemic [15]. Messages will be replicated to any other nodes while nodes roam in the network. Obviously there are maximum replications of messages in opportunistic networks for Epidemic and high messages delivery probability in an ideal environment.

However, there is no energy and storage considered in the above mentioned routing protocols [13–15]. Because of the finite storage constraint of mobile nodes in practice, the congestion phenomenon arises as the time goes on when node buffer is full in Epidemic fashion. So the criterion of selecting messages to drop is very important if congestion occurs. The simplest selection method is according to the time feature of messages [16]. These congestion control strategies do not take the copies number of message into account and are local view of node itself. In order to overcome this shortcoming, GLCCS (game of life based congestion control strategy) [17] scheme is proposed. CLACCS (cellular learning automata based congestion control strategy) [18] is an improvement of GLCCS. Different from GLCCS, messages drop probability is defined in this strategy. It describes the dropping probability of message using the distribution of messages around current neighbor nodes under the rule of learning automata automatically. With the help of this probability, it is very easy to pick up which message to drop when congestion situation.

An optimization in terms of energy consumption based on Epidemic is proposed in [15]. In this scheme, messages will not be transmitted if the number of neighbors less than the threshold n. The classic routing protocol in this type is named n-Epidemic. A novel adaptive adjustment strategy of n-Epidemic routing (ANER) is proposed in [19], which employs the cellular learning automata model to depict the dynamic characteristics of opportunistic networks, and local rule is defined to tune the parameter n of n-Epidemic dynamically according to the energy level of nodes and their neighbors'. EACC [20] is a congestion control scheme under the consideration of energy consumption in Epidemic paradigm. The cellular learning automata model is used in EACC to update the energy level of node and its neighbors. Furthermore, fragmental messages are wholly unused in the opportunistic networks. This is very easy to be prevented in a stable link network environment. As long as the message follows a run-to-completion model on a per-message basis, the message will be received totally. However, messages may be transferred partially in opportunistic networks for the wireless links between nodes are temporary. This may be caused when link connections break down as with the nodes moving. Messages will not be scheduled to forwarding if the left connection duration time is shorter than the messages transfer time.

These above schemes only take partial factor (energy or congestion) into account. However, a complete routing protocol should consider feasibility as many as possible. Our proposal focuses on the fragmental message, congestion and energy consumption in Epidemic paradigm. We introduce CLA to opportunistic networks to deal with the TTL value of messages like EACC when they were replicated. Also the message dropping probability is updated periodically according to the messages stored in the neighbors using the principle of CLA as CLACCS. In the forward phase, fragment message will be cancelled avoiding energy consumption. The proposed algorithm is to balance the delivery and energy concerns associated with Cellular Learning Automata. Our contributions of this paper are the following:

- We take all the factors of the process of store-carry-forward routing paradigm into account.
- We update the message dropping probability and energy level of nodes at the same time using the principles of cellular learning automata in the store and carry phases.
- Connection durations between nodes are calculated according to the historical records in the forward phase.
- The simulation results are implemented comparing with the existing routing algorithms to show the efficient of proposed algorithm.

3 Proposed Routing Algorithm

In opportunistic networks scenario, nodes have distinct levels of remaining energy and messages information of themselves, and can get these information of their current neighbors through the inquiring method. Hence a detrimental replicating decision for adjacent nodes can be canceled ahead of schedule according to the messages dropping probability and nodes' energy status. In the scheme, each node is described as a cellular equipped with multiple number LAs in each cellular. These multiple LAs assigned to a cellular act different roles. We will use two kinds of LAs to describe the message dropping probability and threshold of receiving message associated with energy level respectively in the following scheme. The reinforcement signals of each LAs are independent, and calculated according to the different information from ambient neighbors.

The proposed scheme is based on the original Epidemic routing protocol. Furthermore, it takes the message dropping probability and energy consumption of nodes into account in the following aspects: a) message distribution situation of ambient nodes within nodes' communicate range. b) message dropping probability of each message stored in nodes. c) current energy level of individual node. d) time to live (TTL) of messages before they want to be flooded to the neighbors. e) residual connection duration time between neighbors. The main idea of this paper is that there is a dynamic process to update message dropping probability and adjust ratio criterion on the basis of the remainder energy level of node and its neighbors. Nodes with the more energy retained can receive the wide range of TTL of messages. And message with higher dropping probability will be removed firstly when buffer is full. Furthermore the fragment message transmission can be avoided in advance for energy considerations. This is more energy efficient and much more transmission for the energetic nodes. It is superior for the prime Epidemic routing for receiving any messages from its neighbors without considering energy level of nodes.

In the rest part, we firstly describe message dropping probability, threshold of receiving message and connection duration respectively. Then the detailed description of proposed cellular learning automata based routing algorithm is followed.

3.1 Message Dropping Probability

The message dropping probabilities are updated according to the Ref. [18] using the principle of dynamic irregular cellular multiple learning automata. We think a node as a cellular, and each message buffered in this node equipped with a learning automata. Connections between nodes establish and break can be described as the dynamic process of the DICLA. The variables a_0 and a_1 mean the actions that DICLA can take which indicate discard or keep this message respectively. The probability of each action is p_r or p_d accordingly and the initial value of p_r and p_d is assigned as 0.5. The status of each cellular should be updated periodicity as the fixed interval. At the begining of each interval, every node inquires messages distribution from its neighbors. The reinforcement signal $\beta(n)$ of each learning automata corresponding to a message is given according to the number of neighbors who hold the same message variety.

$$\beta_i(n) = \begin{cases} 1, & \sum_{j=1}^{SUM_i(n)} a_j(n) - \sum_{j=1}^{SUM_i(n-1)} a_j(n-1) > 0 \\ 0, & \text{otherwise} \end{cases} \tag{1}$$

The n is the identifier of current interval. $SUM_i(n)$ is the number of neighbors of node i and $a_i(n)$ is the action of node i which keeps the message at this interval. The message dropping probability is updated according to the $\beta(n)$ and show as Eq. (2) and Eq. (3).

$$p_d(n+1) = p_d(n) + a(n) * (1 - p_d(n)) \tag{2}$$

$$p_d(n+1) = (1 - b(n)) * p_d(n) \tag{3}$$

The $a(n)$ and $b(n)$ are the simulate and punishment parameters. $0 < a(n) < 1, 0 < b(n) < 1$, And they are calculated as Eq. (4) and Eq. (5). φ, ρ are the factors and range in [0,1] in Eq. (4) and Eq. (5). $R_i^m(n)$ is the number of neighbors who store the message m at the nth intervals.

$$a(n) = \phi * R_i^m(n)/SUM_i(n) \tag{4}$$

$$b(n) = \rho * R_i^m(n)/SUM_i(n) \tag{5}$$

If the number of nodes which store a message is increasing relative to the previous time interval, the dropping probability of this message should be increased. That is to say, there is much more nodes store this message. The impact of dropping this message is smaller than other messages at this time. So if the buffer of this node is not enough to store other message from neighbors, it should delete the messages with higher dropping probability to free space to receive the new messages.

3.2 Threshold of Receiving Message

In traditional Epidemic routing strategies, any node accepts any message from its peers randomly. If the buffer is full, the node will remove message with the given criterion from its buffer until there is enough room to store the new coming message. For activity nodes, especially in terms of energy, the efficiency is very low, because activity nodes have more opportunities to meet other nodes. This also accelerates the energy consumption of activity node because there are much more transmissions for activity nodes. It is easy to cause the disproportion energy consumed among nodes.

Some criteria of receiving message have been adopted in EACC [20] to insure energy conservation trade-off among nodes. These criteria neither ignores energy constraints of the nodes themselves, nor neglect the current energy state information of local ambient when making replicate decisions. Some definitions associated with energy have been introduced in EACC.

3.3 Connection Duration Estimation

Because of the indeterminate wireless connection among mobile nodes in the opportunistic networks, many sudden abort of message transmissions caused by unpredictable connection interrupted between nodes will waste the limited resource including buffer and energy. If we can estimate the connection duration time before a transmission, we will decide whether or not to start this transmission so as to avoiding resource wasted.

For this purpose, each node records the begin time and end time for every connection. Then the connection duration time of this connection can be accurately obtained by subtracting the begin time from end time. Also each node records every connection duration time with the other nodes to a historical information database while moving in the network. We consider the connection duration as a discrete random variable X, and the $E(X)$ denotes the expectation of this random variable X. The expectation $E(X)$ of this random variable X can be gained as follows:

$$E(X) = \sum_{k=1}^{\infty} x_k p_k \tag{6}$$

where p_k represents the distributing of random variable $X = x_k$.

Based on this prediction, nodes can make a wise decision whether to start a transmission according to current message size, transmission rate and the expected left time of this connection duration.

3.4 Proposed Routing Algorithm

The flow chat of proposed forwarding algorithm is shown in Fig. 2, and it is explained as follows:

1. Whenever two nodes encounter, and a wireless connection is established between them, they will exchange the message summary information buffered on their storage. Acknowledgments of delivered messages are flooded in the whole network to remove the redundant copies of messages.
2. At the beginning each interval, they update and calculate the *AEL* and *REL* respectively. The *LTL* value can be computed on the basis of current neighbors. This process is identical with the Ref. [20].
3. Each message updates its own dropping probability accordingly to the proportion of its neighbors. This is borrowed from Ref. [18].
4. Nodes record the connect time as the begin time of this connection.
5. Message transmission sequence is made based on the dropping probability. That is message with largest dropping probability will be sent first.
6. If the buffer of peer is full, message replicated to the peer must be check whether the *RTL* of messages is large than the peer's current *LTL* product the initial TTL value when message created.
7. The node will reject any messages from its neighbors if the current value of it *LTL* is less than a fix threshold (THD), which is very useful for balancing the energy consumption among nodes. This means that the remaining energy level between current nodes and its neighbors is very different. Therefore will refuse to receive any messages to reduce energy consumption until the difference exceeds the threshold.
8. Message m transfer time t_m is defined as Eq. (7).

$$t_m = s_m / w \tag{7}$$

where s_m is the size of message m and w is the speed of wireless communication.

9. If the message transfer time is longer than the left connection duration time between peers, this transmission should be canceled. All messages in the buffer are processed in this way in turns.

10. When the connection broken down, each node of this connection records this time. The detailed flow chat of this algorithm is showed in Fig. 1.

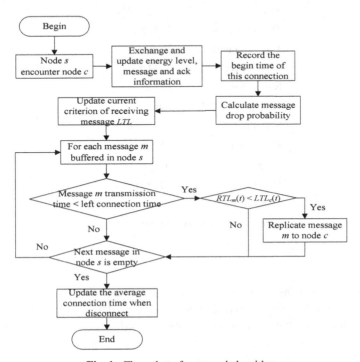

Fig. 1. Flow chat of proposed algorithm

4 Performance Evaluation

In this section, we use the java-based ONE (Opportunistic Network Environment) simulator [21] to evaluate the performance of our routing algorithm and other two other proposed routing algorithms CLACCS [18] and EACC [20] under the Levy Walk mobility model. The proposed scheme named Cellular Learning Automata based Routing Algorithm (CLARA) and routing and energy performances are compared among these three policies. The base routing protocol used in all simulations is Epidemic routing protocol.

4.1 Simulation Parameter Setting

The scenario of our simulation is limited to a region of 800 m x 400 m. Nodes deployed randomly in the range. The number of nodes ranges from 50 to 110 and they are all the same with the initial energy, movement speed and buffer size. The detailed simulation and energy parameter are shown in Table 1.

Table 1. Simulation parameters settings

Map size	800×400 m^2
Transmit speed	2 Mbps
Transmit range	25 m
Nodes speed	0.5–1.5 m/s
Buffer size	70 MB
Time to live (TTL)	300 m
Nodes movement	Levy walk
Message size	500 kB – 700 KB
Initial energy	5000 units
Scan energy	0.1 units
Transmit energy	0.2 units
Scan response energy	0.1 units
Simulation time	10 h

Especially, the routing performance named delivery ratio, overhead ratio and energy performance named average residual energy, standard deviation of residual energy metrics in our experiments are compared to show the efficiency of proposed CLARA.

4.2 Performance Under Different Node Number

Figure 2 and Fig. 3 show the routing and energy performance respectively. As can be seen from Fig. 2(a) and Fig. 2(b), in these compared strategies, the delivery ratio and overhead ratio of our CLARA are almost the best. With the increase in the number of nodes, the delivery ratio of CLACCS and EACC increases. This is because that as the number of nodes increases, the encounter probability of nodes increases. Messages replication between nodes becomes more frequent and there are more message copies in the network. Therefore, messages are more likely to reach their destinations. At the same time, the overhead ratio is also increased.

Although CLACCS policy don't consider energy consumer, it uses the message dropping probability to choose message to remove when buffer is full. This is superior to the in EACC schemes. So CLACCS can obtain a higher delivery ratio. Our CLARA incorporates the two features of EACC and CLACCS. Hence the consequence of delivery ratio is clearly achieved better than the two schemes mentioned above. On the other hand, the goal of these policies is only to increase the delivery ratio by copying as many as possible messages to intermediate nodes. The overhead ratio is arising as the number of node increasing. For there are much more opportunities to exchange messages among

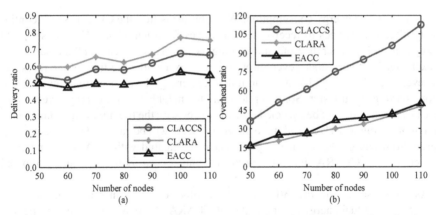

Fig. 2. (a) message delivery ratio and (b) overhead ratio under different number of nodes

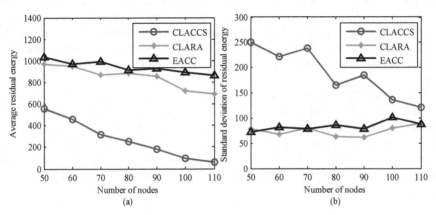

Fig. 3. (a) average residual energy (b) standard deviation of residual energy under different number of nodes

nodes while node moving in the network. Our CLARA gets almost the comparative performance of overhead ratio with EACC. And they are much better than CLACCS does. This is because that EACC and CLARA only receive specific messages rather than arbitrarily accept any message from their peers. This will reduce the copying of some messages that are about to expire between nodes. In addition, these two algorithms periodically adjust the TTL proportion of receiving messages based on the energy level of neighbors. This is of great help to the ping-pong effect of message exchange. Furthermore, EACC and CLARA will propagate the messages with larger TTL to much more intermediate nodes. When the buffer is full, these messages can not be replaced by other messages with smaller TTL values. So the overhead ratio is decline.

It can be clearly seen in Fig. 3(a), the average residual energy of nodes decreases as the nodes number increases. This is due to that as the number of nodes increases, nodes contact with each other more frequently. There are much more messages exchange between pairs and energy consumption. When buffer is full, the CLACCS will continuously discard messages to receive new messages from neighbors. This is especially energy consuming under the Epidemic routing pattern. This is because all messages will be exchanged between nodes even through it may exceed the life time of the message. However, the CLARA and EACC can utilize the energy level of current environment before starting the transfer. Some replications for neighbors with energy levels lower than the launch node will be canceled. The messages with the life time will expire in proportion of the initial TTL according to the energy level will be canceled to avoid wasting energy. So it can get better energy performance compared with CLACCS. Under the same conditions, CLARA and EACC perform a longer network life time than compared others.

As can be seen from Fig. 3(b), with the number of nodes increases, the standard deviation of residual energy among nodes of CLARA and EACC is increases slightly. This is because the energy level is dynamically updated according to the LA rules in these schemes. This will avoid difference latitude changing vibrational among nodes. Nodes with low energy levels still reduce replication times to save energy. In addition, this is an efficient method to prevent the energy from excessively wasting for the given node with conclusive energy left. It is of great significance significant for nodes which are powered by battery and energy consumption unbalance among nodes in the opportunistic networks.

In summary, CLARA can get better performance than EACC and CLACCS policies during the congestion condition in the opportunistic networks. Also it reduces the energy consumed and overhead ratio for messages replicated. It discriminates messages and nodes according to TTL and energy level. Moreover the message dropping probability is calculated according to the status of messages stored in the ambient nodes. This reduces the possibility of dropping the less copies messages. Therefore the messages delivery ratio is enhanced.

5   Conclusions

How to select the appropriate messages to transmit to intermediate node in terms of limited storage capacity and energy resource to improve the message delivery ratio is an eternal topic in the opportunistic networks. If nodes can make intelligent decisions according to the circumstances of current environment, this is an advisable scheme to existing routing algorithms. A novel intelligent approach based on the ambient nodes using DICLA model which is a dynamical system model widely used in the ambient intelligence situations is proposed in this paper. Message density and node energy status are updated dynamically to compute the message dropping probability and criterion of receiving message of each node. Furthermore the connection duration time between nodes is used to choose proper size message to avoid the incomplete message transfer. The simulation results showed that the proposed CLARA scheme can efficiently improve the message delivery ratio and get the balance of congestion and energy consumption. The life time of network is also prolongs accordingly.

References

1. Cao, Y., Sun, Z.: Routing in delay/disruption tolerant networks: A taxonomy, survey and challenges. IEEE Commun. Surveys Tuts. **15**(2), 654–677 (2013)
2. Trifunovic, S., Kouyoumdjieva, S.T., Distl, B., et al.: A decade of research in opportunistic networks: challenges, relevance, and future directions. IEEE Commun. Mag. **55**(1), 168–173 (2017)
3. Mota, V.F.S., Cunha, F.D., Macedo, D.F., et al.: Protocols, mobility models and tools in opportunistic networks: a survey. Comput. Commun. **48**, 5–19 (2014)
4. Vendramin, A.C.K., Munaretto, A., Delgado, M.R., et al.: A social-aware routing protocol for opportunistic networks. Expert Syst. Appl. **54**, 351–363 (2016)
5. Batabyal, S., Bhaumik, P.: Mobility models, traces and impact of mobility on opportunistic routing algorithms: a survey. IEEE Commun. Surveys Tuts. **17**(3), 1679–1707 (2015)
6. Sharma, D.K., Dhurandher, S.K., Agarwal, D., et al.: kROp: k-Means clustering based routing protocol for opportunistic networks. J. Amb. Intell. Hum. Comp. **1**, 1–18 (2018)
7. Sharma, D.K., Kukreja, D., Chugh, S., Kumaram, S.: Supernode routing: a grid-based message passing scheme for sparse opportunistic networks. J. Amb. Intell. Hum. Comp. **10**(4), 1307–1324 (2018). https://doi.org/10.1007/s12652-018-0993-y
8. Yuan, P., Fan, L., Liu, P., et al.: Recent progress in routing protocols of mobile opportunistic networks: A clear taxonomy, analysis and evaluation. J. Netw. Comput. Appl. **62**, 163–170 (2016)
9. Meybodi, M.R., Beigy, H., Taherkhani, M.: Cellular learning automata and its applications. Appl. Soft Comput. pp. 1–18 (2017)
10. Khomami, M.M.D., Rezvanian, A., Meybodi, M.R.: A new cellular learning automata-based algorithm for community detection in complex social networks. J. Comput. Sci. **24**, 413–426 (2017)
11. Wongthanavasu, S., Ponkaew, J.: A cellular automata-based learning method for classification. Expert Syst. Appl. **49**, 99–111 (2016)
12. Ghavipour, M., Meybodi, M.R.: Irregular cellular learning automata-based algorithm for sampling social network. Eng. Appl. Artif. Intell. **59**, 244–259 (2017)
13. Aung, C.Y., Ho, W.H., Chong, P.H.J.: Store-carry-cooperative forward routing with information epidemics control for data delivery in opportunistic networks. IEEE Access **5**(99), 6608–6625 (2017)
14. Zhou, H., Leung, V.C.M., Zhu, C., et al.: Predicting temporal social contact patterns for data forwarding in opportunistic mobile networks. IEEE Trans. Veh. Technol. **66**(11), 10372–10383 (2017)
15. Lu, X., Hui, P.: An energy-efficient n-epidemic routing protocol for delay tolerant networks[C]. In: 2010 IEEE Fifth International Conference on Networking, Architecture and Storage (NAS). pp. 341–347, IEEE (2010)
16. Zhang, D., Yang, M., Cui, L.: Congestion control strategy for opportunistic network based on message values. J. Netw. **9**(5), 1132–1138 (2014)
17. Wang, E., Yang, Y.J., Li, L.: Game of life based congestion control strategy in delay tolerant networks. J. Comput. Res. Dev. **50**(11), 2393–2407 (2014). (in chinese)
18. Zhang, F., Wang, X.M., Zhang, L.C., Li, P.: A cellular-learning-automata-based congestion control strategy in opportunistic networks. J. Sichuan Univ. (Eng. Sci. Edition). **48**(1), 158–165 (2016). (in chinese)
19. Zhang, F., Wang, X.M., Zhang, L.C., Li, P., Wang, L., Yu, W.Y.: Dynamic adjustment strategy of n-epidemic routing protocol for opportunistic networks: a learning automata approach. KSII Trans. Internet Inf. Syst. **11**(4), 2020–2037 (2017)

20. Zhang, F., Wang, X.M., Li, P., Zhang, L.C.: Energy aware congestion control scheme in opportunistic networks. IEEJ Trans. Electrical Electronic Eng. **12**(3), 412–419 (2017)
21. The ONE'. http://www.netlab.tkk.fi/tutkimus/dtn/theone/

Performance Analysis of MPTCP Under High Load Based on SDN Environment

Jiahui Hou[1,2], Dinghui Hou[1,2], Bixin Tao[2], Hui Qi[1,2(✉)], Xiaoqiang Di[1,2,3], Weiwu Ren[1,2], and Ligang Cong[1,2]

[1] School of Computer Science and Technology, Changchun University of Science and Technology, Changchun, China
[2] Jilin Key Laboratory of Network and Information Security, Changchun University of Science and Technology, Changchun, China
qihui@cust.edu.cn
[3] Information Center, Changchun University of Science and Technology, Changchun 130022, China

Abstract. Multipath Transmission Control Protocol (MPTCP) is in a rapid development process. MPTCP allows a network node to utilize multiple network interfaces and IP paths at the same time. It can take full advantage of network resources and provide reliable transmission, which brings advantages to users in terms of performance and reliability. In order to study the performance of MPTCP under high load, this paper uses Mininet to create an SDN environment and compare the performance differences between MPTCP and TCP under high load, and simulates a common Web application network architecture. The performance of MPTCP under this architecture is tested and analyzed. The test results show that MPTCP performs better than traditional TCP under high load. Besides, its performance can be optimized further by adjusting related parameters.

Keywords: MPTCP · Load test · SDN

1 Introduction

With the development of information technology, the online examination system has become an important part of college examinations. However, with the number of students increasing, the response speed of servers becomes much slower, and the examination system is overwhelmed by high load. These problems can be solved with the emergence of MPTCP. MPTCP is a new type of multipath transmission protocol that bridges the gap between multipath networks and single path transmission. It can be seen as an extension of the conventional TCP protocol, providing the ability for both parties to transmit data over multiple paths simultaneously and allowing for the use of multiple paths to transmit a single stream of data between two terminal hosts. The original idea of designing MPTCP is to use plural links in end-to-end communication, so as to increase

W. Li and D. Tang (Eds.): MOBILWARE 2020, LNICST 331, pp. 57–68, 2020.
https://doi.org/10.1007/978-3-030-62205-3_5

the transmission bandwidth, make full use of network resources and improve fault redundancy. SDN separates the control plane and the forwarding plane to improve key features such as system flexibility and scalability, which is the development trend of the future network. SDN network simulation is widely used in networks. For example, Mininet gained popularity for allowing Linux applications to run on emulated networks. This paper designs an MPTCP load test framework under high load performance in SDN environment that is used to test performance of the server and client in the network. At the same time, this paper provides a network framework that uses Mininet to simulate a common Web application and considers multi-threaded and multi-cycle testing. It also analyzes the performance of multipath transmission under this framework. Besides, the results of the experiment are analyzed in depth and the parameters are tuned to make the framework take full advantage of the performance of MPTCP.

The main contributions of this paper:

(1) The performance difference between MPTCP and TCP under high load is compared, and the results are analyzed.

(2) A common Web application network architecture is simulated in the SDN environment, and the multi-path transmission performance under this architecture is analyzed.

The other parts of this paper are structured as follows: The second section introduces the work of this paper and MPTCP. The third section introduces related work. The fourth section describes the test framework and environment for this paper. The fifth section analyzes the experimental results. The sixth section summarizes the paper and introduces future research directions.

2   Background

Standard TCP communication uses a pair of IP addresses to transfer ordered data packets between two communicating parties. Therefore, there is a limit to using one interface, even though multiple interfaces are available at each end of the TCP connection. While MPTCP can use multiple interfaces to establish sub-connection paths between peers at the same time. By making use of all available interfaces at both ends of the communication, MPTCP aims to increase the network's resilience to interface failures (unavailability) and increase throughput. The MPTCP path is defined by two parts, the client IP and the server IP address. The subflow in MPTCP is a single-path standard TCP in which the component obtains fragments from a packet scheduler sent to the receiver. MPTCP is implemented at the transport layer and is supported by the same sockets used for application layer transparency in standard TCP. Each subflow uses standard TCP headers, which is transparent to the network layer.

Table 1 is the traditional TCP protocol and the multipath MPTCP protocol. It can be seen that MPTCP is built on the TCP subflow.

The MPTCP layer is located below the application layer and above the TCP layer in the protocol stack. It provides a standard TCP interface for the application layer to hide multipath, and it needs to manage multiple TCP subflows. The

Table 1. TCP protocol and MPTCP protocol comparison.

Application layer	Application layer		
TCP	MPTCP		
	Subflow 1 (TCP)	Subflow 1 (TCP)	Subflow N (TCP)
Network layer	Network layer		

MPTCP layer has the functions of path management, data packet scheduling, subflow interface, and congestion control.

Load test refers to different network environments, such as LAN, WAN, ATM or their combination. Test traffic is generated by one or more network interfaces of the test equipment. Through the device or network under test, certain indicators of the network or device Tests are performed, mainly including throughput, latency, and frame loss. The premise of all this is the generation of data packets and data streams. For traditional networks, the transport layer load test is mostly targeted at TCP and UDP.

The general method of load testing is to gradually increase the system load, examine the performance change of the system in an overload environment, and find the maximum load that the system can bear without affecting other performance indicators of the system. The load test is performed before the user understands the system performance, response time, and processing power, thereby achieving the purpose of forecasting in advance. It can identify problems through system performance characteristics or behaviors to help improve system performance.

This paper is aimed at the multipath transmission protocol MPTCP. JMeter is used to load test the server under the high-load MPTCP environment.

3   Related Work

With the widespread use of Web applications, Web performance issues have begun to plague users. For example, when a Web page is opened, it often fails to display normally for a long time or even disconnects. Due to people's increasing demand, the network bandwidth cannot meet the application requirements. The way to solve the problem is that designers increase the link bandwidth. In addition to it increasing the link bandwidth by aggregating the bandwidth of multiple physical links is also worked. If the network bandwidth resources of different links can be integrated and used, the utilization of network resources will be increased, and this will also bring higher throughput and better redundancy to the network.

Many researchers have proposed various methods, such as Reliable Multiplexing Transport Protocol, Parallel TCP [1,2] MPTCP [3] (Multipath TCP), and CMT-SCTP [4,5] (Concurrent Multipath Transfer-Stream Control Transmission Protocol). The current MPTCP and CMT-SCTP multipath transmission methods are relatively mature and perfect, but before large-scale deployment and implementation of these methods, a large number of tests still need to be performed to observe whether they can obtain better performance in the existing network structure framework. MPTCP performance testing is very vital for the IETF standardization process. In this paper, the performance of MPTCP under high load is tested and analyzed.

MPTCP has the functions of path management, packet scheduling, sub-flow interface and congestion control. Researchers perform MPTCP performance tests from these aspects. Jinsung Lee et al. [6] considered the MPTCP neutron flow. The slow start (SS) and congestion avoidance (CA) stages accurately perform MPTCP performance analysis, and simulate a real MPTCP network in NS-3. The test results show that the method can accurately predict MPTCP throughput. Vivek Adarsh et al. [7] performed performance tests on MPTCP on heterogeneous subflow paths, focusing on the performance of MPTCP on paths with different characteristics, especially delay and loss rates. Experimental results show that it is difficult to implement MPTCP by using heterogeneous sub-paths. All sub-paths of MPTCP need to be close to the same network conditions in order to make full use of its potential. Yeonsup Lim et al. [8] The experimental results show that the use of the default path scheduler will reduce performance when there are path differences, and the paper proposes a new path scheduling method. The result is better than the existing scheduler. Xavier Corbillon et al. [9] measured the multiple transmissions of 100 MB files from the server to client by deploying MPTCP client and Web server, recording the time of data packet transmission path, and transmission on the network the time of the data packet and the time of the client receiving the data packet were analyzed on the MPTCP network. Feng Zhou et al. [10] deployed the MPTCP protocol to Linux and calculated the send and receive buffer sizes required by MPTCP in the actual Internet test platform NORNET, and tested the network by adjusting the buffer size. The experimental results show that MPTCP can increase payload throughput. Lucas Chaufournier et al. [11] deployed MPTCP in a Linux server and performed performance tests in a data center network. The performance of MPTCP under different congestion control algorithms was tested and compared with TCP. The comparison shows that MPTCP is feasible in the data center network. Slawomir Przylucki et al. [12] used multipath to study a multipath video real-time monitoring system based on an adaptive streaming mechanism. Its transmission network consists of WIFI and LTE units, and it is applied to the operation of a video surveillance system. Jiawei Huang et al. [13] used NS2 simulation test analysis to adaptively adjust the number of sub-flows through real-time network state and transfer the traffic from the congested path to reduce the delay. Yannis Thomas et al. [14] proposed a normalized multipath congestion control algorithm to achieve TCP-friendliness, and experimental evaluation using htsim simulator and real Linux proved that the method can speed up throughput.

At the same time, some researchers have applied MPTCP to the actual environment, studied the performance of MPTCP, and improved the performance of MPTCP from different angles. Karl-Johan Grinnemo et al. [15] used MPTCP to reduce latency and improve the quality of service based on cloud applications. By researching three applications, namely Netflix, Google Maps and Google Docs, they represent typical applications that generate high-intensity, medium-intensity and low-intensity traffic. The results show that MPTCP can significantly reduce the latency of cloud applications, especially for applications such as Netflix and Google Maps. Tongguang Zhang et al. [16] applied MPTCP to an ad hoc network composed of drones or mobile devices. Run MPTCP on drones or MSDs. By improving the MPTCP sub-path establishment algorithm, it has a good performance in improving data throughput. Yuqing Qiu et al. [17] applied MPTCP to the migration of LXC containers. Because the container migration process needs to go through a WAN, congestion or network failure may occur. Therefore, MPTCP protocol is used to solve this problem and improve the flexibility of the migration process, reducing migration time.

Combining MPTCP with SDN is also a good method, which can take advantage of network resources and reduce the occurrence of network congestion. Pengyuan Du et al. [18] studied the performance of MPTCP on LEO satellite networks supporting SDN, and designed an SDN controller that identifies MPTCP substreams attached to the same MPTCP session and splits them into Intersecting paths. The SDN architecture centralizes routing logic, so the system is more scalable and minimizes onboard processing. Simulation results verify the effectiveness of the framework. Behnaz Arzani et al. [19] discussed the effect of initial sub-path selection on performance. And empirical data is used to prove which sub-path to choose to start the MPTCP connection may produce unintuitive results. Subsequently, the numerical results and models confirm the empirical results, which helps to design a better MPTCP scheduler. Navin Kukreja et al. [20] designed an SDN-based MPTCP path manager, implemented an automated test platform for performance evaluation, and analyzed different scheduling algorithms in-depth, and learned how the delay affects the MPTCP protocol. Overall performance. In order to more easily establish the MPTCP simulation environment, Matthieu Coudron et al. [21] implemented MPTCP in the NS3 network simulator, and compared it with the implementation of MPTCP in Linux, confirming that their effects are the same, and that NS3 is used in traffic processing. Aspect has more advantages.

Based on the research on the preliminary work, this paper finds that under high load conditions, there is still a lack of research and analysis of MPTCP performance. In this paper, we conducted a load test and analysis of mptcp in the SDN environment for the performance of mptcp under high load.

4   Experimental Architecture Design

In order to test the performance of MPTCP in a high-load, we simulated a common Web application network framework in the SDN environment for testing.

Figure 1 shows the simulated network architecture in the SDN environment. The Web server is deployed on H2 and the database is deployed on H3. The H1 simulated client is used to access the server and the records are stored in the H3 database. Each host has two IP addresses.

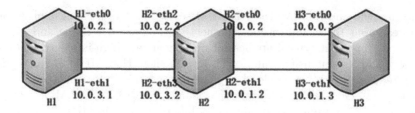

Fig. 1. A common Web application network architecture.

In this section, we will introduce the choice of platform implementation and testing schemes in detail.

Mininet [22]: It is a network emulator connected by some virtual terminal nodes, switches and routers, which can easily create a network supporting SDN. It uses lightweight virtualization technology to make the system comparable to real networks. Mininet uses process-based virtualization and network namespaces to create virtual networks, which are available in the latest Linux kernel. Programs running on Linux can basically run on Mininet, such as Wireshark.

JMeter [23]: The ApacheJMeter^{TM} application is open source software and is a Java application designed to load test functional behavior and measure performance. It was originally designed for testing Web applications, but later expanded to other testing capabilities. Apache JMeter can be used to test the performance of static and dynamic resources, Web dynamic applications. In this paper, it is used to simulate heavy loads on servers and network objects to test their strength or analyze the overall performance under different loads types.

The purpose of the experiment is to study the performance of MPTCP under the common Web application network architecture in the SDN environment. Through the comparison results of MPTCP and TCP in high load test, the performance of MPTCP is analyzed, and the server parameters are adjusted according to the results.

This paper compiled MPTCP on Ubuntu 18.04. The MPTCP scheduler is set as the default scheduler, which makes packet scheduling decisions based on the RTT of the subflow. The congestion control algorithm is CUBIC, which is the default Linux congestion control algorithm.

This paper uses Mininet to simulate the SDN network, the details are as follows:

(1) Under real network conditions, this paper record test cases by visiting the online examination system.

(2) Simulate the network architecture shown in Fig. 1 in the SDN environment. Three hosts H1, H2, H3, deploy servers and databases on H2, H3, and set the link bandwidth to 50M.

(3) Use JMeter to test and compare server access.

5   Analysis

In this experiment, the high load test of MPTCP multi-path transmission and traditional single-path TCP was tested under the experimental architecture, and the multi-path MPTCP and single-path TCP transmission throughput were compared. Observed and analyzed the performance changes of MPTCP and traditional TCP under different loads.

In the throughput test, this paper fixed the number of requests, by reducing the thread startup time, the number of concurrent requests per unit time was increased to simulate the increase in load. In the test experiment, 4000 threads were fixed, and each thread initiated 20 requests. Figure 2 (a) to Fig. 2 (g) shows the actual throughput changes of single-path and multipath MPTCP with a thread start time of 160 s, 150 s, 140 s, 130 s, 120 s, 110 s and 100 s, respectively. Increasing experimental load by continuously reducing startup time. As can be seen from Fig. 2, the throughput of multipath MPTCP is significantly higher than that of traditional single-path TCP under each different loads. As the test load continues to increase, the throughput of multipath MPTCP also increases, and the throughput increases significantly. All MPTCP requests can be completed almost immediately after the thread startup time is over. From the minimum test load to the maximum test load, the throughput has increased by 50%, which has been greatly improved. The traditional single-path TCP transmission throughput also increases with increasing load, but the growth rate is not obvious, and the problem of erroneous requests appears, causing some requests to fail to respond normally. TCP takes longer than the startup time to complete all requests. From the minimum test load to the maximum test load, the throughput increased by only 16%. Figure 3 shows the throughput between hosts under different loads and protocols.

With increasing test load, traditional single-path TCP and multipath MPTCP show different results. Figure 4 shows the change in the number of error requests for traditional single-path TCP under increased load. (Multipath MPTCP increases with parallel requests, and no error requests occur, so the growth of single-path TCP's error requests is plotted separately in Fig. 4). The horizontal axis is the test load, and the vertical axis is the percentage of error requests. With the increase of test load, the throughput of traditional single-path TCP has increased slightly, but generally, it cannot meet the demand, resulting in the appearance of erroneous requests. As the number of wrong requests increases, the server needs extra time to process the wrong requests. As a result, the time for the server to respond to the wrong requests also increases, resulting in an increase in the total running time of the experiment. This is also the reason why the throughput increases but the total running time of the experiment also increases. Figure 5 shows the comparison of the total running time of traditional single-path TCP and multipath MPTCP experiments under different loads. The horizontal axis is the test load, and the vertical axis is the experimental running time. Multipath MPTCP can steadily increase throughput under increasing load without error requests. Because the server only needs to process normal requests,

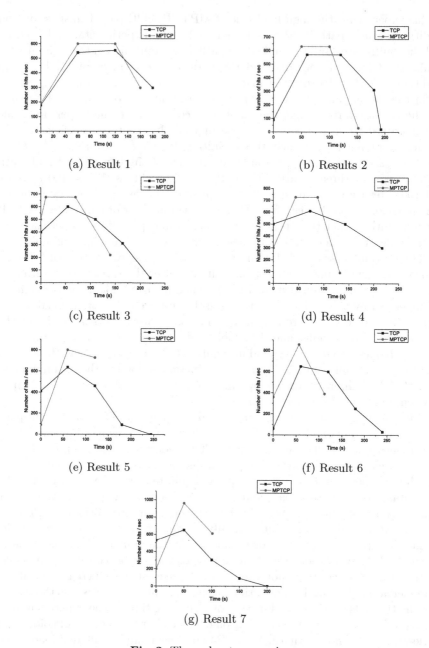

(a) Result 1

(b) Results 2

(c) Result 3

(d) Result 4

(e) Result 5

(f) Result 6

(g) Result 7

Fig. 2. Throughput comparison.

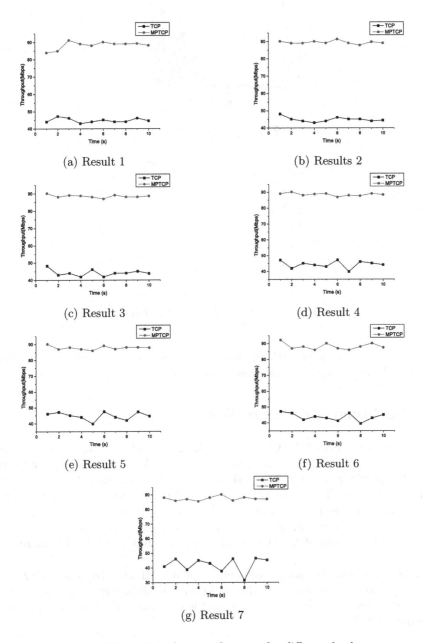

Fig. 3. Throughput between hosts under different loads.

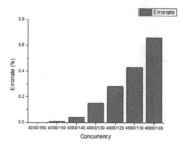

Fig. 4. TCP error rate.

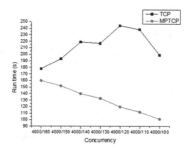

Fig. 5. Comparison of experiment running time.

the throughput increases with the increase of test load, and the experimental run time decreases with the increase of test load.

6   Conclusion and Future Work

This paper introduces MPTCP, uses the Linux kernel to compile MPTCP to implement MPTCP deployment, builds a common Web network framework in the SDN environment, tests the performance of MPTCP under high load and compares it with TCP. Through experimental results, we can see that under low or no load, the performance difference between multi-path MPTCP and traditional TCP is not much different. At the maximum load tested in this paper, the throughput of MPTCP is compared to traditional TCP has increased by 45%.

In future work, this paper considers applying MPTCP to data center networks, spatial information networks, and even combining with SDN, so that it can have better application scenarios, and is committed to improving the performance of MPTCP.

Acknowledgments. The manuscript was supported in part by the National Key Research and Development Program of China under Grant No. 2018YFB1800303 and the Science and Technology Planning Project of Jilin Province under Grant No. 20180414024GH.

References

1. Hacker, T.J., Noble, B.D., Athey, B.D.: Improving throughput and maintaining fairness using parallel TCP. In: IEEE INFOCOM 2004. IEEE, vol. 4, pp. 2480–2489 (2004)
2. Altman, E., Barman, D., Tuffin, B., et al.: Parallel TCP Sockets: Simple Model, Throughput and Validation. In: INFOCOM 2006, pp. 1–12 (2006)
3. Wikipedia. http://en.wikipedia.org/
4. Eklund, J., Grinnemo, K.J., Brunstrom, A.: Using multiple paths in SCTP to reduce latency for signaling traffic. Comput. Commun. **129**, 184–196 (2018)
5. Lai, W.K., Jhan, J.J., Li, J.W.: A cross-layer SCTP scheme with redundant detection for real-time transmissions in IEEE 80211 Wireless Networks. IEEE Access **7**, 114086–114101 (2019)
6. Lee, J., Im, Y., Lee, J.: Modeling MPTCP performance. IEEE Commun. Lett. **23**(4), 616–619 (2019)
7. Adarsh, V., Schmitt, P., Belding, E.: MPTCP Performance over Heterogenous Subpaths. In: 2019 28th International Conference on Computer Communication and Networks (ICCCN). IEEE, pp. 1–9 (2019)
8. Lim, Y., Nahum, E.M., Towsley, D., et al.: ECF: An MPTCP path scheduler to manage heterogeneous paths. In: Proceedings of the 13th International Conference on emerging Networking EXperiments and Technologies, pp. 147–159 (2017)
9. Corbillon, X., Aparicio-Pardo, R., Kuhn, N., et al.: Cross-layer scheduler for video streaming over MPTCP. In: Proceedings of the 7th International Conference on Multimedia Systems, pp. 1–12 (2016)
10. Zhou, F., Dreibholz, T., Zhou, X., et al.: The performance impact of buffer sizes for multi-path TCP in internet setups. In: 2017 IEEE 31st International Conference on Advanced Information Networking and Applications (AINA), pp. 9–16. IEEE (2017)
11. Chaufournier, L., Ali-Eldin, A., Sharma, P., et al.: Performance evaluation of Multi-Path TCP for data center and cloud workloads. In: Proceedings of the ACM/SPEC International Conference on Performance Engineering 2019, pp. 13–24 (2019)
12. Przylucki, S., Czerwinski, D., Sierszen, A.: QoE-oriented fairness control for DASH systems based on the hierarchical structure of SVC streams. In: Gaj, P., Kwiecień, A., Stera, P. (eds.) CN 2016. CCIS, vol. 608, pp. 180–191. Springer, Cham (2016). https://doi.org/10.1007/978-3-319-39207-3_16
13. Huang, J., Li, W., Li, Q., et al.: Tuning high flow concurrency for MPTCP in data center networks. J. Cloud Comput. **9**(1), 1–15 (2020)
14. Thomas, Y., Karaliopoulos, M., Xylomenos, G., et al.: Low latency friendliness for multipath TCP. IEEE/ACM Trans. Netw. **28**(1), 248–261 (2020)
15. Hurtig, P., Grinnemo, K.J., Brunstrom, A., et al.: Low-latency scheduling in MPTCP. IEEE/ACM Trans. Netw. **27**(1), 302–315 (2018)
16. Zhang, T., Zhao, S., Ren, B., et al.: Performance enhancement of multipath TCP in mobile Ad Hoc networks. In: 2017 IEEE 25th International Conference on Network Protocols (ICNP), pp. 1–2. IEEE (2017)
17. Qiu, Y., Lung, C.H., Ajila, S., et al.: LXC container migration in cloudlets under multipath TCP. In: 2017 IEEE 41st Annual Computer Software and Applications Conference (COMPSAC), vol. 2, pp. 31–36. IEEE (2017)
18. Du, P., Nazari, S., Mena, J., et al.: Multipath TCP in SDN-enabled LEO satellite networks. In: MILCOM 2016–2016 IEEE Military Communications Conference, pp. 354–359. IEEE (2016)

19. Arzani, B., Gurney, A., Cheng, S., et al.: Deconstructing MPTCP performance. In: 2014 IEEE 22nd International Conference on Network Protocols, pp. 269–274. IEEE (2014)
20. Kukreja, N., Maier, G., Alvizu, R., et al.: SDN based automated testbed for evaluating multipath TCP. In: 2016 IEEE International Conference on Communications Workshops (ICC), pp. 718–723. IEEE (2016)
21. Coudron, M., Secci, S.: An implementation of multipath TCP in ns3. Comput. Netw. **116**, 1–11 (2017)
22. Mininet. http://mininet.org/
23. JMeter. http://jmeter.apache.org/

Performance Analysis of QUIC-UDP Protocol Under High Load

Lin Qi[1,2], Zhihong Qiao[1,2], Aowei Zhang[1,2], Hui Qi[1,2(✉)], Weiwu Ren[1,2], Xiaoqiang Di[1,2,3], and Rui Wang[1,2]

[1] School of Computer Science and Technology, Changchun University of Science and Technology, Changchun, China
qihui@cust.edu.cn
[2] Jilin Key Laboratory of Network and Information Security, Changchun University of Science and Technology, Changchun, China
[3] Information Center, Changchun University of Science and Technology, Changchun 130022, China

Abstract. The QUIC protocol is currently recognized as a network protocol that is expected to replace TCP. It is characterized by encryption, multiplexing, and low latency. It was proposed by Google in 2013 and aims to improve the transmission performance of HTTPS traffic and achieve rapid deployment and continuous development of transmission mechanisms. QUIC has gone through many versions since its release, and previous researchers have compared the transmission performance of QUIC and TCP. In this paper, the pressure test tool vegeta is modified, and the modified vegeta is used to test the TCP and QUIC protocols in a high load environment and collect the results to evaluate the performance of different protocols. Experiments show that under high load network conditions, the TCP protocol has better performance than the QUIC protocol; IQUIC (IETF QUIC) performs better than GQUIC (Google QUIC) at lower attack frequencies; as the attack frequency increases, IQUIC Performance decreases faster than GQUIC performance.

Keywords: Load test · QUIC · TCP

1 Introduction

1.1 Development Status of QUIC

TCP has been the dominant transport protocol on the Internet for the last decade but several factors could reduce it in the coming years. With the use of TCP, it exposed some shortcomings. First, the Internet contains a variety of middle boxes that make some assumptions on specific TCP variants. Second, there are many in-kernel implementations of TCP and any change requires both engineering effort and negotiations within the IETF.

QUIC is a protocol that is expected to replace TCP. QUIC protocol is a UDP-based transport layer protocol proposed by Google in 2013, and its design goal

© ICST Institute for Computer Sciences, Social Informatics and Telecommunications Engineering 2020
Published by Springer Nature Switzerland AG 2020. All Rights Reserved
W. Li and D. Tang (Eds.): MOBILWARE 2020, LNICST 331, pp. 69–77, 2020.
https://doi.org/10.1007/978-3-030-62205-3_6

is to make the Internet faster and more secure [15–18]. QUIC incorporates the features of protocols including TCP, TLS, HTTP/2, etc., but is based on UDP transmission. One of the main goals of QUIC is to reduce the connection delay. When the client connects to the server for the first time, QUIC only needs 1 RTT (round trip time) delay to establish a reliable and secure connection. Compared to TCP + TLS, it requires 1–3 RTTs, which is faster. After that, the client can cache the encrypted authentication information locally, and can achieve a 0-RTT connection establishment delay when establishing a connection with the server again. QUIC also multiplexes the multiplexing function of HTTP/2 protocol at the same time, because QUIC is based on UDP, it avoids the head-of-line blocking problem of HTTP/2. Because QUIC is based on UDP and runs in the user domain instead of the system kernel, the QUIC protocol can be quickly updated and deployed, thus well solving the difficulties of TCP protocol deployment and update [1].

QUIC has gone through many versions since its inception [19]. With the continuous optimization of QUIC, some new versions of QUIC gradually no longer support Google Chrome. The latest version that supports Google is 0.10, while the version that does not support Googles QUIC is the latest version 0.14. This paper distinguishes GQUIC (supporting Googles version 0.10 QUIC) and IQUIC (IETF 0.14 version of Quic), and conducts experimental analysis separately.

1.2 Vegeta

Stress testing the server is a method of testing network performance. This test can find the performance bottleneck of the server by simulating a large number of requests, so as to make corresponding measures and response capabilities when encountering a large number of requests, and provide experimental basis and theoretical support for future work. This paper selects vegeta as a stress testing tool.

Vegeta is a multifunctional HTTP load test tool written in Go language, which provides command line tools and a development library. Vegeta can initiate requests of different frequencies to a certain website according to users' needs and collect experimental results, such as delay, throughput, etc., and then analyze server performance based on the collected results. Every request under high pressure is like an attack. The original Vegeta can only launch attacks against servers that support the TCP protocol. This paper transforms vegeta and follows the original Vegeta attack method. By changing the underlying protocol called when the request is initiated, the modified vegeta supports QUIC. The modified vegeta code can be downloaded by visiting [21]. In this paper, vegeta is used to test TCP, and the modified vegeta is used to test GQUIC and IQUIC and then observe the performance of these protocols under the same environment and different degrees of pressure.

The rest of the paper is structured as follows: Section 2 reviews related work; Section 3 describes the experiment; Section 4 conclusions, gives the evaluation results and future work.

2   Related Work

The safe and reliable transmission of data has always been a topic of great concern. Nowadays, the demand for networks is constantly increasing. It is very important to be able to transmit data without sacrificing security and reliability. TCP and QUIC are widely used protocols in data transmission and have received much attention in the industry. Since the QUIC protocol was proposed, many researchers have compared the performance of QUIC and TCP, and have related research in terms of throughput and fairness. Because the development of the QUIC protocol is so rapid, the research on the QUIC protocol in different scenarios has become extremely important. In order to study the performance of QUIC in different environments, [3–6,9] configured different network environments (bandwidth, delay, loss) to test the page load time which based on the QUIC protocol. Studies have shown that QUIC has low bandwidth and high latency And high loss network conditions show better performance. Yajun Yu et al. [2] evaluated the performance and fairness between QUIC and TCP. Studies have shown that when QUIC competes with TCP for bandwidth resources, it is affected by data loss rate and path buffer size. When the buffer is small, QUIC shows better performance and can obtain greater throughput; conversely, when the lossless network or larger buffer, QUIC is lower than the throughput obtained by TCP.

Due to the high latency and high loss characteristics of the space network, the research on the QUIC protocol under the space network is also worthy of attention. [11,12,20] According to the improvement of the ground network, the performance of the QUIC under the space network was evaluated. The results show that QUIC can reduce the overall page retrieval time of the spatial network. In the case of extended propagation and high packet loss rate, the performance of QUIC is better than TCP. This also shows the ability and future trend of QUIC protocol to solve space network problems. Sevket Arisu et al. [7] measured the transmission performance of QUIC in media streaming. The results show that when the network is more congested, QUIC can start media streaming better and provide better service and search experience for streaming media. There are other studies, for example [10] evaluated QUIC for the first time in a field scene, and [8] analyzed the performance differences of multiple versions of QUIC in different environments on the transport layer and application layer. In real time communications, such as voice and video conferencing, [14] measures packet loss, delay, and jitter, and proposes a performance measurement method that helps provide better QoE.

In addition to the transmission performance of the QUIC protocol, security and privacy are also guaranteed. QUIC combines the key negotiation function of TLS1.3 to encrypt all connections to prevent the middle box from tampering with the packet information. However, it hinders the future of QUIC protocol Development [13]. QUIC also has congestion control and loss recovery functions similar to TCP, and also provides rich signaling functions. In short, the advantages of QUIC protocol in low bandwidth, high latency and high loss areattributed to the characteristics of QUIC, which can shorten the loading time of the page. Thanks to UDP-based stream multiplexing.

In summary, many studies have evaluated the performance differences of QUIC under different scenarios and different network conditions. Comparing the performance of QUIC and TCP, the QUIC protocol shows better performance in poor network environments. Due to the different network conditions in different scenarios (the bandwidth, delay and packet loss rate are different), the performance of the QUIC protocol will also fluctuate, and the throughput and bandwidth utilization will be greatly affected. Therefore, QUIC Whether the agreement can occupy an important position in the future needs to be continuously improved. There are also some studies to evaluate the fairness and resource utilization between QUIC and TCP. In this paper, we use the vegeta test tool to stress test the QUIC protocol, compare the network performance changes when different protocols are subjected to a large number of attacks, and evaluate the performance of different protocols. Experiments show that the performance of QUIC is lower than that of TCP.

3   Experiment

The experiment of this paper is to build a simulation environment through Ubuntu 18.04, in which the Ubuntu system is configured with 6G memory and a 4-core processor. We through the transformed vegeta, call the client of QUIC and TCP to initiate a request to the QUIC and TCP server. The page size requested in the experiment is 11000 byte. The relevant source code of this paper is on Github[1]. The experiment analyzes the performance of each protocol by continuously increasing the number of attacks per second, observing the average delay, throughput, and success rate under different protocols.

Without using vegeta and initiating only one request, the single delay of TCP, GQUIC and IQUIC and the number of data packets are shown in Table 1. The result is counted by Wireshark (a network packet analysis software). Although the same page is requested, because of using the different protocols, the delay and the total number of packets transmitted are not the same. As can be seen from the table, when requesting the experiment page, the number of data packets that TCP needs to transmit is smaller than GQUIC and IQUIC and IQUIC is slightly higher than GQUIC. In terms of latency, GQUIC and IQUIC are inferior to TCP, and IQUIC has obvious advantages over GQUIC.

Through a lot of experiments, this paper finally collected the experimental results of the stress test frequency range of 50–1000 times per second, and divided these results into three categories according to the performance of each protocol: low-frequency band, medium-frequency band and High-frequency band. The results of the experimental data collected in the low-frequency band are shown in Table 2. It can be seen that the TCP protocol is superior to the QUIC protocol in terms of average delay, throughput, and success rate at low-frequencies of 50–200 attacks per second; QUIC in terms of delay The protocol is 7–8 times

---

[1] https://github.com/qilin7070/quictest.git

Table 1. Single delay and number of packets for different protocols under no pressure.

Protocol	Single delay	Number of packet
TCP	0.0014	26
GQUIC	0.05	40
IQUIC	0.0076	49

Table 2. Average delay, effective throughput and success rate of different protocols under low-frequency attacks.

50 attacks/s	Protocol	Average delay (ms)	Throughput (Mbps)	Success rate (percent)
	TCP	1.05	4.20	100
	GQUIC	7.94	4.20	100
	IQUIC	7.46	4.20	100
100 attacks/s	Protocol	Average delay (ms)	Throughput (Mbps)	Success rate (percent)
	TCP	1.25	8.40	100
	GQUIC	8.40	8.38	99.77
	IQUIC	7.48	8.398	99.98
150 attacks/s	Protocol	Average delay (ms)	Throughput (Mbps)	Success rate (percent)
	TCP	1.26	12.60	100
	GQUIC	8.22	12.57	99.78
	IQUIC	7.59	12.58	99.82
200 attacks/s	Protocol	Average delay (ms)	Throughput (Mbps)	Success rate (percent)
	TCP	0.91	16.80	100
	GQUIC	11.35	16.72	99.55
	IQUIC	10.09	16.71	99.46

that of the TCP protocol, and IQUIC is slightly better than GQUIC in terms of latency. The results of the experimental data collected in the medium-frequency band are shown in Table 3. It can be seen that the TCP protocol is still better than the QUIC protocol in terms of average delay, throughput, and success rate at an intermediate frequency of 250–400 attacks per second, and remains very stable status, but the performance of the QUIC protocol gradually decreases. And it can be seen that IQUIC performance drops faster than GQUIC, so that it starts to be inferior to GQUIC in terms of average delay, throughput, and success rate. The results of the experimental data collected in the high-frequency band range are shown in Table 4. At this time, IQUIC has been unable to collect data normally and frequently reports errors. Therefore, the experimental results of IQUIC have not been added to the table. When the attack frequency is 600–1000 times per second, the performance of the GQUIC protocol drops sharply. This conclusion can be seen from the throughput and success rate of the GQUIC. Although the average GQUIC delay in this band is very low, it does not mean that GQUIC is performing well, because the average delay at this time is the result of a large number of error requests.

The average delay line chart of the experimental results (see Fig. 1). The horizontal axis is the attack frequency and the vertical axis is the average delay time. Because the success rate of the high-frequency band QUIC protocol drops

Table 3. Average delay, effective throughput and success rate of different protocols under medium-frequency attacks.

250 attacks/s	Protocol	Average delay (ms)	Throughput (Mbps)	Success rate (percent)
	TCP	0.87	21.00	100
	GQUIC	10.78	20.98	99.89
	IQUIC	13.95	20.97	99.84
300 attacks/s	Protocol	Average delay (ms)	Throughput (Mbps)	Success rate (percent)
	TCP	0.81	25.20	100
	GQUIC	11.95	25.17	99.87
	IQUIC	19.60	25.06	99.43
350 attacks/s	Protocol	Average delay (ms)	Throughput (Mbps)	Success rate (percent)
	TCP	0.87	29.40	100
	GQUIC	18.56	25.37	99.89
	IQUIC	26.48	25.34	99.37
400 attacks/s	Protocol	Average delay (ms)	Throughput (Mbps)	Success rate (percent)
	TCP	0.95	33.60	100
	GQUIC	28.59	33.49	99.66
	IQUIC	35.06	33.29	99.09

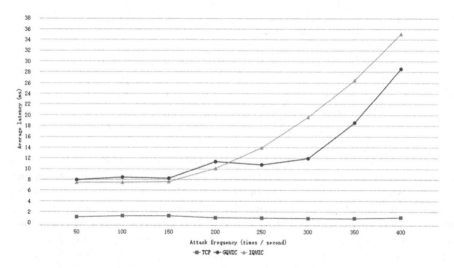

Fig. 1. The average latency of TCP, GQUIC, and IQUIC under different frequency attacks.

sharply, the average delay obtained at this time is the average delay in the case of failure, which has no practical significance, so the line chart only includes the experimental results of low-frequency band and intermediate frequency. It can be seen from the figure that when the attack frequency is less than 150 times per second, the average delay of IQUIC and GQUIC both remain relatively stable, and the average delay of IQUIC is slightly better than GQUIC. When the attack frequency is greater than 150 times per second, the average delay of IQUIC and GQUIC started to increase. The average delay of IQUIC increased significantly

Table 4. Average delay, effective throughput and success rate of different protocols under high-frequency attacks.

600 attacks/s	Protocol	Average delay (ms)	Throughput (Mbps)	Success rate (percent)
	TCP	0.90	50.40	100
	GQUIC	9901	18.07	35.86
800 attacks/s	Protocol	Average delay (ms)	Throughput (Mbps)	Success rate (percent)
	TCP	0.88	67.20	100
	GQUIC	12018	9.07	13.49
1000 attacks/s	Protocol	Average delay (ms)	Throughput (Mbps)	Success rate (percent)
	TCP	0.87	84.00	100
	GQUIC	11895	4.84	5.76

faster than GQUIC and soon exceeded GQUIC, the average delay of GQUIC was more stable. The average delay of the TCP protocol remains very low and stable throughout.

4   Conclusion

Through the pressure test experiments of different protocols by the vegeta test tool, we can see that the TCP protocol is stable and far superior to the QUIC protocol. As an optimized QUIC protocol, IQUIC has better performance under no pressure and low pressure. As the pressure increases, the performance of GQUIC is more stable than that of IQUIC. In theory, because the QUIC protocol is better than TCP in terms of handshake, the QUIC protocol should be superior to TCP in terms of latency. This experimental result is different from the original assumption. In future work, the author will do more indepth research on TCP and QUIC protocols, and explore the reasons leading to this experimental result.

Acknowledgement. The manuscript was supported in part by the National Key Research and Development Program of China under Grant No. 2018YFB1800303 and the Science and Technology Planning Project of Jilin Province under Grant No. 20200401105GX.

References

1. Cui, Y., Li, T., Liu, C., et al.: Innovating transport with QUIC: design approaches and research challenges. IEEE Internet Comput. **21**(2), 72–76 (2017)
2. Yu Y, Xu M, Yang Y.: When QUIC meets TCP: an experimental study. In: 36th International Performance Computing and Communications Conference (IPCCC), pp. 1–8. IEEE (2018)
3. Biswal P, Gnawali O.: Does QUIC make the web faster?. In: 2016 IEEE Global Communications Conference (GLOBECOM), pp. 1–6. IEEE (2017)
4. Carlucci G, Cicco L D, Mascolo S.: HTTP over UDP: an experimental investigation of QUIC. In: Proceedings of the 30th Annual ACM Symposium on Applied Computing, pp. 609–614. ACM (2015)

5. Wang, P., Bianco, C., Riihijärvi, J., Petrova, M.: Implementation and performance evaluation of the QUIC protocol in Linux kernel. In: Proceedings of the 21st ACM International Conference on Modeling, Analysis and Simulation of Wireless and Mobile Systems, pp. 227–234. ACM (2018)
6. Nepomuceno, K., de Oliveira, I.N., Aschoff, R.R., et al.: QUIC and TCP: a performance evaluation. In: 2018 IEEE Symposium on Computers and Communications (ISCC), pp. 00045–00051. IEEE (2018)
7. Arisu, S., Begen, A.: Quickly starting media streams using QUIC. In: Proceedings of the 23rd Packet Video Workshop, pp. 1–6. ACM (2018)
8. Kakhki, A., Jero, S., Choffnes, D., Nita-Rotaru, C., Mislove, A: Taking a long look at QUIC: an approach for rigorous evaluation of rapidly evolving transport protocols. In: Proceedings of the 2017 Internet Measurement Conference, pp. 290–303. ACM (2017)
9. Papastergiou, G., Fairhurst, G., Ros, D., et al.: De-ossifying the Internet transport layer: a survey and future perspectives. IEEE Commun. Surv. Tutorials **19**(1), 619–639 (2017)
10. Rüth, J., Poese, I., Dietzel, C., Hohlfeld, O.: A first look at QUIC in the wild. In: Beverly, R., Smaragdakis, G., Feldmann, A. (eds.) PAM 2018. LNCS, vol. 10771, pp. 255–268. Springer, Cham (2018). https://doi.org/10.1007/978-3-319-76481-8_19
11. Zhang, H., Wang, T., Tu, Y., Zhao, K., Li, W.: How quick Is QUIC in satellite networks. In: Liang, Q., Mu, J., Jia, M., Wang, W., Feng, X., Zhang, B. (eds.) CSPS 2017. LNEE, vol. 463, pp. 387–394. Springer, Singapore (2019). https://doi.org/10.1007/978-981-10-6571-2_47
12. Yang, S., Li, H., Wu, Q.: Performance analysis of QUIC protocol in integrated satellites and terrestrial networks. In: 2018 14th International Wireless Communications and Mobile Computing Conference (IWCMC), pp. 1425–1430. IEEE (2018)
13. Bulgarella, F., Cociglio, M., Fioccola, G., Marchetto, G., Sisto, R.: Performance measurements of QUIC communications. In: Proceedings of the Applied Networking Research Workshop, pp. 8–14. ACM (2019)
14. Jager, T., Schwenk, J., Somorovsky, J.: On the security of TLS 1.3 and QUIC against weaknesses in PKCS 1 v1. 5 encryption. In: Proceedings of the 22nd ACM SIGSAC Conference on Computer and Communications Security, pp. 1185–1196. ACM (2015)
15. Cook, S., Mathieu, B., Truong, P., et al.: QUIC: better for what and for whom? In: 2017 IEEE International Conference on Communications (ICC), pp. 1–6. IEEE (2017)
16. Langley, A., Iyengar, J., Bailey, J., et al.: The QUIC transport protocol: design and internet-scale deployment. In: Proceedings of the Conference of the ACM Special Interest Group on Data Communication, pp. 183–196. ACM (2017)
17. Palmer, M., Krüger, T., Chandrasekaran, B., Feldmann, A.: The QUIC fix for optimal video streaming. In: Proceedings of the Workshop on the Evolution, Performance, and Interoperability of QUIC, pp. 43–49. ACM (2018)
18. Seufert, M., Schatz, R., Wehner, N., Casas, P., Quicker or not?-An empirical analysis of QUIC vs TCP for video streaming QOE provisioning. In: 2019 22nd Conference on Innovation in Clouds, Internet and Networks and Workshops (ICIN), pp. 7–12. IEEE (2019)

19. Casas, P.: Is QUIC becoming the new TCP? On the potential impact of a new protocol on networked multimedia QoE. In: 2019 Eleventh International Conference on Quality of Multimedia Experience (QoMEX), pp. 1–6. IEEE (2019)
20. Lopes, R.H., Franqueira, V.N., Rand, D.: Integration and Evaluation of QUIC and TCP-BBR in longhaul science data transfers. In: EPJ Web of Conferences, vol. 214, p. 08026. EDP Sciences (2019)

A Cross-Domain Secure Deduplication Scheme Based on Threshold Blind Signature

Jinlei Du[1,2], Jide Deng[1,2], Hui Qi[1,2(✉)], Xiaoqiang Di[1,2], and Zhengang Jiang[2]

[1] Jilin Key Laboratory of Network and Information Security, Changchun University of Science and Technology, Changchun, China
[2] School of Computer Science and Technology, Changchun University of Science and Technology, Changchun, China
qihui@cust.edu.cn

Abstract. In the cloud storage environment, client-side deduplication can perform file repetitive detection locally. However, client-side deduplication still faces many security challenges. First, if the file hash value is used as evidence for repetitive detection, the attacker is likely to obtain the entire file information through the hash value of the file. Secondly, in order to protect data privacy, convergence encryption is widely used in the data deduplication scheme. Since the data itself is predictable, convergence encryption is still vulnerable to brute force attacks. In order to solve the above problems, this paper proposes to construct a secure deduplication scheme by using the threshold blind signature method. The generation of the convergence key is coordinated by multiple key servers, ensuring the confidentiality of the convergence key and effectively solving the violent dictionary attack problem. At the same time, since the key center is introduced to centrally manage the keys, the interaction between the key servers is reduced, and the key generation efficiency is improved. In addition, since the key server in this paper can be distributed in multiple independent network domains and interact with the key center through the Internet, the problem of cross-domain deduplication is solved. The experimental results show that the performance of this scheme is greatly improved in terms of system initialization and key generation.

Keywords: Secure deduplication · Encryption · Threshold blind signature · Cross-domain secure deduplication

1 Introduction

Deduplication technology is a special data reduction technology [20,29], which is used to eliminate redundant data and save network bandwidth and storage space in cloud storage systems [12,21]. This technique identifies common data blocks or files, storing only a single instance [26], and duplicate data is replaced with logical pointers [12,24]. Deduplication technology meets the growing demand for storage capacity. Many cloud storage providers, such as Amazon S3, Bitcasa and Microsoft Azure, are using deduplication technology [30] to improve storage efficiency. There are four deduplication strategies, depending on whether deduplication occurs on the client (before upload) or on the server, and whether deduplication occurs at the block or file level. Client-side deduplication is more advantageous than server-side deduplication because it can ensure that multiple uploads of the same content consume only one upload of network bandwidth and storage space.

Data deduplication technology is widely adopted by cloud service providers. The cloud server verifies whether the data uploaded by the user has been stored by random sampling and extraction of hash values. After verification, if the newly uploaded data of the user is the same as the original stored data, the data deduplication is performed [31]. Experimental research shows that data deduplication will save more than half of the storage space, and the deduplication rate will reach 90%–95% [19,33].

Convergent encryption, in which the encryption key is derived from the plaintext, may be a simple and secure solution allowing deduplication. Unfortunately, it was proved unsafe [11]. In addition, a general impossibility result holds stating that classic semantic security is not achievable for schemes implementing plain convergence encryption [13].

Miao et al. proposed a security deduplication scheme based on threshold blind signature [23], which uses n key management nodes to blindly sign H(M) at the same time. The client obtains the encryption key by combining t ($t \leq n$) signatures, thereby solving the single point failure problem and resisting the collusion attack. However, in the initialization process, a large amount of information needs to be exchanged between the key management nodes, and each signature needs to be verified in the process of generating a key, so communication overhead and computational overhead are large. In addition, the solution does not support application scenarios across network domains.

In this paper, we propose a data security deduplication scheme that supports cross-domains. Based on the idea of threshold blind signature, a multi-server-assisted architecture is constructed. The key management nodes are divided into a master key nodes and the multiple sub-key nodes. The digital signature is completed by multiple parties, which improves the difficulty of signature cracking and ensures the security of the key. Communication and computational overhead is reduced by reducing the interaction between key nodes and reducing the number of signatures. In addition, cross-domain scenarios are also supported, and the practical application prospects are greater.

1.1 Contribution of This Article

Our main contributions are summarized as follows:

(1) Support cross-domain application environments. Key nodes can be distributed in separate network domains, and users can still perform deduplication of encrypted data when roaming between network domains. When a user in one domain moves to another domain, the user can recalculate the new key

through the key nodes in the new domain, and perform secure deduplication of the encrypted data.

(2) Reduce the initialization overhead of the key nodes. Miao et al.'s threshold blind signature scheme requires each key node to communicate with other nodes during initialization, and the number of communications is $n(n-1)$. In the scheme of this paper, the master key node interacts with each sub-key node once, the number of communications is n, and each sub-key node does not need to interact with other sub-key nodes.

(3) Reduce the computational overhead of signature verification. In the scheme of Miao et al., the blind signature generated by each key node needs to be verified, and the number of verifications is large, which results in large computational overhead. However, this solution only needs to verify the signature once, which greatly reduces the number of verifications and reduces the computational overhead.

1.2 Organization

The rest of the paper is organized as follows. Section 2 introduces the related work. Section 3 describes the cross-domain problem of threshold blind signature. In the Sect. 4, the system model of the scheme and the goals it achieves are introduced. A detailed description of the scheme can be found in the Sect. 5. The performance evaluation of the scheme is given in the Sect. 6. Finally, we give the conclusion in Sect. 7.

2   Related Work

In order to solve the problem of data security deduplication in cloud storage, researchers have proposed many deduplication schemes [1,3,13,15,16], showing how deduplication is very attractive to reduce the use of storage resources [10]. Most work didn't consider security to be a consideration for deduplication systems. However, recently Harnik et al. [11] have proposed a number of attacks that may lead to data leakage in storage systems where client deduplication is deployed. In order to defend against this attack, Halevi [9] introduced the concept of proof of ownership.

According to the granularity of data, data deduplication is divided into file-level deduplication [5,13,28] and chunk-level (block-level) deduplication [3,6,14,18,35,36]. File-level deduplication was proposed earlier [4], but that technique was subsequently overshadowed by chunk-level deduplication due to the latter's better compression performance [22,37]. The cloud server is honest and curious [32], and it may try to steal users' data information. Therefore, before users upload data to the cloud server, they usually need to encrypt the data to achieve data privacy protection. However, when different users encrypt the same file with their private keys, different ciphertexts will be generated, which is not conducive to the cloud server to de-duplicate the file. Data deduplication based on convergence encryption can well achieve key sharing and is beneficial to deduplication of ciphertext data across users. Therefore, some cloud storage data deduplication methods based on convergence encryption are proposed [3, 6, 8, 15, 16, 34].

Douceur et al. first proposed the Convergent encryption (CE) [7] algorithm, using the hash value of the data as the encryption key, and the same plaintext is encrypted into the same ciphertext. However, the encrypted ciphertext of this scheme relies too much on plaintext information and is vulnerable to offline brute-force attack. Bellare et al. analyzed the security problem of convergence encryption, proposed an abstract Message lock encryption (MLE) scheme [3], and proved the security of the scheme under the random oracle model. Subsequently, they proposed a secure interactive message lock encryption scheme under the standard model [2], and developed a DupLESS system [13] which is mainly consists of clients, cloud storage nodes and a key management node. Since there is only one key management node, there is a single point of failure problem, and once the key management node is compromised, the entire system is broken. Since the DupLESS system was put forward, many scholars have conducted more in-depth research on it and proposed improvements based on it. Miao et al. [23] proposed a multi-server-aided deduplication scheme based on threshold blind signature, which can effectively resist the collusion attack between the cloud server and multiple key servers, and achieve the expected security, but its computational overhead and communication overhead are large during the initialization process. Jan Stanek et al. [27] proposed an enhanced cloud storage security threshold data deduplication scheme, which is based on the original scheme [28] and moves the sensitive data decryption shares and processing of popular state information out of cloud storage. A simpler proof of safety and an easier implementation are given, increasing practicality and increasing efficiency.

3   Cross-Domain Problem of Threshold Blind Signature Scheme

Literature [23] proposed a distributed encryption deduplication scheme based on the idea of threshold blind signature. This scheme is a multi-key server-assisted deduplication architecture, which is mainly composed of clients (users), cloud storage service providers (S-CSP), and multiple key management nodes (K-CSPs), as shown in Fig. 1.

Under this architecture, no key server can obtain the distributed key knowledge among all key servers, which can effectively resist collusion attacks between the cloud server and multiple key servers and solve the problem of single point of failure. However, this solution does not support cross-domain scenarios. As shown in Fig. 2, there are two network domains A and B. Domain A and domain B both have multiple key nodes and users, and generate virtual keys K_a, K_b, respectively. It is assumed that the networks of domain A and domain B cannot communicate with each other, but both domain A and domain B can access the Internet. For example, domain A is a campus network, and domain B is another campus network. When the user of domain A moves to domain B, because the

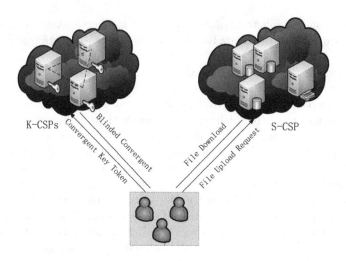

Fig. 1. Architecture of data secure deduplication.

key nodes of the two domains cannot be negotiated, resulting in K_a and K_b being unequal, the data encrypted by K_a and K_b cannot be safely deduplicated. In order to solve the problem of security de-duplication in cross-domain environment, this paper adds a master key node based on the architecture of Fig. 2. As shown in Fig. 3, the master key node is located on the Internet, and the keys of domain A and domain B are allocated by the master key node, so that it is ensured that K_a of domain A and K_b of domain B are equal. In this case, when the user of domain A moves to domain B, the data encrypted by K_a and K_b can be safely deduplicated.

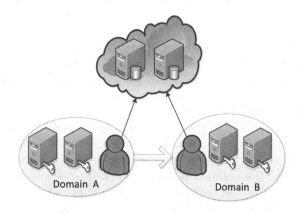

Fig. 2. Cross-domain network topology.

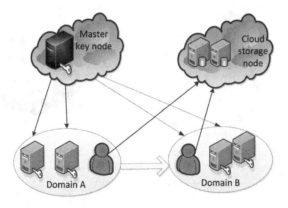

Fig. 3. Supporting cross-domain network topology.

The scheme of this paper introduces the master key node based on the Miao et al scheme [23]. If the master key node is compromised, the entire system will no longer be secure. It appears that there is a single point of failure risk, but since the master key node only communicates with the sub-key node and only distributes the partial key to the sub-key node. After the key distribution is completed, the master key node can be offline and does not receive network requests. Therefore, its security protection is easier than that of the sub-key node, and the possibility of being compromised is also lower. In addition, the scheme of this paper can distribute the sub-key nodes to each network domain, making the key nodes closer to the end users, which can effectively reduce the network communication overhead and shorten the key generation time. It is very suitable for large-scale network environments such as the Internet of Things.

4   System Model

This paper proposes a cross-domain deduplication scheme. Its architecture is shown in Fig. 4. It consists mainly of a master key node, a sub-key node, a client (users) and a cloud storage node. The introduction of each part is as follows.

(1) Master Key Node: The master key node must be secure and trusted. It generates the master key and the public key, exposes the public key, generates part of the private key of each sub-key node, and securely shares it to the sub-key node.

(2) Sub-key Node: There are multiple sub-key nodes, which receive part of the private key generated by the master key node, use it to sign the blind messages of the client, and return the result to the client.

(3) Client (users): The client blinds the message, sends it to the sub-key node, then combines t $(t \leq n)$ blind signatures, obtains the encryption key after unblinding, and then encrypts the data with the encryption key and sends it to the cloud storage node.

(4) Cloud storage node: Stores ciphertext data and safely deduplicates it.

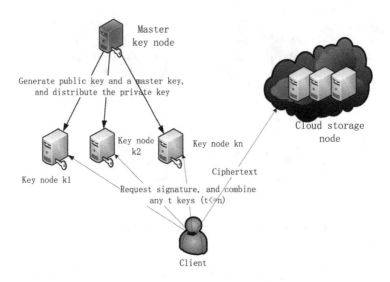

Fig. 4. Data security deduplication architecture.

5   Detailed Plan

In this section, we will introduce this scheme in detail. This scheme adopts threshold blind signature algorithm, which is based on bilinear pairings. Bilinear pairing will be constructed in the following way:

5.1   Bilinear Pairing

Let G_1 be a cyclic addition group generated by P, whose order is prime q; and G_2 be a cyclic multiplication group of the same order q. A bilinear pairing is a map $e : G_1 \times G_1 \rightarrow G_2$ with the following properties:

(1) Bilinear: $e(aP, bQ) = e(P, Q)^{ab}$ for all $P, Q \in G_1$, and $a, b \in Z_q^*$.

(2) Non-degenerate: There exists $P, Q \in G_1$ such that $e(P, Q) \neq 1$.

(3) Computable: There is an efficient algorithms to computed $e(P, Q)$ for all $P, Q \in G_1$.

Based on bilinear mapping, we can get the following definitions.

Define 1: Discrete Logarithms Problem (DLP): Given two group elements P and Q, find an integer n such that Q=nP whenever such an integer exists.

Define 2: Computational Diffe-Hellman problem (CDHP): For $a, b \in Z_q^*$, give P, aP, bP, compute abP.

Define 3: Dicision Diffe-Hellman problem (DDHP): $a, b, c \in Z_q^*$, give P, aP, bP, cP, decide whether $c \equiv ab \bmod q$.

5.2   Detailed Steps

The main steps are as follows: system initialization, key generation, blinding, signature, verification, and encrypted storage.

First, system initialization is performed. The master key node generates the public key and the master key, and publicizes the public key. The n sub-key nodes are numbered $k_1,k_2,...,k_n$, and the $t-1$ degree polynomial is constructed: $f(x)=a_0+a_1x+...+a_{t-1}x^{t-1}$; calculate the partial private key corresponding to each sub-key node: $f(k_1),f(k_2),...,f(k_n)$ and transmit it securely to the sub-key node. The client then blinds the message and sends the blinded message to the sub-key node. The sub-key node signs the message and returns it to the client. The client uploads the ciphertext data to the cloud server. Specific steps are as follows.

System initialization: The master key node selects a cyclic addition group G_1, the generator is p, and the order is prime q; Then select a cyclic multiplication group G_2 of the same order; to generate and a bilinear map e: $G_1 \times G_1 \rightarrow G_2$. The master key node selects an integer $K_M \in Z_q^*$, calculates the system public key

$$Q = K_M P \tag{1}$$

and selects the following strong collision-free hash function $H_1:\{0,1\}^* \rightarrow G_1$, $H_2:\{0,1\}^* \rightarrow Z_q^*$; The master key node then saves K_M as the system private key and exposes the parameters $\{G_1,G_2,e,q,P,Q,H_1,H_2 \}$.

Key generation: The n sub-key nodes are numbered $k_1,k_2,...,k_n$, and a random $t-1$ degree polynomial,

$$f(x) = a_0 + a_1 x + ... + a_{t-1}x^{t-1} \tag{2}$$

is constructed, where $t \leq n$. Let $f(0)=a_0=K_M$, calculate partial private keys $f(k_1),f(k_2),...,f(k_n)$ and Lagrange polynomials $l(k_1),l(k_2),...,l(k_n)$ corresponding to each sub-key node, where

$$l(k_i) = \prod_{k_i \neq k_j} \frac{-k_j}{k_i - k_j} \tag{3}$$

Finally, $f(k_i)$ and $l(k_i)$ are securely transmitted to the sub-key node.

Blinding: The client selects the random number $\alpha \in Z_q^*$ to blind the message $H_1(m)$, obtains the blinded message

$$W = \alpha H_1(m) \tag{4}$$

and then sends W to the sub-key node.

Signature: After receiving the blind message w of the client, the sub-key node k_i performs signature using the partial key $f(k_i)$ calculates

$$\sigma_i = w \times f(k_i) \times l(k_i) \tag{5}$$

and return σ_i to the client. The client combines the t signatures to obtain $\sum_{i=1}^{t} \sigma_i$ and unblinds it by α^{-1} to obtain:

$$\sigma = \alpha^{-1} \sum_{i=1}^{t} \sigma_i$$

$$= \alpha^{-1} W \sum_{i=1}^{t} f(k_i) \times l(k_i) \tag{6}$$

$$= H_1(m) \sum_{i=1}^{t} f(k_i) \times l(k_i)$$

where

$$\sum_{i=1}^{t} f(k_i) \times l(k_i) = a_0 = f(0) = K_M \tag{7}$$

so that $\sigma = K_M H_1(m)$ is obtained.

Verification: The client calculates $e(\sigma, P)$ and $e(H_1(m), Q)$. If they are equal, it proves that σ is obtained by K_M encryption. The left side of the equation is:

$$e(\sigma, P) = e(\alpha^{-1} \sum_{i=1}^{t} \sigma_i, P)$$

$$= e(\alpha^{-1} W \sum_{i=1}^{t} f(k_i) \times l(k_i), P)$$

$$= e(H_1(m) \sum_{i=1}^{t} f(k_i) \times l(k_i), P) \tag{8}$$

$$= e(H_1(m) K_M, P)$$

$$= e(H_1(m), K_M P)$$

$$= e(H_1(m), Q)$$

6 Performance Evaluation

The data deduplication scheme in this paper is essentially a threshold blind signature scheme, and its security is similar to that of [23]. This section mainly evaluates the computational performance of the proposed scheme, and compares it with Miao et al.'s scheme in terms of system initialization time and key generation time.

6.1 Experimental Method

Since the network transmission performance will vary greatly in practical applications, this difference should be ignored during the experiment. For this reason, this paper carries out simulation experiments on a physical computer. The master key node, each sub-key node, the client, and the cloud storage are simulated by separate threads, and the communication between the nodes is simulated by the Socket communication interface. Since the local communication jitter between multiple threads on the same physical computer is extremely small, this method can effectively shield the impact of network transmission on experimental results.

6.2 Experimental Environment

The experimental hard ware consists of a 2.5 GHz Intel Core i5-4200 CPU processor and 4G memory. The software is based on the Windows operating system and the Eclipse integrated development environment. The experimental program is implemented by the Java programming language, and the cryptographic operations mentioned in Sect. 5.2 are performed using the JPBC (Java Pairing-Based Cryptography) library.

6.3 Experimental Results and Analysis

As with the experiment by Miao et al., experiments were performed with 5 to 10 key node. In order to accurately calculate the time and reduce the error, the average of ten experimental data was taken. The time comparison of system initialization consumption is given in Fig. 5.

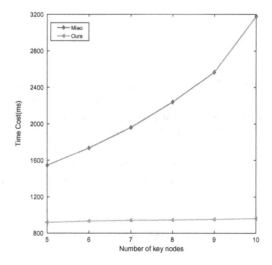

Fig. 5. Time comparison of system initialization consumption.

It can be seen from Fig. 5 that the initialization time of the scheme of Miao [23] increases approximately as a power function with the increase of the number of key nodes, and the scheme proposed in this paper increases linearly. Because Miao et al.'s scheme needs to communicate with other nodes during the system initialization, the total number of communications is $n(n-1)$. However, in the scheme proposed in this paper, the master key node only needs to communicate with n sub-key nodes for n times to complete initialization, which reduces communication and computational overhead. The experimental results show that the average performance is increased by 54.83%. Figure 6 gives a comparison of the time to generate the key.

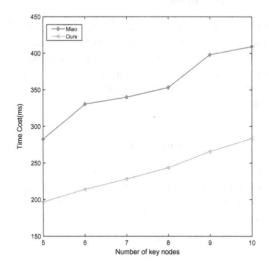

Fig. 6. Generate key time comparison.

As can be seen from Fig. 6, as the number of key nodes increases, the time to generate the key increases linearly. In the scheme of Miao et al. [23], the user needs to verify the signatures of all key nodes. If the verification passes, the blind signature is calculated and verified again. However, in this scheme, the client does not need to verify the signature of each sub-key node, and the client only needs to verify once, reducing the verification and computational overhead. The experimental results show that the average performance is improved by 32.24%.

7   Conclusion and Future Work

In order to solve the problem of cloud storage data security, the predecessors have done a lot of research work. An existing security deduplication scheme based on threshold blind signature requires a large amount of information to be exchanged between key management nodes, and the computational cost of verifying the signature is large. In addition, cross-domain scenarios are not supported. In this paper, a new threshold blind signature scheme is proposed. The key management node is divided into a master key node and multiple sub-key nodes. The key of the sub-key node is generated and allocated by the master key node, so that the number of communications is reduced from $n(n-1)$ times to n times, and the verification is reduced from multiple times to once. The scheme of this paper supports secure deduplication in a cross-domain environment in addition to ensuring data encryption security, preventing brute force attacks, and satisfying convergence key security. The experimental results show that the performance of the scheme is improved in terms of system initialization and key generation, and it is more suitable for computing resource-constrained application scenarios, such as the Internet of Things.

Acknowledgment. This work is supported in part by the National key research and development plan of China under Grant No. 2018YFB1800303 and the 13th Five-Year Science and Technology Research Project of the Education Department of Jilin Province under Grant No. JJKH20190598KJ.

References

1. Anderson, P., Zhang, L.: Fast and secure laptop backups with encrypted deduplication. In: van Drunen, R. (ed.) Uncovering the Secrets of System Administration: Proceedings of the 24th Large Installation System Administration Conference, LISA 2010, San Jose, CA, USA, 7–12 November 2010. USENIX Association (2010)
2. Bellare, M., Keelveedhi, S.: Interactive message-locked encryption and secure deduplication. In: Katz, J. (ed.) PKC 2015. LNCS, vol. 9020, pp. 516–538. Springer, Heidelberg (2015). https://doi.org/10.1007/978-3-662-46447-2_23
3. Bellare, M., Keelveedhi, S., Ristenpart, T.: Message-locked encryption and secure deduplication. In: Johansson, T., Nguyen, P.Q. (eds.) EUROCRYPT 2013. LNCS, vol. 7881, pp. 296–312. Springer, Heidelberg (2013). https://doi.org/10.1007/978-3-642-38348-9_18
4. Bolosky, W.J., Douceur, J.R., Ely, D., Theimer, M.: Feasibility of a serverless distributed file system deployed on an existing set of desktop pcs. In: Brandwajn, A., Kurose, J., Nain, P. (eds.) Proceedings of the 2000 ACM SIGMETRICS International Conference on Measurement and Modeling of Computer Systems, Santa Clara, CA, USA, 18–21 June 2000, pp. 34–43. ACM (2000)
5. Cao, Z., Wen, H., Ge, X., Ma, J., Diehl, J., Du, D.H.C.: TDDFS: a tier-aware data deduplication-based file system. TOS **15**(1), 4:1–4:26 (2019)
6. Chen, R., Mu, Y., Yang, G., Guo, F.: BL-MLE: block-level message-locked encryption for secure large file deduplication. IEEE Trans. Inf. Forens. Secur. **10**(12), 2643–2652 (2015)
7. Douceur, J.R., Adya, A., Bolosky, W.J., Simon, D., Theimer, M.: Reclaiming space from duplicate files in a serverless distributed file system. In: Proceedings of the 22nd International Conference on Distributed Computing Systems (ICDCS'02), Vienna, Austria, 2–5 July 2002, pp. 617–624. IEEE Computer Society (2002)
8. González-Manzano, L., Orfila, A.: An efficient confidentiality-preserving proof of ownership for deduplication. J. Netw. Comput. Appl. **50**, 49–59 (2015)
9. Halevi, S., Harnik, D., Pinkas, B., Shulman-Peleg, A.: Proofs of ownership in remote storage systems. In: Chen, Y., Danezis, G., Shmatikov, V. (eds.) Proceedings of the 18th ACM Conference on Computer and Communications Security, CCS 2011, Chicago, Illinois, USA, 17–21 October 2011, pp. 491–500. ACM (2011)

10. Harnik, D., Margalit, O., Naor, D., Sotnikov, D., Vernik, G.: Estimation of dedu-
    plication ratios in large data sets. In: IEEE 28th Symposium on Mass Storage
    Systems and Technologies, MSST 2012, 16–20 April 2012, Asilomar Conference
    Grounds, Pacific Grove, CA, USA, pp. 1–11. IEEE Computer Society (2012)
11. Harnikand, D., Pinkasand, B., Shulman-Peleg, A.: Side channels in cloud services:
    deduplication in cloud storage. IEEE Secur. Privacy 8(6), 40–47 (2010)
12. Hovhannisyan, H., Qi, W., Lu, K., Yang, R., Wang, J.: Whispers in the cloud
    storage: a novel cross-user deduplication-based covert channel design. Peer-to-Peer
    Netw. Appl. 11(2), 277–286 (2016). https://doi.org/10.1007/s12083-016-0483-y
13. Keelveedhi, S., Bellare, M., Ristenpart, T.: Dupless: server-aided encryption for
    deduplicated storage. In: King, S.T. (ed.) Proceedings of the 22nd USENIX Secu-
    rity Symposium, Washington, DC, USA, 14–16 August 2013, pp. 179–194. USENIX
    Association (2013)
14. Kumar, N., Antwal, S., Jain, S.C.: Differential evolution based bucket indexed data
    deduplication for big data storage. J. Intell. Fuzzy Syst. 34(1), 491–505 (2018)
15. Li, J., Chen, X., Li, M., Li, J., Lee, P.P.C., Lou, W.: Secure deduplication with
    efficient and reliable convergent key management. IEEE Trans. Parallel Distrib.
    Syst. 25(6), 1615–1625 (2014)
16. Li, J., Li, Y.K., Chen, X., Lee, P.P.C., Lou, W.: A hybrid cloud approach for
    secure authorized deduplication. IEEE Trans. Parallel Distrib. Syst. 26(5), 1206–
    1216 (2015)
17. Li, J., Qin, C., Lee, P.P.C., Li, J.: Rekeying for encrypted deduplication storage.
    In: 46th Annual IEEE/IFIP International Conference on Dependable Systems and
    Networks, DSN 2016, Toulouse, France, June 28 - July 1, 2016, pp. 618–629. IEEE
    Computer Society (2016)
18. Li, M., Qin, C., Li, J., Lee, P.P.C.: CDStore: toward reliable, secure, and cost-
    efficient cloud storage via convergent dispersal. IEEE Internet Comput. 20(3),
    45–53 (2016)
19. Liu, J., Asokan, N., Pinkas, B.: Secure deduplication of encrypted data without
    additional independent servers. In: Ray, I., Li, N., Kruegel, C. (eds.) Proceedings of
    the 22nd ACM SIGSAC Conference on Computer and Communications Security,
    Denver, CO, USA, 12–16 October 2015, pp. 874–885. ACM (2015)
20. Ma, J., et al.: Lazy exact deduplication. TOS 13(2), 11:1–11:26 (2017)
21. Mandagere, N., Zhou, P., Smith, M.A., Uttamchandani, S.: Demystifying data
    deduplication. In: Douglis, F. (ed.) Middleware 2008, ACM/IFIP/USENIX 9th
    International Middleware Conference, Leuven, Belgium, 1–5 December 2008, Com-
    panion Proceedings, pp. 12–17. ACM (2008)
22. Meyer, D.T., Bolosky, W.J.: A study of practical deduplication. In: Ganger, G.R.,
    Wilkes, J. (eds.) 9th USENIX Conference on File and Storage Technologies, San
    Jose, CA, USA, 15–17 February 2011, pp. 1–13. USENIX (2011)
23. Miao, M., Wang, J., Li, H., Chen, X.: Secure multi-server-aided data deduplication
    in cloud computing. Pervasive Mobile Comput. 24, 129–137 (2015)
24. Paulo, J., Pereira, J.: A survey and classification of storage deduplication systems.
    ACM Comput. Surv. 47(1), 11:1–11:30 (2014)
25. Puzio, P., Molva, R., Önen, M., Loureiro, S.: Cloudedup: secure deduplication with
    encrypted data for cloud storage. In: IEEE 5th International Conference on Cloud
    Computing Technology and Science, CloudCom 2013, Bristol, United Kingdom,
    2–5 December 2013, vol. 1, pp. 363–370. IEEE Computer Society (2013)
26. Shin, Y., Koo, D., Hur, J.: A survey of secure data deduplication schemes for cloud
    storage systems. ACM Comput. Surv. 49(4), 74:1–74:38 (2017)

27. Stanek, J., Kencl, L.: Enhanced secure thresholded data deduplication scheme for cloud storage. IEEE Trans. Dependable Sec. Comput. **15**(4), 694–707 (2018)
28. Stanek, J., Sorniotti, A., Androulaki, E., Kencl, L.: A secure data deduplication scheme for cloud storage. In: Christin, N., Safavi-Naini, R. (eds.) FC 2014. LNCS, vol. 8437, pp. 99–118. Springer, Heidelberg (2014). https://doi.org/10.1007/978-3-662-45472-5_8
29. Tian, Y., Khan, S.M., Jiménez, D.A., Loh, G.H.: Last-level cache deduplication. In: Bode, A., Gerndt, M., Stenström, P., Rauchwerger, L., Miller, B.P., Schulz, M. (eds.) 2014 International Conference on Supercomputing, ICS'14, Muenchen, Germany, 10–13 June 2014, pp. 53–62. ACM (2014)
30. Wang, J., Chen, X.: Efficient and secure storage for outsourced data: a survey. Data Sci. Eng. **1**(3), 178–188 (2016)
31. Xia, W., et al.: A comprehensive study of the past, present, and future of data deduplication. Proc. IEEE **104**(9), 1681–1710 (2016)
32. Xiong, J., Li, F., Ma, J., Liu, X., Yao, Z., Chen, P.S.: A full lifecycle privacy protection scheme for sensitive data in cloud computing. Peer-to-Peer Netw. Appl. **8**(6), 1025–1037 (2014). https://doi.org/10.1007/s12083-014-0295-x
33. Xiong, J., Zhang, Y., Li, X., Lin, M., Yao, Z., Liu, G.: Rse-pow: a role symmetric encryption pow scheme with authorized deduplication for multimedia data. MONET **23**(3), 650–663 (2018)
34. Yan, F., Tan, Y., Zhang, Q., Wu, F., Cheng, Z., Zheng, J.: An effective raid data layout for object-based de-duplication backup system. Chin. J. Electron. **25**(5), 832–840 (2016)
35. Zhang, C., et al.: MII: a novel content defined chunking algorithm for finding incremental data in data synchronization. IEEE Access **7**, 86932–86945 (2019)
36. Zhang, Y., et al.: A fast asymmetric extremum content defined chunking algorithm for data deduplication in backup storage systems. IEEE Trans. Comput. **66**(2), 199–211 (2017)
37. Zhu, B., Li, K., Patterson, R.H.: Avoiding the disk bottleneck in the data domain deduplication file system. In: Baker, M., Riedel, E. (eds.) 6th USENIX Conference on File and Storage Technologies, FAST 2008, 26–29 February 2008, San Jose, CA, USA, pp. 269–282. USENIX (2008)

The Spatiotemporal Traffic Accident Risk Analysis in Urban Traffic Network

Chijun Zhang[1,2,5], Jing jin[1,2,5], Qiuyang Huang[3(✉)], Zhanwei Du[2], Zhilu Yuan[4], Shengjun Tang[4], and Yang Liu[1,2,5]

[1] School of Management Science and Information Engineering, Jilin University of Finance and Economics, Changchun 130117, China
[2] Jilin Province Key Laboratory of Fintech, Jilin University of Finance and Economics, Changchun 130117, China
[3] College of Computer Science and Technology, Jilin University, Changchun 130012, China
huangqy17@mails.jlu.edu.cn
[4] Research Institute for Smart Cities and Shenzhen Key Laboratory of Spatial Information Smart Sensing and Services, School of Architecture and Urban Planning, Shenzhen University, Shenzhen, People's Republic of China
[5] Jilin Big Data Research Center for Business, Jilin University of Finance and Economics, Changchun 130117, China

Abstract. Traffic accidents seriously threaten people's lives and property all over the world. Therefore, it is of great significance to human society to have a long-term traffic accidents data with detail temporal and geographic information in a specific space, which can be used for traffic accident hotspots identification to reduce the incidence of traffic accidents. Here, we obtain a one-year dataset of traffic accidents of the city center in Changchun, Northeast China, in 2017. In this paper, we analyze the risk of traffic accident in urban area, and then discover the characteristics of traffic accidents at the temporal and spatial aspect. We construct a traffic network, which takes crossings as nodes and road sections as edges and weighted by the total number of traffic accidents. In addition, we integrate road structure data and meteorological data to explore the characteristics of the traffic network.

Keywords: Traffic accident · Urban traffic network · Risk analysis

1 Introduction

With the development of urbanization and the growth of urban population and vehicles, people are facing many problems such as traffic congestion, air pollution, traffic accidents, etc. Among them, traffic accidents pose a great threat to people's lives and property. According to the World Health Organization's Road Traffic Injury Report, more than 3,400 people die in traffic accidents every day, and tens of millions of people are injured or disabled each year. Therefore, how to reduce the traffic accidents and the corresponding loss has become a hot topic [1–5].

© ICST Institute for Computer Sciences, Social Informatics and Telecommunications Engineering 2020
Published by Springer Nature Switzerland AG 2020. All Rights Reserved
W. Li and D. Tang (Eds.): MOBILWARE 2020, LNICST 331, pp. 92–97, 2020.
https://doi.org/10.1007/978-3-030-62205-3_8

If the early incidents and risk can be recognized and predicted, early warning or intervention could be made to reduce the possibility of traffic accident [6–8]. However, it's difficult to predict the risk of a traffic accident because the causes of road traffic accidents are complex and it can be affected by many factors [9–14], such as driving habits, road structure, bad weather, traffic condition, human mobility, etc. With the development of big data and machine learning, many researchers have focused on using new method to predict traffic accident risk and identify the key factors associated with traffic accident. For example, Chen *et al.* [15] proposed a matrix factorization method to estimate accident risk; Xiong *et al.* [6] combined SVM and HMM method to predict vehicle collision; Chen *et al.* [16] and Zhidan, L. *et al.* [17] utilized deep learning to predict traffic accident risk. However, because of the lack of data associated with traffic accidents, effective prediction of the traffic accident risk dynamically is still a challenge problem.

In this paper, we obtain a one-year dataset of traffic accidents of the city center in Changchun, Northeast China, conducted by an open-data program in Changchun Municipal Engineering Design & Research Institute. Specifically, the dataset contains 5831 traffic accident records and covers 1077 roads in Changchun city center area during one-year period since 1 January 2017. Each record in the raw file contains longitude, latitude and time of the accident. According to the location information, the accidents are divided into four types (crossing, road section, residential area and roundabout), and we match all records to the traffic network, so each record corresponds to a road ID.

In order to explore the influence of different factors and the characteristics of traffic accidents at the temporal and spatial aspect, we construct a traffic network which takes crossings as nodes and road sections as edges, and weighted by the total number of traffic accidents.

2 Original Data Sources

We obtain one-year traffic accident data in a specific space of Changchun city center. The dataset contains 5831 traffic accident records and covers 1077 roads during one-year period since 1 January 2017. Each record in the raw file contains longitude, latitude and timestamp of the accident. In order to explore the influence of different factors and the characteristics of traffic accidents at the temporal and spatial aspect, we integrate road structure data and meteorological data to construct our dataset.

We first count the total number of traffic accidents occurred on each road; And then extract the length of each road, whether it is a one-way lane and the degree of each node from the road structure data; Finally, we construct the traffic network through our dataset by taking crossings as nodes and road sections as edges, and weighted by the total number of traffic accidents.

3 Defining Traffic Network

Traffic network refers to the road system which is composed of various roads in a certain area and interweaves into a network distribution. Through OpenStreetMap platform, we get the road structure data of Changchun city, then take crossings as nodes and road sections as edges. After that, we integrate the traffic accidents data with road structure data to extract the weight of each edge.

The traffic network is defined as a directed graph $G(V, E, W)$, where V is a set of vertices representing the crossings with accurate longitude and latitude in the road network, and E is a set of edges representing road sections, each edge connects two nodes. W is the weight of each edge, in this paper the weight is defined as the total number of traffic accidents occurred on each edge.

4   Spatial and Temporal Aspects Analysis

We construct the weighted traffic network to explore the influence of different factors and the characteristics of traffic accidents at the temporal and spatial aspect, it largely depends on the reliability of the source traffic accidents data. We visualize the location information of traffic accidents data, as shown in Fig. 1.

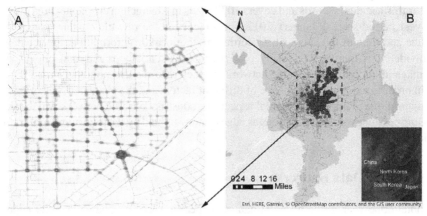

Fig. 1. Geographical distribution and heat map of traffic accidents. (A) The heat map of traffic accidents on the road network. (B) Geographical distribution of traffic accidents in Changchun city.

The heat map of the traffic accident data is shown in Fig. 1A and the geographical distribution of traffic accidents in Changchun city is shown in Fig. 1B. We integrate one-year traffic accident records occurred on the city center in Changchun in 2017. There are totally 5831 traffic accidents occurred on 1077 roads, statistics found that, 54.91% occurred on the crossings, 15.47% occurred on roundabouts, the other occurred on road Sects. (15.29%) and residential area (14.32%) respectively. From Fig. 1B, we can intuitively find that roundabouts and crossings are high-risk areas for traffic accidents.

According to the time of each traffic accident, we count the number of accidents in each hour and find that it is highly similar to people's travel patterns. It can be found that the number of accidents happened in the daytime is significantly higher than that in the night, and there are two peaks, the morning peak (7:00–8:00) and the evening peak (4:00–5:00), as shown in Fig. 2A.

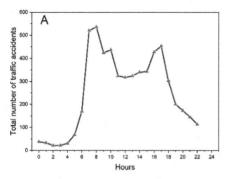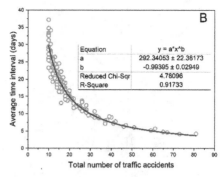

Fig. 2. Temporal aspects of the traffic accidents. (A) The number of traffic accidents happened in different hours. The X-axis represents the 24 h, and the Y-axis represents the total number of traffic accidents happened on each hour in 2017. (B) Average time interval between traffic accidents of each road. The X-axis represents the total number of traffic accidents, and the Y-axis represents the average time interval (days) between the accidents of each road.

Specially, in Fig. 2B, the X-axis represents the total number of traffic accidents, and the Y-axis represents the average time interval (days) between the accidents of each road. We fit it by using the power-law, validated by the chi-square goodness-of-fit test, and find it follows $f(x) = (292.34053 \pm 22.38173) * x^{(-0.99395\pm0.02949)}$ with r^2 as 0.91733.

We first analysis the weights of the traffic network. In our dataset, the traffic accidents are distributed on 1077 roads, the weights of the network are defined as the count of traffic accidents in each road. We divide the roads into 5 levels, the red edges represent the road with highest risk of accidents, which happened 41 to 81 traffic accidents in 2017, as shown in Fig. 3A. Then we calculate the percentage of roads with different weights, and fit it by using the power-law distribution, as shown in Fig. 3B. It follows $f(x) = (394.01205 \pm 3.83406) * x^{(-1.28262\pm0.01619)}$ with r^2 as 0.99601.

Road structure is an important factor affecting traffic conditions of the traffic network. We calculated the average number of traffic accidents on each road type in 1077 roads, as shown in Fig. 3C, it is obviously higher on truck roads. Finally, we calculate the average number of traffic accidents happened in different kinds of weather conditions. As shown in Fig. 3D, the average number of accidents in moderate snow is obviously higher than others. However, it is lowest in heavy snow, one of the most possible reasons is some roads will be closed when it snows heavily in Changchun.

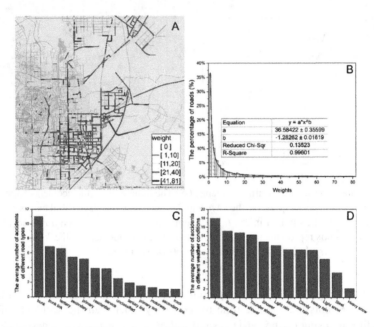

Fig. 3. Network characteristics analysis. (A) The weights of the traffic network. According to the weights, the roads are divided into 5 levels, as shown in the legend. (B) The percentage of roads with different weights in the traffic network. We calculate the percentage of roads with different weights, and fit it by using the power-law distribution. (C) The average number of accidents of different road types. (D) The average number of accidents in different weather conditions.

Acknowledgements. This work was supported by the National Social Science Foundation of China (grant no. 16BGL180), The Foundation of Jilin Provincial Science & Technology Department (grant no. 20180101332JC, 20180101337JC), Changchun Philosophy and Social Science Planning Project (grant no. CSKT2019ZX-053), Jilin University of Finance and Economics Doctoral Fund Project (grant no. 2018B15), Open Fund of Key Laboratory of Urban Land Resources Monitoring and Simulation, MNR (No. KF-2019-04-034), NSFC under Grant 71901147, 41801392 and Grant 41701187, China Postdoctoral Science Foundation under Grant 2018M640821, Grant 2018M633133 and Grant 2018M643150.

References

1. Ryder, B., Gahr, B., Egolf, P., Dahlinger, A., Wortmann, F.: Preventing traffic accidents with in-vehicle decision support systems - the impact of accident hotspot warnings on driver behaviour. Decis. Support Syst. **99**, 64–74 (2017)
2. Chung, Y., Recker, W.W.: Spatiotemporal analysis of traffic congestion caused by rubbernecking at freeway accidents. Ieee T. Intell. Transp. **14**, 1416–1422 (2013)
3. Deb, R., Liew, W.C.: Missing value imputation for the analysis of incomplete traffic accident data. Inform. Sci. **339**, 274–289 (2016)
4. Weiming, H., Xuejuan, X., Xie, D., Tieniu, T., Maybank, S.: Traffic accident prediction using 3-D model-based vehicle tracking. IEEE T. Veh. Technol. **53**, 677–694 (2004)

5. Ki, Y.K., Lee, D.Y.: A traffic accident recording and reporting model at intersections. IEEE T Intell. Transp. **8**, 188–194 (2007)
6. Xiong, X., Long, C., Liang, J.: A new framework of vehicle collision prediction by combining SVM and HMM. IEEE T. Intell. Transp. **19**, 699–710 (2018)
7. Cheol, O., Jun-Seok, O., Ritchie, S.G.: Real-time hazardous traffic condition warning system: framework and evaluation. IEEE T Intell. Transp. **6**, 265–272 (2005)
8. An, J., Fu, L., Hu, M., Chen, W., Zhan, J.: A novel fuzzy-based convolutional neural network method to traffic flow prediction with uncertain traffic accident information. IEEE Access **7**, 20708–20722 (2019)
9. Moriya, K., Matsushima, S., Yamanishi, K.: Traffic risk mining from heterogeneous road statistics. IEEE T Intell. Transp. **19**, 3662–3675 (2018)
10. Eboli, L., Mazzulla, G., Pungillo, G.: Measuring the driver's perception error in the traffic accident risk evaluation. IET Intell Transp Syst. **11**, 659–666 (2017)
11. Yu, R., Abdel-Aty, M.A., Ahmed, M.M., Wang, X.: Utilizing microscopic traffic and weather data to analyze real-time crash patterns in the context of active traffic management. IEEE T Intell Transp. **15**, 205–213 (2014)
12. Zhang, W., Deng, H., Wang, X.: Safety factor analysis for traffic accident scene based on computer simulation. In: Proceedings of the International Conference on Computer Design and Applications, pp. 260–263 IEEE Computer Society (2010)
13. Huang, Q., et al.: The temporal geographically-explicit network of public transport in Changchun City. Northeast China. Sci Data. **6**, 190026 (2019)
14. Du, Z., et al.: The temporal network of mobile phone users in changchun municipality. Northeast China. Sci Data. **5**, 180228 (2018)
15. Chen, Q., et al.: A context-aware nonnegative matrix factorization framework for traffic accident risk estimation via heterogeneous data. In: Proceedings of the IEEE Conference on Multimedia Information Processing & Retrieval, pp. 346–351. IEEE Computer Society (2018)
16. Chen, Q., Song, X., Yamada, H., Shibasaki, R.: Learning deep representation from big and heterogeneous data for traffic accident inference. In: Proceedings of the Thirtieth AAAI Conference on Artificial Intelligence, pp. 338–344. AAAI (2016)
17. Liu, Z., Li, Z., Wu, K., Li, M.: Urban traffic prediction from mobility data using deep learning. IEEE Netw. **32**, 40–46 (2018)

Identifying Climatological Interactions in Global Influenza Across Temperate and Tropical Regions

Zhilu Yuan[1], Shengjun Tang[1], Qiuyang Huang[1,2(✉)], Chijun Zhang[3],
Zeynep Ertem[4], Zhanwei Du[5], and Yuan Bai[5]

[1] Research Institute for Smart Cities and Shenzhen Key Laboratory of Spatial Information Smart Sensing and Services, School of Architecture and Urban Planning, Shenzhen University, Shenzhen, People's Republic of China
[2] College of Computer Science and Technology, Jilin University, Changchun 130012, China
huangqy17@mails.jlu.edu.cn
[3] School of Management Science and Information Engineering, Jilin University of Finance and Economics, Changchun 130117, China
[4] Marshall School of Business, The University of Southerm California, California, USA
[5] Key Laboratory of Urban Land Resources Monitoring and Simulation, MNR, Shenzhen, China

Abstract. Recently, global epidemic models that uses climatological factors have been shown to explain influenza activities for both temperate and tropical regions. In this paper, we extend these global models by including interactions of climatological factors. We find that countries in Europe and Australia have higher forecast skill, indicating the stronger relationship of influenza with climatological factors, than regions in other continents. The influenza activities of 47 (83%) countries can be explained with a closer match using multi-factor interactions along with original factors than only using the original factors.

Keywords: Multi-factor interaction · Influenza · Climatological factor

1 Introduction

Influenza outbreaks are affected by climatological factors, such as relative humidity [12], absolute humidity [11], temperature [7] and precipitation [16]. The survival and transmission rates of influenza outbreaks are affected by climatological factors. Due to geographic variations, different countries exhibit different climatological properties due to geographical variations [1,6]. The seasonality of influenza has been well studied in temperate regions, which are characterized by significant seasonal changes in climatological factors [15]. In contrast, tropical regions have much weaker annual climatological cycles with weak seasonality [9,10]. Climatological factors of absolute humidity and temperature were shown to improve the global models of influenza outbreaks, with different influence in different regions [16].

© ICST Institute for Computer Sciences, Social Informatics and Telecommunications Engineering 2020
Published by Springer Nature Switzerland AG 2020. All Rights Reserved
W. Li and D. Tang (Eds.): MOBILWARE 2020, LNICST 331, pp. 98–103, 2020.
https://doi.org/10.1007/978-3-030-62205-3_9

When researchers drill down to the relationships between climatological factors and influenza, they find that climatological factors may interact with each other and thus eventually affect the influenza dynamics [1,16]. For example, the effect of absolute humidity on influenza was mediated by temperature with a U-shaped pattern [1]. In addition, the synthetic conditions of specific humidity and temperature were associated with the activity of influenza [16]. Previous studies enlighten us for the global phenomenon of climatological factors' interactions. However, the combined influences of factors' interactions on influenza transmission is not yet understood. Due to the geographic variations of climatological factors across different countries [4,5,8,14], factor interactions can be heterogeneous across countries. This study aims to identify all possible interactions of climatological factors in each country and to what extent these interactions are useful to explain the observed influenza epidemics than factors' main effects.

2   Methods

2.1   Study Design

We conduct a retrospective time series study of global influenza to highlight the major interactions of climatological factors across countries via the relationships of weekly influenza cases with climatological factors.

2.2   Data

Our data include both influenza incidences and climatological factors for 79 countries over at least 208 weeks (4 years), and such countries geographically cover an area of <1.5 million mi^2 [1]. In these countries, totally 57 countries have the concurrent period of weekly influenza cases and temperature, absolute/relative humidity and precipitation. More details can be found in the following subsections of influenza and climatological data.

Influenza Data. We use the open-access influenza data, released by the World Health Organization for the weekly laboratory confirmed influenza cases of type A and B on April 2014 in country level in the period of January 1, 1996 to March 26, 2014 [1]. To infer the risk of influenza, we use the incidence density (per capita) as the influenza index, which is estimated via counting the estimated population size and reporting rates.

Climatological Data. In the open-access climatological data , weekly temperature (T) and absolute humidity (AH) data are calculated for each country by taking the average value of all available stations in National Oceanic and Atmospheric Administration Global Surface Summary of the Day. Given the temperature and absolute humidity of a region, the relative humidity (RH) is calculated by assuming standard atmospheric pressure. In addition, the precipitation (PRCP) values of a region are taken from the combined National Centers for Environmental Prediction Climate Forecast System (http://cfs.ncep.noaa.gov/).

2.3   Forecast Analysis

The forecast skill refers to the accuracy of association of prediction to an observation. Here, it is represented in terms of the Pearson correlation between the predicted index and the observed influenza index. In order to calculate the forecast skill, we used the model-free method of multi-view embedding (MVE) to forecast, which is particularly effective in the scenario of noisy time series. This kind of methods is also popular in the relationship analysis of influenza and climatological factors.

Baseline models are taken as MVE with the four climatological factors as input together or separately through their main effects. A forecast is estimated via the average of the nearest neighbors of attractors, built from lags of factors [2,3,13] to enable influenza dynamics reconstructed.

To be specific, MVE is defined as:

$$y_{t+1} = \frac{1}{k} \sum_{i=1}^{k} y_{nn^i(t)+1} \tag{1}$$

where y_{t+1} represents the prediction at time $t + 1$. $y_{nn^i(t)+1}$ is the i-th factor's attractor, ordered by the time index $nn^i(t)$.

As for the interactions of multiple factors, we consider the method of tensor product interaction (ti) [17], which uses different smoothing bases for factors and has a huge advantage of flexibility in comparison to the usage of single smoothing base. The factors are divided into two sets. One is M, involving the factors with only main effects. Another is TI with only multi-factor interactions. Thus, the influenza prediction can be written as

$$\frac{1}{4} \Big(\sum_{M_k \in M} y_{nn^{M_k}(t)+1} + \sum_{ti_l \in TI} y_{nn^{ti_l}(t)+1} \Big) \tag{2}$$

where M_k infers the main effect of the k-th factor in M and ti_l denotes the l-th multi-factor interaction in TI.

3   Results

We, first, study the forecast analysis of influenza across countries by choosing the best model in all 21 possible combinations of the four climatological factors with the highest forecast skill for forecasting, as shown in Fig. 1, ordered by the latitude.

The X axis represents the forecast skill, starting from 0 to 0.9, and the Y axis represents the latitude. We find that the higher the latitude of a country

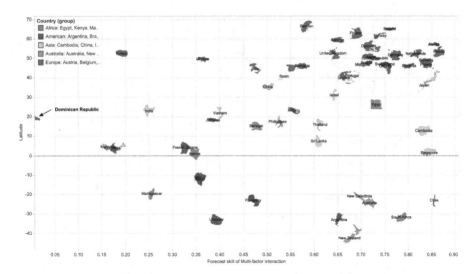

Fig. 1. Overview of the forecast skill over countries. Countries are ordered by with the latitude and colored by continents. For each country, we show its highest forecast skill for forecasting over 21 possible combinations of the four climatological factors as input together or separately. The X axis represents the forecast skill, starting from 0 to 0.90, and the Y axis denotes the latitude. There are 25 European countries with average forecast skill of 0.68, 5 African countries with 0.52, 12 American countries with 0.43, 12 Asian countries with 0.57, and 3 Australian countries with 0.70.

the higher the forecasting skill of the corresponding influenza forecasts. Most countries that are north of the 30° latitude appear to have forecast skill values around 0.75 with relatively small variation. In contrast, countries that are south of the 30° latitude show high variation in their forecast skill values. When we examine the results for countries in each continent separately, we find that the 25 European countries have an average forecast skill of 0.68; the 12 American countries have an average forecast skill of 0.43; the 12 Asian countries have an average forecast skill of 0.52; and the 3 Australian countries have an average forecast skill of 0.70. Forecasts for European countries exhibit high levels (0.55 to 0.85) of forecast skill, such as Netherlands, Slovenia, Ireland and France.

In Fig. 2, we show the relative improvement in forecast skill for each country by including the climatological interaction terms. The brighter the red color, the more the improvement in forecast skill for the corresponding country. We find that, including multi-factor interaction terms of climatological factors in our modeling results in improved forecast skill values for countries except part of Europe. Among the 57 countries, the epidemics dynamics for 47 (~83%) countries can be explained with a closer match using additional multi-factor interactions. The mean forecast skill of the 47 countries is enhanced by 8.54% from 52.28% to 60.82%.

Fig. 2. Overview of the forecast skill enhanced. The forecast skill is enhanced by the best multi-factor interactions, in the contrast with the main effects of climatological factors. The redder the color, the greater the country's forecast skill is. Forecast with multi-factor interaction exhibits better forecast skills in most countries in North/South America, Africa, Asia and Australia. Among the 57 countries, the epidemics dynamics for 47 (~83%) countries can be explained with a closer match using additional multi-factor interactions. The mean forecast skill of the 47 countries is enhanced by 8.55% from 52.28% to 60.82%.

4   Conclusion

Interactions of climatological factors correlate with influenza at the country level, which result in higher values of forecast skill than models that exclude interactions terms. Including multi-factor interactions increases the explanation of observed influenza time series, indicating the common interactions of climatological factors across countries. Tropical countries benefit from the interaction of absolute humidity and precipitation. In the contrast, temperate countries in the northern hemisphere benefit from by temperature and humidity. Our work extends previous studies from the analysis of multiple climatological factors to their additional interactions, revealing the disparity of different countries in the view of multi-factor interactions. to get better influenza surveillance and control through monitoring climatological factors and their interactions.

Acknowledgments. This work was supported by the Open Fund of Key Laboratory of Urban Land Resources Monitoring and Simulation, MNR (No. KF-2019-04-034), NSFC under Grant 71901147, 41801392 and Grant 41701187, China Postdoctoral Science Foundation under Grant 2018M640821, Grant 2018M633133 and Grant 2018M643150, National Social Science Foundation of China (grant no. 16BGL180),

The Foundation of Jilin Provincial Science & Technology Department (grant no. 20180101332JC, 20180101337JC).

References

1. Deyle, E.R., Maher, M.C., Hernandez, R.D., Basu, S., Sugihara, G.: Global environmental drivers of influenza. Proc. Natl. Acad. Sci. **113**(46), 13081–13086 (2016)
2. Deyle, E.R., Sugihara, G.: Generalized theorems for nonlinear state space reconstruction. PLoS One **6**(3), e18295 (2011)
3. Dixon, P.A., Milicich, M.J., Sugihara, G.: Episodic fluctuations in larval supply. Science **283**(5407), 1528–1530 (1999)
4. Jóhannesson, T., Jónsson, T., Källén, E., Kaas, E.: Climate change scenarios for the nordic countries. Clim. Res. **5**(3), 181–195 (1995)
5. Karagiannidis, A.F., Karacostas, T., Maheras, P., Makrogiannis, T.: Climatological aspects of extreme precipitation in Europe, related to mid-latitude cyclonic systems. Theor. Appl. Clim. **107**(1–2), 165–174 (2012)
6. Liu, Y., Huang, L.: A novel ensemble support vector machine model for land cover classification. Int. J. Distrib. Sens. Netw. **15**(4), 1550147719842732 (2019)
7. Lowen, A.C., Mubareka, S., Steel, J., Palese, P.: Influenza virus transmission is dependent on relative humidity and temperature. PLoS Pathog. **3**(10), 1470–1476 (2007)
8. Menzel, A., Jakobi, G., Ahas, R., Scheifinger, H., Estrella, N.: Variations of the climatological growing season (1951–2000) in germany compared with other countries. Int. J. Clim. **23**(7), 793–812 (2003)
9. Moura, F.E.: Influenza in the tropics. Curr. Opin. Infect. Dis. **23**(5), 415–420 (2010)
10. Moura, F.E., Perdigão, A.C., Siqueira, M.M.: Seasonality of influenza in the tropics: a distinct pattern in northeastern brazil. The American Journal of Tropical Medicine and Hygiene **81**(1), 180–183 (2009)
11. Qi, L., et al.: The burden of influenza and pneumonia mortality attributable to absolute humidity among elderly people in chongqing, china, 2012–2018. Sci. Tot. Environ. **716** 136682 (2020)
12. Salomon, A., et al.: Influenza increases invasive meningococcal disease risk in temperate countries. Clin. Microbio. Infect. (2020)
13. Sauer, T., Yorke, J.A., Casdagli, M.: Embedology. Journal of statistical. Physics **65**(3–4), 579–616 (1991)
14. Stagge, J.H., Kohn, I., Tallaksen, L.M., Stahl, K.: Modeling drought impact occurrence based on climatological drought indices for four European countries. In: EGU General Assembly Conference Abstracts. EGU General Assembly Conference Abstracts, vol. 16, p. 15425 (May 2014)
15. Tamerius, J., Nelson, M.I., Zhou, S.Z., Viboud, C., Miller, M.A., Alonso, W.J.: Global influenza seasonality: reconciling patterns across temperate and tropical regions. Environ. Health Perspect. **119**(4), 439–445 (2011)
16. Tamerius, J.D., et al.: Environmental predictors of seasonal influenza epidemics across temperate and tropical climates. PLOS Pathog. **9**(3), 1–12 (2013)
17. Wood, S.N.: Low-rank scale-invariant tensor product smooths for generalized additive mixed models. Biometrics **62**(4), 1025–1036 (2006)

Measuring the Impact of Public Transit on the Transmission of Epidemics

Yuan Bai[1], Qiuyang Huang[2(✉)], and Zhanwei Du[1]

[1] Department of Integrative Biology, University of Texas at Austin,
Austin 78705, USA
[2] College of Computer Science and Technology, Jilin University,
Changchun 130117, China
huangqy17@mails.jlu.edu.cn

Abstract. In many developing countries, public transit plays an important role in daily life. However, few existing methods have considered the influence of public transit in their models. In this work, we present a dual-perspective view of the epidemic spreading process of the individual that involves both contamination in places (such as work places and homes) and public transit (such as buses and trains). In more detail, we consider a group of individuals who travel to some places using public transit, and introduce public transit into the epidemic spreading process. Our simulation results suggest that individuals with a high public transit trip contribution rate will increase the volume of infectious people when an infectious disease outbreak occurs by affecting the social network through the public transit trip contribution rate.

Keywords: Community structure · Subway system · Early prediction

1 Introduction

Epidemiological research is complex and involves aspects such as public policies [1]. There are an increasing number of applications and tools that support real-world decisions in public health epidemiology. It is critical to use mathematical models to analyze epidemic spreading in public health epidemiology, to help overcome the problems of sparse observations, inference with missing data, and so on [1,2]. These models can describe the spreading mechanisms of viruses, quantify the interventions' effects, and identify key factors related to the course of an outbreak [2]. Infectious disease spreading models are powerful tools for controlling the development of infectious diseases [2]. Mathematical and computational models have proven useful when addressing the 2014 Ebola outbreak, the 2009 H1N1 outbreak, and so on.

Consider the difference between urban transport in China and other Western countries; people would like to choose public transit for their daily travel needs. In contrast, in some cities in China, such as Beijing and Shanghai, the average public transit trip contribution rate can be as high as 40%. However,

© ICST Institute for Computer Sciences, Social Informatics and Telecommunications Engineering 2020
Published by Springer Nature Switzerland AG 2020. All Rights Reserved
W. Li and D. Tang (Eds.): MOBILWARE 2020, LNICST 331, pp. 104–109, 2020.
https://doi.org/10.1007/978-3-030-62205-3_10

individual-based models are important tools for studying the transmission mechanism of pandemic influenza [3]. With regards to individual-based models, many of these models ignore the possible risk inherent in commuting. For example, a heterogeneous graph modeling method was used by Dongmin et al. to describe the dynamic process of influenza virus transmission using clinical data [4]. The VirusTracker app simulates the spread of a virus and highlights the critical role of vaccinations in combating a disease outbreak [5]. Dynamic Behavior Visualizer is a tool for visualizing people's dynamic behaviors and movements in a disaster [6]. However, these aforementioned models primarily assume that people are infected at a fixed location. Public transit, as a high-risk place where different crowds contact each other, is often neglected. This overlook can be understood, particularly in some developed countries (such as the United States) where almost ninety percent of the people travel by private vehicles and few travel by public transit or other modes of public transportation [7].

These methods cannot describe the infection risk due to crowded public transit, such as that in large cities in China. Thus, we can see that the intervention of public transit can affect the trend of epidemic diseases to some extent and enlarge the transmissibility threshold to some extent (see the analysis of the transmissibility threshold in the Methods section). In this regard, a new model is needed that considers urban public transit. In this respect, our work may provide a means for modeling the impact of public transit trips and for estimating the effectiveness of infection controls during public transit trips.

2   Materials and Methods

We use the data of a resident in Blacksburg from http://ndssl.vbi.vt.edu/synthetic-data/ to construct the social network. We know when and where the resident is for one day. Moreover, the public transit information data can be obtained from http://www.gtfs-data-exchange.com/agency/blacksburg-transit/. With the public transit information, we can schedule people's daily trips with the help of Google Maps. The resident information includes resident identification, start time of resident activity, resident location, the duration in this location, and so on. The public transit information includes public transit stops, trips, stop times, routes, and so on. Then, we propose a novel modeling framework for describing the dynamic process of individuals transmitting influenza virus by integrating public transit. In this model, we use the chain-binomial model in susceptible-exposed-infected-recovered (SEIR) models based on [8] to simulate the disease transmission process in public transit.

2.1   Methods

We use a general computational approach for networked epidemiology based on [10], which can generate a social contact network of the region under consideration. Three main steps are involved in the process of constructing synthetic populations [10]: Step 1 constructs an artificial population with open-source databases. Step 2 connects daily activities to individuals for each household through daily surveys [10,11]. Step 3 assigns public-transit-based activities between the two activity locations. Demographics and home locations are considered here. The social contact graph is constructed with activity information for each person. Google Maps can be used here to compute the public-transit-based activities between the two activity locations.

Individual-Based Model. We embedded an individual-based model in the PTF model to denote the virus transmission mechanism by considering the travel of an individual using public transit. The individual-based model of an epidemic features a dynamic process, including factors such as individuals visiting places, visiting public transits, and daily infection transmission.

To model this process, we defined the following functions. The subject's infection risk at location p is defined as:

$$\tau(i,j,p) = \beta \cdot c \cdot t(i,j) \qquad (1)$$

where β indicates the infection rate. t(i, j) represents the contact time between individual i and individual j at location p. c represents the contact rate and is set as two different values according to the current location, which belongs to the public transit set $S_{\text{public transits}}$ or the place set S_{places}. It is assumed that if someone remained near a symptomatic patient for more than h hours in the public transit, then the infection rate for this person is 100% of c_p, where a is the infectiousness at a certain location. If the person remained at some location for h hours, then the probability decreases proportionally to the duration.

$$c = \begin{cases} \alpha \cdot c_p \; if \; p \in S_{public \; transits} \\ c_p \; if \; p \in S_{places} \end{cases} \qquad (2)$$

The infection force of susceptible individual i caused by the infected neighbors $j(j = 1, ..., S_i)$ at location p: $\lambda(i,p) = 1 - \prod_{S_i}^{j=1}(1 - \tau(i,j,p))$

where $\tau(i,j,p)$ is the infectivity of infected contact j at location p, capturing the probability of infected individual j infecting others.

3   Results

Our PTF considers the process. To measure the effect of an individual visiting public transit during the epidemic, the following experiments are conducted by setting different public transit trip contribution rates in the different basic reproductive number R0 (see Figs. 1, 2 and 3). From these three figures, we can see that as the number of people who take public transit is reduced, less people will be infected. In each figure, a higher R0 corresponds to a larger infected population. In each subplot, a larger time threshold h corresponds to a lower infected population. Moreover, when only 10% of people take public transit, the infected population is almost the same for the different h values (30, 150 and inf), as shown in Fig. 1. This means that when there are only a few people who

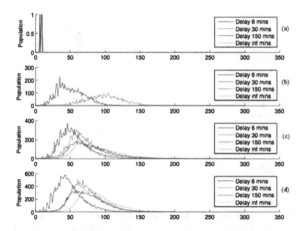

Fig. 1. Simulation of the influenza epidemic curve with 50% PTTCR. The number of people who take public transit is reduced by 50%. Additionally, seven scenarios were simulated for this intervention. In the four scenarios, the time threshold h (see Methods) in public transit is increased by 6 min, 30 min, 150 min and an infinite number of minutes, and the basic reproductive number R0 is increased by (a) R0 = 0.9, (b) R0 = 2.1, (c) R0 = 4.0, and (d) R0 = 4.5

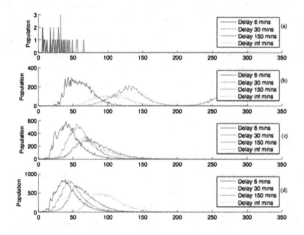

Fig. 2. Simulation of the influenza epidemic curve with 30% PTTCR. The number of people who take public transit is reduced by 30%. Additionally, seven scenarios were simulated for this intervention. In the four scenarios, the time threshold h (see Methods) in public transit is increased by 6 min, 30 min, 150 min and an infinite number of minutes, and the basic reproductive number R0 is increased by (a) R0 = 0.9, (b) R0 = 2.1, (c) R0 = 4.0, and (d) R0 = 4.5

take public transit, the intervention performance of public transit cannot play a large role in the epidemic process. Regardless of how much effort is expended here, we cannot obtain a substantial improvement.

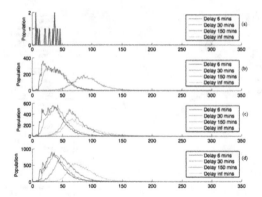

Fig. 3. Simulation of the influenza epidemic curve with 0% PTTCR. The number of people who take public transit is reduced by 0%. Additionally, seven scenarios were simulated for this intervention. In the four scenarios, the time threshold h (see Methods) in public transit is increased by 6 min, 30 min, 150 min and an infinite number of minutes, and the basic reproductive number R0 is increased by (a) R0 = 0.9, (b) R0 = 2.1, (c) R0 = 4.0, and (d) R0 = 4.5

Rather, when approximately 20% of people take public transit, the infected population is different for the different h values (30, 150 and inf), as shown in Fig. 3. This means that when there are many people who take public transit, the intervention performance of public transit will play an important role in the epidemic process. We can obtain a substantial improvement if we can control the spreading in public transit. School closure is a common intervention in an epidemic.

4   Conclusion

Our simulation results suggest that individuals with high public transit trip contribution rates will increase the number of infectious people when there is an infectious disease outbreak, similar to the school closure intervention, guiding similar research in other fields. We conclude that the public transit trip contribution rates will have an impact on the process of the spread of an infectious disease because they can affect the social network. In this respect, our work provides a means for modeling the impact of public transit trips and for estimating the effectiveness of infection controls for public transit trips.

Acknowledgments. This work was supported by the Open Fund of Key Laboratory of Urban Land Resources Monitoring and Simulation, MNR (No. KF-2019-04-034).

References

1. Marathe, M., Vullikanti, A.K.S.: Computational epidemiology. Commun. ACM **56**(7), 88–96 (2013)
2. Lofgren, E.T., Halloran, M.E., Rivers, C.M., et al.: Opinion: mathematical models: A key tool for outbreak response. Proc. Natl. Acad. Sci. **111**(51), 18095–18096 (2014)
3. Ohkusa, Y., Sugawara, T.: Application of an individual-based model with real data for transportation mode and location to pandemic influenza. J. Infect. Chemother. **13**(6), 380–389 (2007)
4. Guo, D., Li, K.C., Peters, T.R., et al.: Multi-scale modeling for the transmission of influenza and the evaluation of interventions toward it. Sci. Rep. **5** (2015)
5. VirusTracker. http://ndssl.vbi.vt.edu/apps/virustracker/
6. DBV. http://ndssl.vbi.vt.edu/apps/dbv/
7. Santos, A., McGuckin, N., Nakamoto, H.Y., et al.: Summary of Travel Trends: 2009 National Household Travel Survey (2011)
8. Hladish, T., Melamud, E., Barrera, L.A., et al.: EpiFire: an open source C++ library and application for contact network epidemiology. BMC Bioinf. **13**(1), 76 (2012)
9. Swarup, S., Eubank, S.G., Marathe, M.V.: Computational epidemiology as a challenge domain for multiagent systems. In: Proceedings of the 2014 International Conference on Autonomous Agents and Multi-agent Systems. International Foundation for Autonomous Agents and Multiagent Systems, pp. 1173–1176 (2014)
10. Eubank, S., Guclu, H., Kumar, V.S.A., et al.: Modelling disease outbreaks in realistic urban social networks. Nature **429**(6988), 180–184 (2004)
11. Barrett, C.L., Beckman, R.J., Khan, M., et al.: Generation and analysis of large synthetic social contact networks. In: Winter Simulation Conference. Winter Simulation Conference, pp. 1003–1014 (2009)

Evaluation Method for Water Network Connectivity Based on Graph Theory

Yujia Zhou[✉], Yannan Shi, Hui Wu, Yifan Chen, Qiong Yang, and Zhongshuai Fang

Key Laboratory of Disaster Prevention and Reduction,
Zhejiang Institute of Hydraulics and Estuary, Hangzhou 310020, China
zhouyujia77@126.com

Abstract. Water network connectivity plays a pivotal role in water security and ecological civilization, which also has been viewed as an important part for water comprehensive improvement. Using graph theory, the water network can be modeled as an undirected graph with multiple interconnected elements which represent rivers by edges and junctions by nodes. In this paper, the weight on edge represents the simplified river cross-section area which can be equivalent to flow capacity between two adjacent nodes. In order to obtain the flow capacity between any two nodes, a maximum flow evaluation scheme is designed by using Boykov-Kolmogorov algorithm. Then by using the maximum flow between nodes before and after dredging based on node degree features, a solution is assayed for average flow capacity of each node and water network connectivity. The proposed approach has been tested on the river network of Xiacheng District in Hangzhou with dredging data in year 2016. The result shows that the water network connectivity is improved by 7.89% over the whole area and more than 40% in part region by dredging, and significant influenced by intersect density and dredging extent.

Keywords: Water network · Graph theory · Connectivity · Dredging

1 Introduction

In the recent studies of water resources and hydrological cycle, water networks represent an important and fundamental class due to their simple structures. The connectivity of the water networks has an important impact on the regional flood and drought disaster resilience, water resources allocation and river-lake health protection, and be significant for water resources management. The distribution of natural rivers generally appears to be a network or treelike shape, and water can flow through the channel with the function of flood prevention, water resources regulation and improvement of water eco-environment [1]. Deficiency of network connectivity caused by river channel shrinkage and disappearance may lead to serious problem for water shortage and series disasters. However, numbers of engineering measures as dredging and artificial drainage can be used to improve water connectivity, which can be helpful to optimize water resources allocation, improve water supper, and promote water ecological civilization [2, 3].

W. Li and D. Tang (Eds.): MOBILWARE 2020, LNICST 331, pp. 110–118, 2020.
https://doi.org/10.1007/978-3-030-62205-3_11

Numbers of methods including graph theory method, hydrologic and hydraulic method, landscape ecology method, biological method, and comprehensive index method are used to evaluate water network connectivity. Graph theory is helpful to simplify water system, which comprises of nodes for features at river interchange and links for river or pipe between nodes [4–6]. It can be utilized to calculate connectivity of the water network by analysis connectivity of graph with edge weight given by specify physical attributes such as river length, river width or hydrodynamic factor. From Xia Jihong's summarize, the meaning of edge weight between any two nodes could be guarantee rate of streamflow from one node to another under certain water level and discharge [7]. Gao Yuqin used graph theory to develop a methodology for calculating connectivity with edge weight by dynamic flow passing capacity [8]. Another evaluation method for river network connectivity was proposed by Xu Guanglai which can be calculated by edge weight allocated with the reciprocal of hydraulic resistance, thus flow capacity of any two nodes, average flow capacity of each node, and connectivity of river network can be obtained [9, 10]. It was proved to be suitable for assessment of connectivity of the water network which influenced by hydraulic engineering as dredging and artificial river. On the other hand, water network was considered as internet of things due to the function of water supply and delivery by perception and intelligent dispatching based on the connected structure [11]. Two important ways to increase water supply and delivery are links added and flow capacity added. Compare to links added by artificial river, flow capacity added by dredging appears a more practical measure to increase the connectivity of water network.

In this paper, flow capacity and connectivity change by dredging will be detail analysis, where graph is established by rivers of Xiacheng District in Hangzhou, while edge weight references to flow capacity by river cross-section area, average flow capacity of node references to ability for one node to other nodes, connectivity of river network references to average flow capacity of all nodes.

2 Methodology

2.1 Graph of Water Network

According to graph theory, water network is represented as a mathematical graph $G = G(V, E, W)$ in which V is the set of all graph nodes with n elements, E is the set of graph edges with m elements and W is the set of graph edge weights between any two nodes which can be defined as adjacency matrix $W = \left(w_{ij}\right)_{n \times n}$. It is common to represent rivers or pipes by graph edges E, junctions such as pipe intersections, reservoirs and consumers by graph nodes V and edge weights by flow capacity W. Here w_{ij} has the meaning of flow capacity from node i to j, and $(i, j) \in E$ is out-degree neighbors for j to i, otherwise $(j, i) \in E$ is in-degree neighbors for i to j which means node i can supply water for nose j. It is equal for out-degree and in-degree for undirected graph. With such representations, connectivity of the water network can be evaluated by connectivity of graph [12].

2.2 Edge Weight of Water Network

Edge weight w of graph is represented by the degree of patency within a river channel can be estimated by the reciprocal of hydraulic resistance in the plain as slope of river bed is usually neglected. Hydraulic resistance of trapezoid channel can be expressed as a function of channel length l, roughness n and bottom width b, water depth h and slope coefficient m [9], the formula can express as

$$H = ln \left[\frac{(b+mh)h}{b+2h\sqrt{1+m}} \right]^{-\frac{2}{3}} \tag{1}$$

Then edge weight follows as $w = 1/H$.

For the rectangular channel, m equals zero and river cross-section area added Δa by dredging can be computed by

$$\Delta a = \Delta hb = \frac{q}{l}, \tag{2}$$

where Δh represents added depth and q represents river dredging volume.

As length and roughness is constant for the same river, ratio of the degree of patency within a river channel w' after dredging to w before dredging is calculated as

$$\frac{w'}{w} = \left[1 + \frac{\Delta hb}{h(b+2h+2\Delta h)} \right]^{\frac{2}{3}} \tag{3}$$

In the condition of the flat land, roughness can be ignored, the degree of patency within a river channel can be instead by flow capacity in simple, more easy formula is adopted for evaluating ratio of flow capacity w' after dredging to w before dredging as [1]

$$\frac{w'}{w} \approx \frac{a+\Delta a}{a} = \frac{h+\Delta h}{h}, \tag{4}$$

which only need the parameter of the increased river cross-section area or increased water depth to compute connectivity change.

2.3 Connectivity of Water Network

Connectivity algorithms for graph usually refer to node connectivity and edge connectivity which means the graph will be disconnected by removing with fewest nodes or edges. However, it usually appears as a sparse network graph while water network is not so dense compared with personal networks and power network, the result of node connectivity and edge connectivity often show 1 which cannot be utilized to evaluation water network connectivity exactly. As the graph of water network can clearly express river channel and intersect, node degree could be obtained with number of river channel connected with intersect, and higher node degree implies the more important position in the network. Thus, it is easy to get average node degree for assessing the connectivity of water network as a basic method with meaning of higher average node degree better connectivity.

Graph edge weights w with flow capacity for adjacent nodes can be represented by river cross-section area, and non-adjacent nodes can be expressed by maximum flow by given the hypothesis that indirectly connected nodes can be reached to each other through middle nodes. Maximum flow of two nodes can be obtained by the principle that flow capacity will be limited by the smallest flow capacity of middle links. There is a calculation example for the directed graph with a given graph by 5 nodes and 6 edges (see Fig. 1). According to this graph, there are 3 paths from node 1 to node 5 refer to ① v1-v2-v4-v5, ② v1-v2-v3-v5 and ③ v1-v3-v5, and the maximum flow of path is limited by the minimum edge weight which represents flow capacity of link. Thus, the maximum flow through path ① is 3, path ② is 2, and path ③ is 2. Considering path ② and path③ share edge v3-v5, so the maximum flow can pass is limited by edge weight v3-v5 which equals 2. Finally, maximum flow from node 1 to node 5 equals 5. In addition, for the undirected graph of double bidirectional flow may contains more paths, but it also follows the basic principle that the maximum flow between two nodes is limited by the minimum flow capacity of the edge along the path and the flow of each edge does not exceed the capacity.

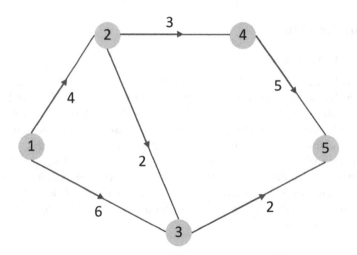

Fig. 1. Example of maximum flow between nodes

Connectivity of water network is calculated as follows:

Step 1: Boykov-Kolmogorov method is used to calculate maximum flow between any two nodes by MATLAB. The mathematical expression follows as [13]

$$\left(f_{ij}\right)_{n \times n} = \text{maxflow } w_{ij}; \text{i}, \text{j} = 1, 2, \ldots, \text{n} \tag{5}$$

Where, f_{ij} represents maximum flow from node i to node j, and the result appears the matrix of maximum flow by traveling node method.

Step 2: Average flow capacity of node D_i can be obtained by

$$D_i = \frac{1}{n-1} \sum_{i \neq j}^{n} f_{ij}; \text{i}, \text{j} = 1, 2, \ldots, \text{n} \tag{6}$$

Step 3: Connectivity of water network D is actually the average maximum flow of all nodes as

$$D = \frac{1}{n} \sum_{i=1}^{n} D_i \tag{7}$$

The flowchart of connectivity algorithm is as follows (Fig. 2):

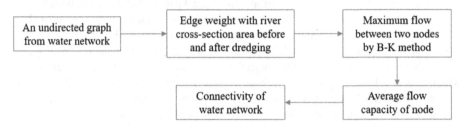

Fig. 2. The flowchart of connectivity algorithm

3   Application Study

3.1   Region Introduction

Hangzhou is located in the northern part of Zhejiang Province and in the downstream region of the Qiantang River. It is the starting point of south for the Beijing-Hangzhou Grand Canal and considered as an important city of the Yangtze River Delta. It is a plain city with developed water system with river density of more than 10 km/km². Benefit from abundant water resources, rivers play an important vector to meet the needs of irrigation, power generation, drainage, shipping, breeding, production and domestic water. According to the statistics, water network of Xiacheng District in Hangzhou consists of 31 main rivers with width from 10 to 100 m and depth from 2 to 3 m. Affected by urbanization, the cross-sections of most rivers appear as rectangle by artificial modification.

3.2   Node Degree and Flow Capacity

Xiacheng District is so flatland that water network is suitable for undirected graph. It is a connected graph with 52 nodes and 71 edges (excluding beheaded river due to boundary restriction, see Fig. 3) by node connectivity and edge connectivity both equal 1. According to the statistics, there are 42 nodes with a degree value of 3 and a high percent of 80.77%, the maximum node degree is 4, the minimal node degree is 1, and the average node degree is 2.73. Nodes of degree 1 or 2 may be the beheaded river or boundary limit.

According to the data obtained, there are 8 rivers dredged with total 175,500 cubic meters over river length more than 19 km in the year 2016 in Xiacheng District. The cross-section area of dredged river increased by 2.92–28.93 m², ratio of $\Delta a/a$ ranges from 11.67% to 100.62%. As a result, a total of 18 graph edges have weight added (see Table 1).

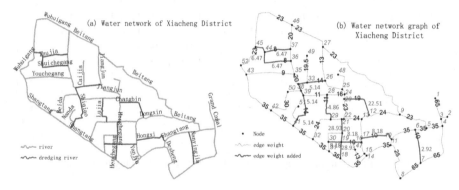

Fig. 3. Water network and graph

Table 1. Edge weight added by dredging

Name	l (m)	b (m)	h (m)	a (m²)	q (m³)	Δa (m²)	E (Δa)
Nanyingjia	1200	10	2.5	25	3500	2.92	8
Changbin	1777	19	2.5	47.5	40000	22.51	18
Hongxi	3300	10	2.5	25	27000	8.18	15, 26, 30
Henghegang	1400	11.5	2.5	28.75	40500	28.93	27, 29, 32
Lujia	1850	11	2.5	27.5	9000	4.86	44
Shiqiao	7100	14	2.5	35	36500	5.14	42, 50, 53, 60, 62, 64
Zhujia	1546	8	2.5	20	10000	6.47	59, 70
Shuichegang	1513	8	2.5	20	9000	5.95	57

Note: E (Δa) refers to edges with area added.

3.3   Average Flow Capacity and River Network Connectivity

The maximum flow between any two nodes is calculated as formula (1) ,and ratio matrix of maximum flow after dredging F' to maximum flow before dredging F shows in Fig. 4, As F is a symmetric matrix, where $F = (f_{ij})_{n \times n}, f_{ij} = f_{ji}$, it can be expressed as upper triangular. Thus, the maximum flow calculation consists of 1326 node pairs, of which 765 increased and 561 unchanged. Among the increasing node pairs, there are 7 node pairs whose maximum flow f reaches 69.04%, including (12, 19), (14, 19), (18, 19), (19, 31), (19, 32), (19, 41), (19, 42). As node 19 with node degree value 4 is so important that each of the 7 node pairs with maximum flow increasing contain node 19. It is found 42 nodes pairs whose value f is equal or greater than 60%, and 40 of them has relationship with nodes 19 and 20, which is due to the higher node degree of 19 and mass dredging of the two nodes.

Average flow capacity added of each node is calculated by average maximum flow added for the point to all others. As shown in Table 2, there are 9 nodes with an increase of average flow capacity more than 10%, 27 nodes with an increase of 5% to 10%, 12 nodes with an increase of 0 (excluding 0) to 5%, and 4 nodes unchanged. According to data

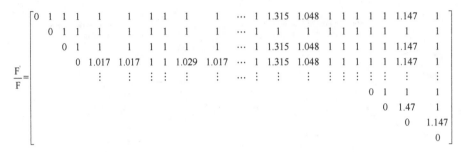

$$\frac{F'}{F} = \begin{bmatrix} 0 & 1 & 1 & 1 & 1 & 1 & 1 & 1 & 1 & 1 & \cdots & 1 & 1.315 & 1.048 & 1 & 1 & 1 & 1 & 1 & 1.147 & 1 \\ & 0 & 1 & 1 & 1 & 1 & 1 & 1 & 1 & 1 & \cdots & 1 & 1 & 1 & 1 & 1 & 1 & 1 & 1 & 1 & 1 \\ & & 0 & 1 & 1 & 1 & 1 & 1 & 1 & 1 & \cdots & 1 & 1.315 & 1.048 & 1 & 1 & 1 & 1 & 1 & 1.147 & 1 \\ & & & 0 & 1.017 & 1.017 & 1 & 1 & 1.029 & 1.017 & \cdots & 1 & 1.315 & 1.048 & 1 & 1 & 1 & 1 & 1 & 1.147 & 1 \\ & & & & \vdots & \vdots & \vdots & \vdots & \vdots & \vdots & \cdots & \vdots & \vdots & \vdots & \vdots & \vdots & \vdots & \vdots & \vdots & \vdots & \vdots \\ & & & & & & & & & & & & & & & 0 & 1 & 1 & & 1 \\ & & & & & & & & & & & & & & & & 0 & 1.47 & & 1 \\ & & & & & & & & & & & & & & & & & 0 & & 1.147 \\ & & & & & & & & & & & & & & & & & & & 0 \end{bmatrix}$$

Fig. 4. Ratio matrix of maximum flow between nodes dredging to original

analysis,Henghegang has the highest river cross-section area added by dredging, and the average flow capacity of the 4 middle nodes within it (18, 19, 20, and 21) increased by 6.93%, 40.42%, 44.01%, and 13.72%. Especially, the middle two nodes 19 and 20 which surrounded by dredging river links have the maximum increase. Average flow capacity of 4 nodes (2, 47, 48, 49) maintain zero while they are only connected with one edge and namely with node degree 1, and limited by it.

Table 2. Average flow capacity added for nodes

1–9		10–18		19–27		28–36		37–45		46–52	
No	D_i (%)	No	D_i (%)	No	D_i (%)	No	D_i (%)	No	D_i (%)	No	D_i (%)
1	4.53	10	6.37	19	40.42	28	5.68	37	6.41	46	4.58
2	0.00	11	6.25	20	44.01	29	5.92	38	9.75	47	0.00
3	4.53	12	8.58	21	13.72	30	8.46	39	10.11	48	0.00
4	6.06	13	4.90	22	5.83	31	6.13	40	13.64	49	0.00
5	6.24	14	6.42	23	13.27	32	6.51	41	6.05	50	1.87
6	6.22	15	1.64	24	1.87	33	13.99	42	6.05	51	13.64
7	6.06	16	7.38	25	0.16	34	8.62	43	4.63	52	3.84
8	6.08	17	7.38	26	5.84	35	2.58	44	29.25		
9	5.46	18	6.93	27	3.93	36	6.10	45	6.56		

The distribution of the average flow capacity of each node before dredging is shown in Fig. 5(a). Nodes of the better average flow capacity before dredging are 4 to 13, which belong to the Grand Canal, Shangtang River, Beitang River, Desheng River and Nanyingjia River with large river cross-section area and high discharge passing capacity. Node of the worse average flow capacity before dredging are 4 nodes (47, 48, 49 and 51) with node degree 1, and node 44 with node degree 3. For node 44, although it is with node degree 3 but the total weight of the three connected edges is still one of the minimum values among the entire river network. The distribution of the average flow capacity added of each node is shown in Fig. 5(b). Henghegang region is with the highest increase of the average flow capacity, and node 44 connected with Zhujia River and Shuichegang followed by. Although the average flow capacity of node 44 before dredging is worse than most nodes, but all of the three connected links are dredged with cross-section area added by 88.88%, which leads to a high increase. It also shows minor increase of Beitang River because there are no dredged rivers connected to it including itself. Analysis indicated that nodes with more dredging and higher node degree appear to be more the average flow capacity added. With the dredging data of the study region, the connectivity of water network is computed to add by 7.89%.

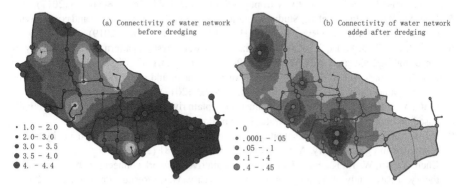

Fig. 5. Average flow capacity of node before dredging and its increase rate after dredging

4   Conclusion

Connectivity of water network declines with reduction of river cross-section by construction of urbanization, which may lead to problems as frequent flooding and bad quality of water. Dredge can be useful to solve the problem by improving river network patency.

(1) This paper presents a method by using river cross-section area as edge weight to calculate average flow capacity of nodes and water network connectivity, which may be helpful to find a better dredging scheme.

(2) The concept of network flow is applied to the water flow, namely maximum flow, which is used as river flow capacity between two nodes with the principle of the maximum flow of the path between two nodes is limited by the minimum flow capacity of the middle links in path and the flow of each link does not exceed its own capacity.

(3) It will be a continues job to research on sensitivity, redundancy and robustness of edges in the water network, and simultaneously consider hydraulic engineering as an essential factor to evaluate flow capacity and connectivity in further study.

Acknowledgments. This work was financially supported by the science and technology plan of Zhejiang province (2016IM020100-4), and the water science and technology plan of Zhejiang Province (RC1908, RC1906).

References

1. Ru, B., Chen, X., Zhang, Q., et al.: Evaluation of structural connectivity of river system in plain river network region. Water Resour. Power **1**(5), 9–12 (2013)
2. Zhao, J., Dong, Z., Zhai, Z., et al.: Evaluation method for river floodplain system connectivity based on graph theory. J. Hydr. Eng. **42**(5), 537–543 (2011)
3. Yazdani, A., Jeffrey, P.: Complex network analysis of water distribution systems. Chaos (Woodbury N.Y.) **21**(1), 016111 (2011)
4. Zhao, J., Dong, Z., Yang, X., et al.: Connectivity evaluation technology for plain river network regions based on edge connectivity from graph theory. J. Hydroecol. **38**(5), 1–6 (2017)
5. Dou, M., Yu, L., Jin, M., et al.: Study on relationship between box dimension and connectivity of river system in Huaihe River Basin. J. Hydr. Eng. **50**(6), 670–678 (2019)
6. Huang, C., Chen, Y., Li, Z., et al.: Optimization of water system pattern and connectivity in the Dongting Lake area. Adv. Water Sci. **30**(5), 661–672 (2019)
7. Xia, J., Chen, Y., Zhou, Z., et al.: Review of mechanism and quantifying methods of river system connectivity. Adv. Water Sci. **28**(5), 780–787 (2017)
8. GAO, Y., Xiao, X., Ding, M., et al.: Evaluation of plain river network hydrologic connectivity based on improved graph theory. Water Resour. Protect. **34**(1), 18–23 (2018)
9. Xu, G., Xu, Y., Wang, L.: Evaluation of river network connectivity based on hydraulic resistance and graph theory. Adv. Water Sci. **23**(6), 776–781 (2012)
10. Chen, X., Xu, W., Li, K., et al.: Evaluation of plain river network connectivity based on graph theory: a case study of Yanjingwei in Changshu City. Water Resour. Protect. **32**(2), 26–29 (2016)
11. Wang, Z., Wang, G., Wang, J., et al.: Developing the internet of water to prompt water utilization efficiency. Water Resour. Hydropower Eng. **44**(1), 1–6 (2013)
12. Chen, Y.: Connectivity mechanism and prediction and evaluation model of alluvial river system (2019)
13. Yuri, B., Vladimir, K.: An experimental comparison of min- cut/ max- flow algorithms for energy minimization in vision. IEEE Trans. Pattern Anal. Mach. Intell. **26**(9), 1124–1137 (2004)

A Study on the Error Characteristics of Smartphone Inertial Sensors

Huifeng Li[✉]

School of Computer, HulunBuir University, HulunBuir, China
33288653@qq.com

Abstract. The inertial sensors embedded in current smartphones are being used in a variety of applications, including motion monitoring, safe driving, panoramic roaming, Pedestrian Dead Reckoning (PDR), etc. Since the performance of these sensors has significant influences on these applications, it is of great value to comprehensively understand how the measurements returned by these sensors are statistically distributed. Most existing studies assume white Gaussian noises in sensor measurements, which is not experimentally confirmed in realistic and dynamic scenarios with commercial off-the-shelf (COTS) smartphones. In this paper, we study the statistical error characteristics of sensor measurements through extensive experiments in practice. The experimental results reveal that, when the device is stationary, the sensor measurement errors fully obey the standard Gaussian distribution; when the speed of smartphones increases, the sensor measurement errors begin rising, and the discrepancy between its distribution and the Gaussian distribution is enlarged. This paper establishes foundation for studying the statistical characteristics of the measurement errors of smartphone inertial sensors.

Keywords: Sensor errors · Smartphones · Gaussian distribution

1 Introduction

With the explosive growth of mobile devices in the past decade, the application scenarios based on smartphone sensors have become more and more widespread. For example, a smartphone can exploit the direction sensor to identify its trajectory to automatically control the moving direction of a game character, so that users are provided with excellent gaming experiences; a smartphone is able to improve its localization accuracy by inferring its user's trajectory based on PDR [7].

At present, by using the inertial sensors embedded in commercial off-the-shelf (COTS) smartphones, i.e. accelerometer, gyroscope and magnetometer, researches on smartphone sensors have achieved outstanding progress in human motion, game development, panoramic roaming, safe driving, etc. [2,3,5]. In [4], a variety of smartphone sensors were employed to design a monitoring algorithm which detects the falling event of elders. In [15], an effective method was proposed

© ICST Institute for Computer Sciences, Social Informatics and Telecommunications Engineering 2020
Published by Springer Nature Switzerland AG 2020. All Rights Reserved
W. Li and D. Tang (Eds.): MOBILWARE 2020, LNICST 331, pp. 119–130, 2020.
https://doi.org/10.1007/978-3-030-62205-3_12

to detect the movement of the user's body and head with accelerometers and gyroscopes to control the natural visualization of three dimensional game objects in smartphones. In [6], the direction sensor embedded in smartphones was used to realize the rotation and translation of the panorama. In [14], a smartphone was employed to identify the driving status of a vehicle, such as going straight-forward, turning and emergency braking, simply based on the accelerometer embedded in a smartphone.

More importantly, different step counting algorithms were proposed to accurately count pedestrian steps by only using an accelerometer. For instances, in [8,11], gyroscope was employed to implement more accurate step counting algorithms; in [16], pedestrian heading was estimated by efficiently fusing all the three inertial sensors. In these application scenarios, sensor measurements are often assumed to be corrupted by white Gaussian noises [5], which has not been investigated in practice.

However, there are few studies in the literature on understanding the statistical characteristics of sensor measurement errors in practical environments. In order to enhance the feasibility of the existing studies relying on Gaussian distributed sensor measurements, we study the statistical characteristics of sensor measurement errors by making the following contributions.

- We develop an APP, named Sensor Data Collector, to collect the real measurements of various smartphone sensors.
- We employ the Xsens MTw to obtain the ground truth of sensor measurements, so that we can evaluate the measurement errors of smartphone sensors.
- We process and analyze the sensor measurement errors by using MATLAB Toolbox to obtain the statistical characteristics of different sensor errors.
- We conduct extensive experiments involving different smartphones under various scenarios, including stationary, low speed (i.e. smartphone is held by a walking person) and high speed (i.e. smartphone is held by a running person). The results reveal that, when the device is stationary, the sensor measurement errors fully obey the standard Gaussian distribution; when the speed of smartphones increases, the sensor measurement errors begin rising, and the discrepancy between its distribution and the Gaussian distribution is enlarged.

The rest of the paper is organized as follows. Section 2 introduces the work related to calibration of inertial sensor measurements, as well as studies on offsetting and compensating these sensor measurement errors. Section 3 presents the design details of the Sensor Data Collector (SDC). Section 4 provides details of the experiments in this paper, and gives a subtle analysis of the experimental results. Finally, Sect. 5 gives a conclusion about the statistical characteristics of the sensor measurement errors.

2   Related Work

In this section, we mainly present some researches related to the calibration of inertial sensor measurement errors, including accelerometer measurement errors, gyroscope measurement errors and magnetometer measurement errors.

Researchers utilized noise sources to reduce the accelerometer measurement errors. Yin et al. [17] proposed a comprehensive calibration scheme. They quantified the random noise term through the Allan variance, and used the least squares method to calculate a deterministic calibration coefficient to reduce the interference of random noise. Zhang et al. [18] analyzed the error sources of accelerometer through a large number of repetitive static experiments and established a mathematical model of the error compensation that affects the positioning accuracy of the navigation system.

Qiao et al. [12] utilized the Allan variance to identify the noise coefficient of a gyroscope, and designed the Kalman filter for dynamic simulation on the basis of the error model about the micro-machined gyroscope. The simulation results showed that the exportable mean value of the gyroscope is significantly higher than the original value and calibration value. Li et al. [9] proposed a posterior compensation method for the gyroscope measurement errors. Firstly, the coning compensation was calculated by using angle increment of a gyroscope to output the compensation without error, and then compensating the output errors of the gyroscope at the updating rate of coning compensation.

Li et al. [13] established the compass correction model to analyze the measurement errors of a magnetometer, and derived a calculation formula of the magnetic deviation coefficient. They reduced the heading errors of the magnetometer through some effective methods, such as elliptic hypothesis method, constrained least squares method, etc. Liu et al. [10] proposed a real-time calibration method based on the least square method and the "8" figure calibration method to effectively solve the problem of magnetic interference in the method of magnetometer calibration.

Undoubtedly, the work mentioned above has made outstanding contributions to the research on the sensor measurement errors, and various methods proposed by researchers have effectively decreased the impact of different sensor measurement errors. However, researchers do not propose an unified and effective model to explain the statistical characteristics of the sensor measurement errors in practical environments. Hence, this paper studies the statistical characteristics of the sensor measurement errors in depth and provides a theoretical basis for future research.

3   Sensor Data Collector

In order to study the statistical characteristics of the measurement errors about three sensors (i.e. accelerometer, gyroscope and magnetometer), we firstly need to develop an Android APP to collect real measurements of various smartphone sensors. In this section, we expound the architecture and implementation details of the Android APP, named Sensor Data Collector (SDC).

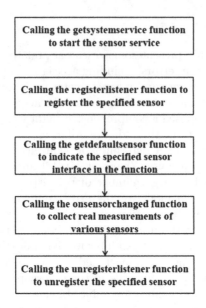

Fig. 1. The sensor invocation mechanism on the Android platform.

The Sensor Data Collector is able to collect X, Y, and Z triaxial measurements of the three sensors and their detailed parameters in real time. These parameters are device name, device version, device vendor, sensor resolution, and minimum collection delay of the sensor. These parameters can help us determine whether the range of different sensor measurement errors is reasonable. In these parameters, the pervious three pieces of these parameters describe the hardware information of a specific sensor. The sensor resolution represents the minimum resolution of the measurements collected by a sensor, and the minimum delay is related to the maximum sample frequency of the sensor. We choose Android Studio as the development tool, and the specific process for calling a specified sensor is shown in Fig. 1.

To be specific, the SDC should obtain management privileges by the Sensor Manager class at first. And then, it registers the specified sensor type (e.g. TYPE_MAGNETIC_FIELD, TYPE_ACCELEROMETER and TYPE_GYROSCOPE) through the registerListener function. Next, it calls the onSensorChanged function to collect real measurements from the specified sensor. Finally, the specified sensor is logged out by the unregisterListener function. We set the sensor sampling frequency of the SDC to 60 HZ, and store three kinds of sensor measurements in a txt file.

4   Experimental Results

In this section, we find out the statistical characteristics of the sensor measurement errors by using the toolbox in MATLAB.

4.1   Experiment Setup

Our experiments are only carried out on the flat road. In the course of the experiments, we ordered an experimenters to carry smartphones and xsens MTW to do a standing motion, walking motion or running motion, these motions correspond to the stationary scenario, the low speed scenario and the high speed scenario, respectively. Smartphones used in our experiments are Nexus5 and Huawei P7. Another device used in the experiments is Xsens MTw, an inertial-magnetic motion tracker made by Xsens [1]. The Xsens MTw can collect highly accurate and real-time 3D measurements with multiple sensors. We set all sensors sampling frequency to 60 Hz and collect 10, 000 data in each motion.

Three different scenarios considered in the experiments include the stationary, low speed and high speed. Specifically, in the stationary scenario, the smartphones are placed on a table; in the low speed scenario, the smartphones are held by a pedestrian who walks at a normal speed of around 1 m/s; in the high speed scenario, the smartphones are held by a person who runs in the playground at a speed of around 4 m/s.

In order to collect real and effective sensor measurements of smartphones and the Xsens MTw, we firstly align one Xsens sensor with the smartphone, such that their coordinate systems are overlapping, and then bind them together using double-side adhesive tape. Finally, we process the sensor measurements obtained by the two devices to calculate the sensor measurement errors used in the experiments. In addition, the magnetometer measurement units about two devices are inconsistent. The magnetometer measurement unit in a smartphone is μT, and the magnetometer measurement unit in MTw is Gauss. According to the unit conversion relationship between Tesla and Gauss, we reduce the magnetometer measurement of the former by 100 times to make the two magnetometer units consistent. Since two electromagnetic devices interfere with each other, we only collect the magnetometer measurement errors under the stationary scenario in a relatively non-magnetic interference environment.

4.2   Sensor Measurement Errors Under the Stationary Scenario

When a mobile device is stationary, we use the dfittool toolbox provided by Matlab to check the statistical characteristics of the sensor measurement errors. Due to the space limit, we have shown the probability density function plot of the different measurement errors collected by two devices in Fig. 2. The horizontal axis of Fig. 2 represents the range of sensor measurement errors, and the vertical axis represents density. Density depends on the group spacing and frequency of different elements. In Fig. 2, 'hw' and 'n5' respectively represent the HUAWEI P7 and NEXUS5. Looking carefully at Fig. 2, we find that the probability density function plot of sensor measurement errors conforms to the Gaussian distribution characteristics, and satisfies the boundedness, unimodality, symmetry and compensation. These characteristics can be judged that the sensor measurement errors obey the Gaussian distribution.

To further illustrate this discovery, we use the normplot function provided by MATLAB to draw some normal probability plots of various sensors, as shown in Fig. 3 and Fig. 4. Therein, the horizontal axis denotes the measurement errors and the red dashed lines measure the linear coincidence degree. It can be observed that the sensor measurement errors nearly always obey Gauss distributions.

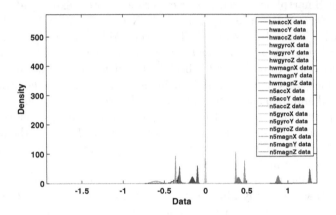

Fig. 2. The probability density function plot in stationary scenario.

4.3   Sensor Measurement Errors Under the Low Speed Scenario

When a device moves in a low speed, the magnetometers in the smartphones and Xsens MTw will interfere with each other, and affect the authenticity of the observed magnetometer measurements. Therefore, in the low speed scenario, we only study the statistical characteristics of accelerometer measurement errors and gyroscope measurement errors. As shown in Fig. 5, we can still observe that the probability density plots of various sensor measurement errors all conform to the Gaussian distribution characteristics.

In addition, Fig. 6 and Fig. 7 illustrate the normal probability plots of various sensor errors with respect to Nexus5 and HWP7, respectively. As can be seen, the various sensor measurements errors also obey the Gaussian distribution in most time, but there are also some outliers appearing in the head and tail of the sensor measurement errors. Thus, it can be concluded that the errors of accelerometer measurements and gyroscope measurements approximately obey the Gaussian distribution in the low speed scenario.

4.4   Sensor Measurement Errors Under the High Speed Scenario

The method of verifying the statistical characteristics of the sensor measurement errors in the high speed scenario is the same as the method mentioned before, and the conclusions are consistent with the sensor measurement errors in low

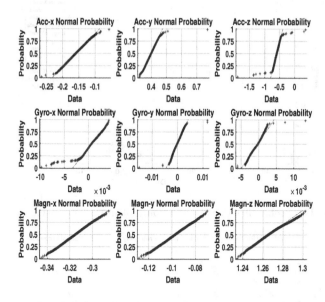

Fig. 3. The normal probability plot of various sensor measurement errors in Nexus5 in the stationary scenario.

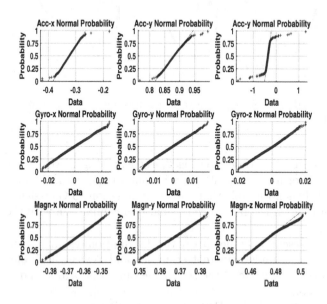

Fig. 4. The normal probability plot of various sensor measurement errors in HUAWEI P7 in the stationary scenario.

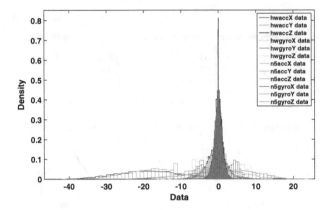

Fig. 5. The probability density function plot in the low speed scenario.

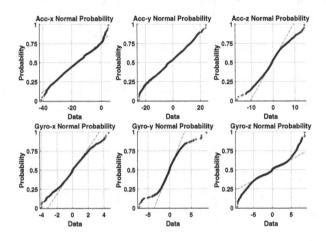

Fig. 6. The normal probability plot of various sensor measurement errors in Nexus5 in the low speed scenario.

speed scenario. However, observing Fig. 2, Fig. 5 and Fig. 8, we can conclude that the range of sensor measurement errors becomes larger with the increase of the moving speed. It is noticeable that the approximation to Gaussian distribution becomes degrading in the high speed scenario in comparison with the low speed scenario.

Finally, we present a detailed list of the distribution results of different sensor measurement errors under different scenarios and devices in Table 1, where μ represents the sample mean of the sensor measurement errors, and σ represents the sample standard deviation of the sensor measurement errors. 'HW' and 'N5' respectively represent the HUAWEI P7 and NEXUS5.

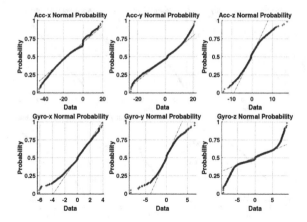

Fig. 7. The normal probability plot of various sensor measurement errors in HUAWEI P7 in the low speed scenario.

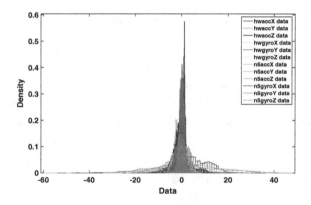

Fig. 8. The probability density function plot in the high speed scenario.

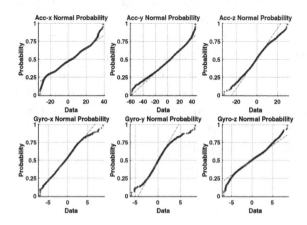

Fig. 9. The normal probability plot of various sensor measurement errors in Nexus5 in the high speed scenario.

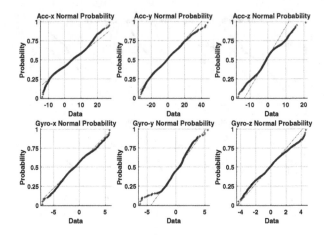

Fig. 10. The normal probability plot of various sensor measurement errors in HUAWEI P7 in the high speed scenario.

Table 1. The results of three sensors in different smartphones under different scenarios.

Results (μ/σ)	HW standing	HW walking	HW running
ACC-X	$-0.323/0.015$	$-16.303/10.214$	$4.760/7.005$
ACC-Y	$0.881/0.016$	$1.128/7.941$	$-0.924/11.035$
ACC-Z	$-0.363/0.053$	$-0.496/2.534$	$-0.525/4.101$
GYRO-X	$-2e{-}5/0.007$	$0.004/1.118$	$-0.832/1.832$
GYRO-Y	$-2e{-}4/0.005$	$-0.073/1.153$	$0.443/1.101$
GYRO-Z	$2e{-}4/0.006$	$0.021/4.556$	$-0.114/1.272$
MAGN-X	$-0.364/0.005$	–	–
MAGN-Y	$0.367/0.005$	–	–
MAGN-Z	$0.474/0.007$	–	–
Results (μ/σ)	N5 Standing	N5 Walking	N5 Running
ACC-X	$-0.159/0.018$	$-16.384/7.834$	$2.942/13.494$
ACC-Y	$0.399/0.019$	$-2.247/7.488$	$3.372/16.168$
ACC-Z	$-0.600/0.056$	$-0.504/3.021$	$-0.742/6.846$
GYRO-X	$7e{-}4/0.001$	$0.085/0.931$	$-0.638/1.832$
GYRO-Y	$-1e{-}4/0.001$	$-0.043/1.083$	$0.147/1.244$
GYRO-Z	$-4e{-}4/0.001$	$0.002/3.735$	$-0.066/2.760$
MAGN-X	$-0.315/0.007$	–	–
MAGN-Y	$-0.097/0.007$	–	–
MAGN-Z	$1.265/0.009$	–	–

5   Conclusion

In this work, we obtained the error characteristics of smartphone inertial sensors by making the following contributions. First of all, we developed an Android APP, named Sensor Data Collector, to collect the measurements of smartphone inertial sensors. The measurements collected by the Xsens MTw was used as the ground truth to evaluate sensor measurement errors. Finally, based on the experiments carried out under different scenarios, the sensor measurement errors were processed and analyzed by using the MATLAB Toolbox.

The experimental results show that the statistical characteristics of the sensor measurement errors are dependent on the moving speed of smartphones. To be specific, when the device is stationary, the sensor measurement errors fully obey the standard Gaussian distribution; when the speed of smartphones increases, the sensor measurement errors begin rising, and the discrepancy between its distribution and the Gaussian distribution is enlarged. Our studies not only confirm the assumptions of Gaussian distributed measurements of inertial sensor in many existing algorithms, but also provide more accurate descriptions of error characteristics of inertial sensor measurements in smartphones, which will definitely benefit future researches.

References

1. Mtwawinda whitepaper. https://www.xsens.com/download/pdf/MTwAwinda_ WhitePaper.pdf
2. Chen, G.L., Li, F., Zhang, Y.Z.: Pedometer method based on adaptive peak detection algorithm. J. Chin. Inert. Technol. **23**(3), 315–321 (2015)
3. Chen, G.L., Zhang, Y.Z., Yang, Z.: Realization of pedometer with auto-correlation analysis based on mobile phone sensor. J. Chin. Inert. Technol. **22**, 794–798 (2014)
4. Cheng, Y., Li, D., Zhang, X.: Research and implementation of fall detection based on android phone. Electron. Design Eng. **24**(14), 181–183 (2016)
5. Harle, R.: A survey of indoor inertial positioning systems for pedestrians. IEEE Commun. Surv. Tutor. **15**(3), 1281–1293 (2013). https://doi.org/10.1109/SURV. 2012.121912.00075
6. Hu, X., Zhao, Z.: The construction of panorama roaming system based on android sensors. Inf. Commun. **11**, 106–107 (2015)
7. Huang, B., Qi, G., Yang, X., Zhao, L., Zou, H.: Exploiting cyclic features of walking for pedestrian dead reckoning with unconstrained smartphones. In: ACM International Joint Conference, pp. 374–385 (2016)
8. Kang, X., Huang, B., Qi, G.: A novel walking detection and step counting algorithm using unconstrained smartphones. Sensors **18**(1), 297 (2018)
9. Li, Z.T., Wu, T.J., Ma, L.H.: A sins coning compensation algorithm based on gyro error post-compensation. J. Shanghai Jiaotong Univ. **45**(3), 388–392 (2011)
10. Liu, Y., Chen, Y.W., Yong-Le, L.U., Ding, Q.X., Yao, L.I.: Research on error compensation and calibration of magnetometer based on least square method. Navigat. Position. Timing (2018)
11. Qi, G., Huang, B.: Walking detection using the gyroscope of an unconstrained smartphone. In: Chen, Q., Meng, W., Zhao, L. (eds.) ChinaCom 2016. LNICST, vol. 210, pp. 539–548. Springer, Cham (2018). https://doi.org/10.1007/978-3-319-66628-0_51

12. Qiao, H.: A high precision compensation method for micro-mechanical gyro error. Foreign Electron. Meas. Technol. **31**, 18–20 (2012)
13. Simin, L.I., Cai, C., Wang, Y., Cao, Z.: Error calibration method of magnetic deviation for hand-held mems magnetometer. Chin. J. Electron. Devices (2017)
14. Song, Y.: Research on the key technology of driving event recognition based on android smartphone sensors. Ph.D. thesis, Ocean University of China (2014)
15. Tolle, H., Pinandito, A., Adams, J.E.M., Arai, K.: Virtual reality game controlled with user's head and body movement detection using smartphone sensors. J. Eng. Appl. Sci. **10**(20), 9776–9782 (2015)
16. Yang, X., Huang, B., Miao, Q.: A step-wise algorithm for heading estimation via a smartphone. In: Control and Decision Conference, pp. 4598–4602 (2016)
17. Yin, H., Zhang, W., Yuan, L.: An error analysis and calibration method of mems accelerometer. Chin. J. Sens. Actuat. **27**(7), 866–869 (2014)
18. Zhang, P.F., Long, X.W.: Research on compensating error model of quartzose flexible accelerometer. Chin. J. Sens. Actuat. **19**(4), 1100–1102 (2006)

Study on Ruminant Recognition of Cows Based on Activity Data and Long Short-Term Memory Network

Shuai Hou$^{(\boxtimes)}$ (ID), Xiaodong Cheng (ID), and Mingshu Han (ID)

College of Electronic Information Engineering, Inner Mongolia University,
Hohhot 010021, China
495830389@qq.com, cxd0808@imu.edu.cn, 657910531@qq.com

Abstract. In this paper, the collected activity data with ruminating status label is used as the data set, based on the long short-term memory network in the recurrent neural network, in order to identify and judge the ruminating process of dairy cows. This paper analyzes the advantages of selecting activity data as input data and long short-term memory network as core algorithm, introduces the hardware design and composition of the self-developed activity data acquisition system, and describes the characteristics of long short-term memory network structure. It is innovative to combine cow activity data with long short-term memory network to identify ruminating in the time period of cow activity data. The experimental results show that the long short-term memory network has different recognition effects on dairy cows of different individuals through the learning of activity data, and the accuracy of ruminating recognition of the whole data is 0.78. This method is effective and feasible. It can provide ideas for the related research of intelligent animal husbandry.

Keywords: Rumination of cows · Activity data · Long Short-Term memory

1 Introduction

Today, the total number of dairy cows in China is about 13.766 million, and the total annual raw milk production is about 38.5 million tons, ranking third in the world [1]. Since 2010, in order to improve the hygienic quality and breeding efficiency of milk, large-scale dairy farming has been carried out in China. In the past, family farms with only a few dozen cows were gradually replaced by large-scale farms with 500, 000 cows. The main production tasks in large-scale pastures are cow feeding, milk production (milking), cow reproduction (estrus monitoring) and disease prevention. With the significant increase in the number of dairy cows in the pasture, the workload in farm production has been increased. It is basically impossible to complete these tasks manually, and there is an urgent need to use mechanization and information means to replace them.

W. Li and D. Tang (Eds.): MOBILWARE 2020, LNICST 331, pp. 131–144, 2020.
https://doi.org/10.1007/978-3-030-62205-3_13

Ruminating activity is very important to the metabolic activity of dairy cows, and it is an important detection index in the process of disease prevention and supervision of dairy cows. Cow ruminating stimulates the secretion of saliva and digestive enzymes, which ensures the activity of rumen cellulose decomposition. Lack of related enzymes, cows will have symptoms such as indigestion, acidosis, limb ulceration, poor state, and finally lead to death. When there was ruminating disorder, the dairy cows showed that the number of ruminating decreased, the duration of ruminating was short or delayed, and even stopped ruminating [2].

Ruminating time is an important index to reflect the health of ruminants. The rhythm and time of ruminants are closely related to health status. Through the collection, processing and analysis of ruminant signals, ruminant health status can be more accurately detected and found. If there is a sudden decline in ruminant activity compared to the normal level, it indicates that the animal loses appetite or is sick, and long-term loss of appetite is a sign that the animal is in a state of disease. As long as there is no change in the health of daily feeding, pasture feeding and ruminants, ruminant activity is in a very stable state. When there are problems with feeding and breeding, the ruminating of the herd will change accordingly. For farm workers, early information on potential health problems of ruminants can be diagnosed and treated as soon as possible to recover losses for pastures. Therefore, the application prospect of cow ruminant recognition is very broad.

In the research of behavior recognition algorithm, Paula Martiskainen et al. (2012) studied a SAAR (Semantic Annotation and Activity Recognition) system, which uses SVM (Support Vector Machine) support vector machine technology to identify the three-axis acceleration of dairy cows [3]. M. Alsaaod et al. (2015) collected the motion information of dairy cows through pedometer, and developed a new RumiWatch algorithm to judge cow behavior, which is used to improve the automatic feeding and management system of dairy cows [4]. Jorge A. V á zquez Diosdado et al. (2015) developed a decision tree algorithm, which uses a three-axis accelerometer installed from the neck of a cow to collect data to classify cow behavior and detect the transition between lying and standing behavior [5]. C Arcidiacono et al. (2016) defined and implemented a new open source algorithm, using statistically defined thresholds to calculate cow steps to improve cow health benefits [6]; Md. Sumon Shahriar et al. (2016) used unsupervised learning method to study the dairy cow fever event detection system based on animal sensor, and used K-means algorithm to group the time series segmentation window to improve the observation sensitivity of dairy cow fever event [7].

Reith et al. (2012) [8] studied the relationship between daily ruminating time and estrus in four dairy farms. The HR-Tag system was used to record 349 estrous cycles of 279 dairy cows. Finally, the milk production data and reproduction data of 265 estrous cycles of 224 dairy cows were used for statistical analysis. The mixed mathematical model of SAS software was used to analyze the relationship between ruminating time and estrus. The experiment showed that 94% of the cows were related to the decrease of ruminating time. Chung et al. (2013) [9] proposed a data mining algorithm for cow estrus detection. In this algorithm, the Mel frequency cepstrum coefficient is extracted from cow sound, and the support vector data description method (SVDD) is used to realize early anomaly monitoring. Daniel. of the University of Minnesota in 2015. A.N.

et al. [10] the ruminating behavior of dairy cows with uterine diseases and metabolic diseases was studied by using the ruminating remote recorder of Israeli company, and it was found that the ruminating behavior of diseased dairy cows decreased greatly. it provides a theoretical basis for the effect of rumination on the health status of dairy cows. G á sp á rdy et al. [11] by monitoring the daily ruminating behavior and actual body weight of 96 dairy cows, it was proved that the ruminating behavior of dairy cows is an important factor affecting the health status and production performance of dairy cows. Clark (2015) et al. [12] by monitoring the hourly activity and ruminating data of each cow by wearing Israeli-produced SCR HR LD Tags for 27 cows and fitting them with a linear mixed model, it was determined that the ruminating behavior and activity of dairy cows were the predictive indexes of calving behavior of dairy cows. Kaufman et al. (2016) [13] the SCR ruminant collar was used to monitor the ruminating behavior of dairy cows 24 h a day to verify the relationship between ruminating time and subclinical ketosis. It is concluded that monitoring the ruminating time of dairy cows can identify the risk of subclinical ketosis in multiple dairy cows after calving.

The activity data of dairy cows refers to the data containing all kinds of behaviors of dairy cows, including feeding, ruminating, running, fighting with other cattle and so on. We use a wearable collector designed by ourselves to fix the collector on the neck of the cow to extract the activity data of the cow. Other data commonly used in cow ruminating research are sound data, body temperature data, video surveillance data and so on, of which the most commonly used is sound data, which is usually due to the complex composition of noise in the environment. Sound feature extraction requires a combination of multiple algorithms, so it is difficult to strike a balance between algorithm optimization and recognition accuracy. Because of the large amount of data and random cow activity, high-definition video data is difficult to achieve automatic identification, so it is generally used for manual observation to verify the recognition results of other data; compared with audio data and high-frequency video data, activity data not only contains rich motion information, but also a small amount of data is easy to train in the deep network after preprocessing. Therefore, we choose the activity data as the data of cow ruminant recognition research.

After extracting the activity data of dairy cows, it is necessary to select an appropriate neural network model to analyze and identify the activity data. Ruminating refers to the physiological activity in which some animals return semi-digested food from their stomach to their mouth and chew again after eating for a period of time [14]. Generally, the ruminating lasts for 40 min and 50 min at a time. Although the time sequence correlation of cow rumination is not the same as the stock price problem, compared with the classical cat and dog classification problem, cow rumination has a certain time series relationship, assuming that the proposed minimum time measure is one minute. then if the judgment of this minute is ruminating, the next minute probability is still ruminating, so we use the long short-term memory (LSTM) model of recurrent neural network as the core algorithm. Recurrent neural network is a kind of neural network which takes sequence data as input, recurses in the evolution direction of sequence and all cells are connected by chain [15]. Recurrent neural network has the characteristics of memory, parameter sharing and Turing completeness, so it is most suitable to make prediction according to the input time series. In the recurrent neural network, the long short-term memory network is the most common neural network. Compared with the ordinary recurrent neural network, the long short-term memory networks can solve the problem of gradient disappearance to a certain extent [16]. Based on the above discussion, we choose the long short-term memory network as the algorithm model of cows ruminant recognition.

2 Data Collection and Simple Processing

2.1 Data Collection System

The activity collection system mainly includes three parts: the activity collector, the base station and the host computer (PC). As shown in Fig. 1.

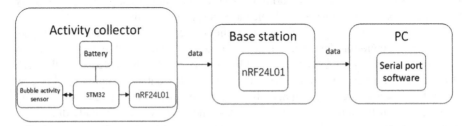

Fig. 1. Activity data collection system

Activity Collector

When ruminating, the cow will retch the food ball directly up to the mouth, chew carefully in the mouth, and then swallow back to the stomach, this process is repeated. There was a continuous fluctuation in the neck of the cow during the whole ruminating process, and the ruminating condition was determined by detecting the fluctuation. The activity collector is worn in the form of a collar on the neck of the cow, which is used to collect the activity data of the cows in real time. As shown in Fig. 2.

The collector consists of a microcontroller, a bubble activity sensor, a wireless transceiver module and a battery. The microcontroller is an ultra-low power 32-bit processor STM32L151C8T6, based on the ARM Cortex-M3 core. It has a data bus width of 32bit and a working power supply voltage of 1.65 V-3.6 V [17]. It has the characteristics of ultra-low power consumption and can meet the needs of products that have been used for a long time. The wireless transceiver module is a monolithic wireless transceiver chip nRF24L01 of 2.4 GHz to 2.5 GHz ISM band produced by Nordic Company. nRF24L01 connected to MCU, through SPI interface has the characteristics of small size, low power consumption, communication radius of about 80 m, etc. [18], it can cover the test environment. The CTRL pin in the sensor is connected to the MCU timer output pin PA1; OUT pin is connected to the MCU modular (AD) sampling channel PA0 [19]. The reference voltage of the AD conversion is set to 3.3 V, the sampling frequency is set to 10 Hz, and the sampling precision is set to 12 bits.

Fig. 2. A cow wearing an activity collector

Bubble sensor is a new type of ultra-low power consumption activity sensor based on the principle of liquid sloshing, which is composed of transparent cavity, infrared emitting diode and infrared receiving diode. The transparent cavity contains a certain amount of silicone oil and air (called bubbles). When the sensor shakes, the movement of the bubble causes the change of the medium between the infrared emitting diode and the receiving diode, which leads to the change of the induced current of the infrared receiving diode, so the movement trend is recorded as an electrical signal. The power consumption of the activity collector is only 1550.5 mAh per year. The two 2600 mAh lithium batteries can be used continuously for 6.87 years in ideal condition, which can meet the use conditions of the collector.

Base Station and PC
The base station includes the nRF24L01 wireless transceiver module, whose main function is to receive the data sent by the activity collector, connect the host computer through the serial port and send the data to the host computer. The host computer has serial port receiving software to receive the data sent by the base station. In the whole process of data acquisition from the activity collector to the host computer, the transmission rate is 8 pieces of data per second.

2.2 Labeling

When collecting the activity data of dairy cows, it is necessary to calibrate the real-time ruminating of dairy cows as a comparison of the results of subsequent model recognition. At present, the more commonly used method is to shoot through the live camera and analyze the video to get the ruminating state of the cow when collecting data. However, this method has some disadvantages, such as too high requirements for hardware, and may not be able to accurately track and observe an individual. Considering the field environment, we adopt the method of manually calibrating the collected data through manual observation in the field. The calibrated state is ruminant and non-ruminant state, non-ruminant state is calibrated to 0, ruminant state is calibrated to 1. We want the time to identify the results to be accurate to minutes, so when labeling, the minimum length of time is one minute.

We collected a total of more than 50 h of data from 6 cows, and finally selected about 40 h of data as the data set, considering the integrity of the data and labels.

2.3 Simple Processing

After obtaining the activity data, simple data processing and analysis are needed for follow-up work. We use matlab2016a to draw a graph of each minute's data to find the difference between ruminant and non-ruminant. As shown in Figs. 3 and 4. The two pictures are the data curves of ruminating and non-ruminating of the same cow, and the time is one minute. Figure 3 is the data curve of ruminating, and Fig. 4 is the data curve of non-ruminating. It can be seen from the picture that when cows do not ruminate, their activity data remain in a steady trend with little fluctuation. When ruminating, the activity data fluctuated greatly, which was obviously different from that

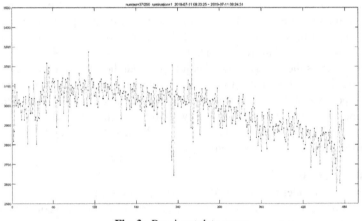

Fig. 3. Ruminant data curve

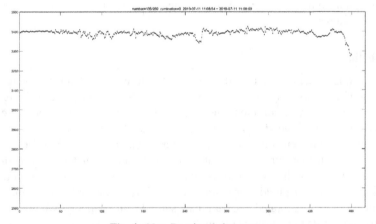

Fig. 4. Non-Ruminant data curve

of non-ruminating. This is because cows do not have too much vibration in their neck when they are not ruminating and eating, so the data extracted by the activity collector fluctuates more smoothly. When it ruminates and chews, the neck vibration is large, which is reflected in the large fluctuation of the data.

3 Long Short-Term Memory Network

Traditional recurrent neural networks are affected by short-term memory. If a sequence is long enough, it will be difficult for them to transfer information from an earlier time step to a later time step. Therefore, if you want to try to process a piece of text for prediction, the recurrent neural network may miss important information from the beginning.

During the period of back propagation, the recurrent neural network will face the problem of gradient disappearance. The gradient is used to update the weight value of the neural network. The vanishing gradient problem means that when the gradient propagates over time, the gradient will decrease. If the gradient value becomes very small, it will not continue to learn. One of the key points of recurrent neural network is that they can be used to connect previous information to the current task, such as using past video clips to infer the understanding of the current segment. If recurrent neural network can do this, they become very useful, but traditional recurrent neural network has long-term dependence problems. As an effective method to solve the long-term dependence problem of general recurrent neural network, long short-term memory network is widely used.

The standard neural network is divided into three layers: input layer, hidden layer and output layer. Input layer can get the data from our custom variables, perform matrix operations on the data, apply it to the activation function, and then store the results in the variables. Hidden layer can get the data from the variables output from the input layer, and after calculating and using the activation function, output the results to the variable for the next hidden layer to use. This process will be iterated several times according to the number of hidden layers you defined. In output layer, the data is obtained from the output variables of the last hidden layer, and the corresponding number of output results are obtained according to the need after operation and using the activation function.

As shown in Fig. 5, the input layer has a cell for reading and transmitting activity data. There are two hidden layers, the number of cells in each layer is 10, the weights of cells between the hidden layers can be transmitted to each other. And the output layer has two cells, representing 0 and 1 respectively. In the long short-term memory network, the core is a hidden neural layer cell, including various gate parameters and activation functions, before and after the cell, each needs input and output network layer. The hidden layer contains three gates for the realization of memory– the forgetting gate, the input gate and the output gate.

3.1 Forgetting Gate

The forgetting gate can decide which information should be discarded or retained. The information from the previously hidden state and the current input are entered into the Sigmoid function at the same time, the output value is between 0 and 1, the closer to 0

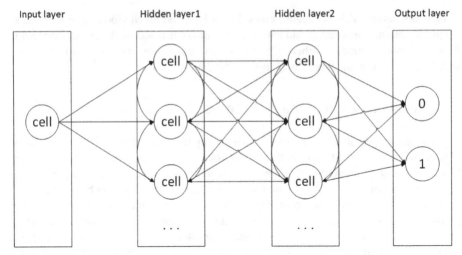

Fig. 5. LSTM structure

means the more should be forgotten, and the closer to 1 means that the more should be retained.

$$f_t = \sigma\left(W_f\left[h_{t-1}, x_t\right] + b_f\right) \tag{1}$$

The calculation of the forgetting gate is shown in formula (1). h_{t-1} is the hidden layer output of the last moment, x_t is the input value of this moment, W_f is the weight matrix of the amnesia gate, b_f is the biases value of the forgetting gate, σ represents the sigmoid function, and f_t represents the output of the forgetting gate.

3.2 Input Gate

The input gate is used to update the cell status. Firstly, the information of the hidden state of the previous layer and the information of the current input are passed to the sigmoid function. Adjust the value to between 0 and 1 to determine which information to update. 0 means unimportant, 1 means important.

Secondly, the information of the hidden state of the previous layer and the information of the current input are passed to the tanh function to create a new candidate vector. Finally, the output value of sigmoid is multiplied by the output value of tanh, and the output value of sigmoid determines which information in the output value of tanh is important and needs to be retained.

$$i_t = \sigma\left(W_i\left[h_{t-1}, x_t\right] + b_i\right) \tag{2}$$

$$C_t' = \tanh\left(W_c\left[h_{t-1}, x_t\right] + b_c\right) \tag{3}$$

In formula (2), W_i and b_i represent the weights matrix and biases value of the input gate respectively, and the output of the input gate can be obtained at this time. In formula

(3), W_c and b_c represent the weight matrix and biases value of neurons respectively. Through the operation of tanh activation function, the value of an intermediate state of cell output can be obtained.

$$C_t = f_t * C_{t-1} + i_t * C'_t \qquad (4)$$

The output of the forgetting gate at this time is multiplied by the output of the cell at the previous moment. Then the product of the intermediate state of the input gate and the output of the cell is calculated. And the two parts are added, that is, the output of the cell at that time, as shown in formula (4).

3.3 Output Gate

The output gate is used to determine the value of the next hidden state, which contains the previously entered information. Firstly, the previous hidden state and the current input are passed to the Sigmoid function. Secondly, the newly obtained unit state is passed to the Tanh function. Thirdly, the Tanh output and the Sigmoid output are multiplied to determine the information that the hidden state should carry. Finally, the hidden state is taken as the current unit output, and the new unit state and the new hidden state are transferred to the next time step.

$$o_t = \sigma\left(W_o\left[h_{t-1}, x_t\right] + b_o\right) \qquad (5)$$

$$h_t = o_t * \tanh(C_t) \qquad (6)$$

In formula (5), W_o and b_o represent the weights matrix and biases value of the output gate, and the output at this time can be obtained by calculation. Then the output of the hidden layer is calculated by formula (6).

3.4 Activation Function

If there is no activation function in the neural network, then the output of each layer is a linear function of the upper input. It is easy to know that no matter how many layers there are in the neural network, the output is a linear combination of input, which has the same effect as no hidden layer. It makes the hidden layer meaningless. After introducing the nonlinear function as the excitation function, the neural network is no longer a linear combination of input and can approach any function. The activation function Tanh is a commonly used nonlinear activation function, which is used to help adjust the value of flow through the network. The tanh function always limits the value to between -1 and 1. The mathematical definition of the tanh function is shown in formula (7) (Figs. 6 and 7).

$$\tanh x = \sinh x / \cosh x \qquad (7)$$

The sigmoid function, also known as the Logistic function, is used to calculate the output of cells in the hidden layer. Because it can map a real number to an interval of 0 to 1, it can be used for binary classification. The effect is better when the feature difference is more complex or the difference is not very large. As an activation function, Sigmoid has many advantages, such as smooth, easy to derive, very good symmetry, insensitive to input beyond a certain range, and so on.

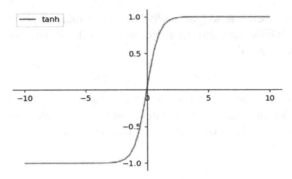

Fig. 6. Tanh activation function graph

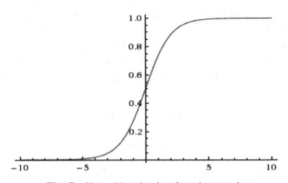

Fig. 7. Sigmoid activation function graph

4 Experiment and Result Analysis

4.1 Experimental Environment

The data collection site was selected from a cattle farm in a village in Hohhot, Inner Mongolia Autonomous Region, in July 2019. A total of about 40 h of activity data of six cattle were collected, with a total of more than 1 million data.

The design language is Python, and its version is 3.6.4. Tensorflow version is 1.13.1.

The initial learning rate is set to 0.0005, and the batch size and time step are both 480. If the learning rate is too large, it will lead to the problem that the possible loss function does not converge; the batch size and time step are set to 480 because the minimum length of manual labels is one minute, while the amount of data in one minute is 480.

4.2 Dataset Partition

The data collected each time is saved in the txt documents, which include year, month, day, hour, minute, second, activity data and manual labels. The minimum time length of manual labels is one minute, ruminating state is labeled as 1, non-ruminating state is labeled as 0, and the ratio of 0 and 1 in all data labels is about 7:3. As the duration of the data collected in each activity is different, in order to make it more convenient for the model to read the data, the data collected in the first three hours are fed into the model, and the data more than three hours in every document are discarded. In order to prevent the over-fitting of the model to a single individual, six Holstein cows were selected, and the amount of data of each cow was also different, ranging from 3 h to 12 h.

We send the data of the first three hours of each txt document into the model one by one, in which there are 57600 pieces of data in the first two hours as the train data set and 28400 pieces of data in the third hour as the test data set. So that the ratio of the train data set to the test data set is 2:1, which is close to the standard proportion of 7:3, and the partition is reasonable. The training effect is measured by the value of loss function, and the test effect is measured by the accuracy.

4.3 Experimental Results

The loss function is also called the cost function, which is the objective function of neural network optimization. The process of neural network training or optimization is the process of minimizing the loss function. The smaller the value of the loss function is, the closer the predicted result is to the real result. The effect of the neural network model and the goal of optimization are defined by the loss function. The loss function between the expected value and the real value can be obtained by calculating the cross entropy. Then the regularization loss of the model is calculated. The total loss is equal to the sum of regularization loss and cross-entropy loss. The expected effect is that the loss function decreases gradually with the increase of the number of iterations. As shown in Fig. 8.

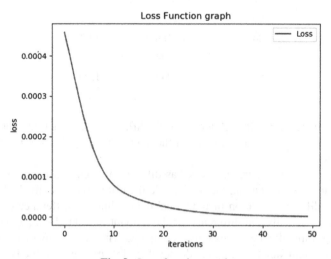

Fig. 8. Loss function graph

The document data of different individuals are identified and determined, and the result is shown in Table 1.

Table 1. The accuracy of different individuals

Number of cows	Duration of data/hours	Accuracy
01	6	0.70
02	6	0.73
03	9	0.80
04	12	0.73
05	3	0.94
06	6	0.78

In Table 1, the duration of the data of the six cows varies, depending on the status of the data we collected at that time and the integrity of the data obtained. We believe that the activity data of different individuals are different, which leads to different recognition effects of long short-term memory networks. Table 2 contains some mathematical eigenvalues of dairy cows activity data.

Table 2. Mathematical eigenvalues of different individuals

Number of cows	Average	Max	Min
01	3110	3511	1602
02	3064	3689	1531
03	2998	3497	1551
04	3188	3717	1488
05	2994	3619	1329
06	2947	3578	1551

As shown in Table 2, although there is little difference in the activity data values of different individuals, it is enough to affect the degree of recognition of the data by the neural network.

We believe that the neural network has different recognition results for different individuals, and the influencing factors include the difference of individual data value itself and the different duration of individual data, while the difference of individual data duration is actually the difference of the amount of data. Take No.05 cow with the best recognition effect as an example, compared with other individuals, its average value and maximum value are in a middle level, and its minimum value is the smallest of all individuals, which may be one of the influencing factors. The No.05 duration of data is the least among all individuals, and we think that this will more or less affect the recognition effect of the model. If No.05 has more activity data, will its accuracy of recognition be close to the level of other individuals? Unfortunately, due to environmental constraints, there is no more individual data No.05 to support this point. However, we select any three-hour data of other individuals, and the accuracy of recognition is lower than that of No.05. As shown in Table 3, we output the data of other individuals every three hours. Based on the comprehensive analysis of all individual data, it is concluded that the recognition accuracy of long short-term memory network is 0.78. We think this is an acceptable result.

Table 3. The accuracy of different individuals every three hours

Number of cows	Accuracy
01	0.68; 0.72
02	0.69; 0.77
03	0.92; 0.82; 0.67
04	0.71; 0.73; 0.76; 0.73
05	0.94
06	0.85; 0.71

5 Conclusion

The experimental results show that the activity data can also be used as the data set of cow ruminating recognition, and the long short-term memory network can effectively identify the activity data of dairy cows ruminating. Compared with sound data or video analysis, activity data is more convenient to extract, less noise, and can be effectively recognized by neural network, and get a more ideal effect.

Due to environmental limitations, this study can also be improved in some aspects. Later, we can continue to collect activity data, improve the data set, specifically, we can add more new individuals, expand the amount of data of all individuals, make the amount of data of all individuals sufficient and close, balance the proportion of 0, 1 labels, and so on.

From the analysis of experimental results, this study has a certain feasibility; from the practical analysis, this study combines cow activity data with long short-term memory network to provide reference ideas for intelligent animal husbandry.

Acknowledgment. This work was funded by Project of Natural Science Foundation of Inner Mongolia Autonomous Region: Research on Automatic Detection Technology of Dairy Cow Ruminant (Project number: 2019MS06011).

References

1. Dongsheng, L.: Study on template matching Dairy Cow recognition based on Dairy Cow activity data and convolution Neural Network. Inner Mongolia University (2019)

2. Hong, W.: Differential diagnosis of ruminant disorders in dairy cows. Herbivores (2015)
3. Martiskainen, P., Järvinen, M., Skön, J.P., et al.: Cow behaviour pattern recognition using a three-dimensional accelerometer and support vector machines. Appl. Anim. Behav. Sci. **119**(1-2), 32–38 (2009)
4. Alsaaod, M., Niederhauser, J.J., Beer, G., et al.: Development and validation of a novel pedometer algorithm to quantify extended characteristics of the locomotor behavior of dairy cows. J. Dairy Sci. **98**(9), 6236–6242 (2015)
5. Diosdado, J.A.V., Barker, Z.E., Hodges, H.R., et al.: Classification of behaviour in housed dairy cows using an accelerometer-based activity monitoring system. Anim. Biotelemetry **3**(1), 15 (2015)
6. Arcidiacono, C., Porto, S.M.C., Mancino, M., et al.: Development of a threshold-based classifier for real-time recognition of cow feeding and standing behavioural activities from accelerometer data. Comput. Electron. Agric. **134**, 124–134 (2017)
7. Shahriar, M.S., Smith, D., Rahman, A., et al.: Detecting heat events in dairy cows using accelerometers and unsupervised learning. Comput. Electron. Agric. **128**, 20–26 (2016)
8. Reith, S., Hoy, S.: Relationship between daily rumination time and estrus of dairy cows. J. Dairy Sci. **95**(11), 6416–6420 (2012)
9. Chung, Y., Lee, J., Oh, S., et al.: Automatic detection of cow's oestrus in audio surveillance system. Asian-australasian J. Anim. Sci. **26**(7), 1030–1037 (2013)
10. Daniela, N.L.: Characterization of peripartum rumination and activity of cows diagnosed with metabolic and uterine diseases. J. Dairy Sci. **98**(10), 6812–6827 (2015)
11. Gáspárdy, A., Efrat, G., Bajcsy, Á., Fekete, S.: Electronic monitoring of rumination activity as an indicator of health status and production traits in high-yielding dairy cows. Acta Vet. Hung. **62**(4), 452–462 (2014)
12. Clark, C.E.F., Lyons, N.A., Millapan, L., et al.: Rumination and activity levels as predictors of calving for dairy cows. Anim. Int. J. Anim. Biosci. **9**(4), 691–695 (2015)
13. Kaufman, E.I., Leblanc, S.J., McBride, B.W., et al.: Association of rumination time with subclinical ketosis in transition dairy cows. J. Dairy Sci. **99**(7), 5604–5618 (2016)
14. Yonghong, J.: Ruminant teaching method in physics teaching in senior high school. Navigation of Arts and Sciences (in the middle) (6), p. 77
15. Ma, Q., Zheng, Q., Peng, H., et al.: Chaotic time series prediction based on dynamic recurrent neural network model. Comput. Appl. **27**(1), 40–43 (2007)
16. Wei, X.: Problem classification based on deep learning model. Hunan University
17. Yuquan, G., Weihua, Y.: Power monitoring system based on ARMCortex-M3. Electronic production (2014)
18. Lin, L., Hongying, Yu., Jiang, S., et al.: Design of nRF24L01 device driver based on Linux. Electronic Test **11**, 61–64 (2012)
19. Huijuan, W., Fengshan, B., Zhaonan, Z., Xiaodong, C., Daoerji, F.: Research on Cow Rumination Monitoring Based on New Activity Sensor. pp. 199–204 (2019). https://doi.org/10.1109/icist.2019.8836709

Design the Tunable Wideband Filter
for DDS+PLL Hybrid Frequency Synthesizer

Yuxin Zhou, Shaoting Cheng, and Xuemei Lei[✉]

Inner Mongolia University, Hohhot 010021, China
ndlxm@imu.edu.cn

Abstract. In this paper, the tunable wideband bandpass filter is designed, which is used in hybrid frequency synthesizer of PLL+DDS mixing in the outside of the feedback loop. The channels of tunable wideband bandpass filter is chosen by two ADGM1304 single-pole, four-throw (SP4T) MEMS switch. And they are integrated on a high-frequency board with a substrate of Ro4350B.The central frequency of bandpass filter is 2.32 GHz, 2.38 GHz, 2.44 GHz and 2.5 GHz respectively. A wideband filter with adjustable center frequency is designed and the bandwidth is up to 240 MHz. Finally, physical tests show the spurious components and unwanted spectral components, especially near-end spurs at the center frequency are removed basically by the tunable broadband bandpass filter.

Keywords: Phase-lock-loop (PLL) · Direct digital synthesis (DDS) · Bandpass filter · Mixer · SP4T MEMS switch

1 Introduction

With the development of communication and remote sensing technology, it is light weight, low cost and easy processing that microstrip filters are widely used in microwave plane circuits and even microwave integrated circuits [1]. Bandpass filter is a fundamental component of wireless communication system that delivers signal within its bandwidth and attenuates signals outside its bandwidth, enhancing the desired frequency component [2]. And the high performance and compact bandpass filters have been widely used in modern communication systems. This kind of filters can be realized by using the methods of high selectivity and harmonic suppression [3]. A multi-layered substrate filter structure is observed that if the split gap width of the microstrip line increases, there is a better suppression of harmonics in the response of the bandpass filter in [4]. In modern wireless communication systems, compact bandpass filters with low insertion loss, dual-band frequency responses and high frequency band selectivity have gained more attention in recent years, which can reduce the complexity and cost of front-end systems [5]. Expecially parallel coupled microstrip line structures have gained great interests in modern communication systems [6]. Parallel coupled microstrip line can realize narrow band filter. Characteristic impedance is the most important feature of microstrip line [7]. Parallel coupled microstrip bandpass filter has become one of the

W. Li and D. Tang (Eds.): MOBILWARE 2020, LNICST 331, pp. 145–155, 2020.
https://doi.org/10.1007/978-3-030-62205-3_14

most commonly used filters for RF front end because of its planar structure and simple design method [8].

Frequency synthesizer is a key component of modern electronic equipment, which can provide a large number of local oscillator signals and carrier signals with high accuracy and fast conversion for communication equipment. It is an important part in modern electronic systems. PLL is good at spurious behavior and there is a shortage in frequency switch speed and frequency resolution [9]. DDS has the advantages of high frequency resolution and short frequency conversion time. Thus, the hybrid frequency synthesizer technology of combine PLL and DDS has become a new research field. And the hybrid frequency synthesizer of PLL+DDS mixing in the outside of the feedback loop can make full use of the characteristics of DDS's high resolution, PLL's high spectral purity, and high stability. But the obvious shortcomings of the structure hybrid frequency synthesizer is the output signal of DDS include spurious frequency and harmonic components so that the frequency components are very complex after mixing with the output signal of PLL so that the near-end spurious of DDS varies with the frequency of the output signal and it is difficult to filter out.

In this paper, we focus on the study of the tunable wideband bandpass filter in DDS+PLL hybrid frequency synthesizer with external loop mixing, mixer output, which include ADGM1304 SP4T MEMS switch and the microstrip line bandpass filter. The hybrid frequency synthesizer consists the mixer so that the spectrum has some new spur. And the near-end spurs are relatively large at the center frequency. Therefore, the bandwidth of the bandpass filter provided cannot be too wide, and stop-band suppression are high. So we design a parallel coupled microstrip line bandpass filter with adjustable center frequency and its stopband attenuation amplitude is greater than 50 dB. The design of the tunable wideband filter applied in the hybrid frequency synthesizer of PLL+DDS mixing in the outside of the feedback loop can remove the spurious and unwanted spectral components to improve the spectral purity of the hybrid frequency synthesizer.

2   Analysis the Hybrid Frequency Synthesizer of PLL+DDS

The hybrid frequency synthesizer mixing in the outside of the feedback loop is mainly composed of phase-locked loop (PLL) module, direct digital frequency synthesizer (DDS) module, mixer (Mixer) module and band-pass filter (BPF) module (see Fig. 1).

The mixer plays the role of spectrum shift in the system, SP4T MEMS switches act as strobe filters for test channels. The last-stage bandpass filter determines the output bandwidth and ability of spurious suppression in entire system.

The phase locked loop (PLL) adopts ADF4351 chip, which a fundamental output frequency range is from 35 MHz to 4400 MHz. The input reference clock of ADF4351 is provided by the active crystal oscillator with a frequency of 25 MHz. The chip is operating with a power supply of 3 V to 3.6 V. The main objective is to provide a communication transceiver with low cost and lower power dissipation [10].

The direct digital synthesis (DDS) adopts AD9910 chip. The AD9910 supports sampling rates up to 1 GSPS. The output frequency range of DDS is from 400 MHz to 6 GHz. The DDS provides fast frequency hopping and frequency tuning resolution with its 32-bit accumulator. AD9910 uses the voltage of 1.8 V and 3.3 V to supply power.

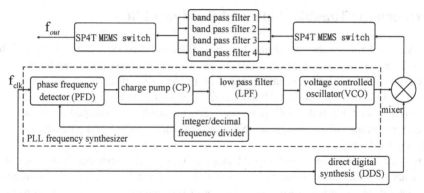

Fig. 1. The hybrid frequency synthesizer structure of PLL+DDS mixing in the outside of the feedback loop

The mixer adopts the ADL5375 chip, which only one input is mixed with the local oscillator and the other is connected to 50 Ω load. PLL provides local oscillator (LO) signal and DDS provides intermediate frequency (IF) signals for mixer. ADL5375 is powered by a 5 V ADP3334 low-dropout regulator (LDO), which reduces the effect of power management on the phase noise of the device.

The SP4T MEMS switch uses the ADGM1304 chip. The SP4T switch provides optimum performance in terms of bandwidth, power handling capability and linearity for RF applications. The power supply voltage needs to be 3.1 V to 3.3 V, the working frequency range is from 0 Hz/dc to 14 GHz, the switching time is 30 μs and the resistance of the conduction is 1.6 Ω.

The indicators of the hybrid frequency synthesizer and tunable wideband bandpass filter are provided in Table 1 and Table 2. These indicators demonstrate that it is necessary for the bandpass filter to have a steep transitional zone and high selectivity. Therefore, the difficulty of the bandpass filter in design is increased.

Table 1. The specific indicators of the hybrid frequency synthesizer

Parameters	Values
The adjustable resolution of the output frequency	1 Hz
The modulation period	us
The single point stability	1 Hz
The range of output power	−76 dBm ∼ −64 dBm

Table 2. The design indicators of the tunable wideband bandpass filter

Parameters	Values
The center frequency of the tunable bandpass filter	2.32 GHz, 2.38 GHz, 2.44 GHz, 2.5 GHz
Stopband rejection of the filter	≥50 dBc (within 65 MHz)
The tunable passband range of the filter	2410 MHz ± 120 MHz

3 Design the Tunable Wideband Bandpass Filter

The design of the tunable wideband bandpass filter is based on a low-pass filter. The lumped parameter components and distributed parameter components can be obtained by a series of model transformations based on the low-pass filter. Since the center frequencies of the tunable wideband bandpass filters designed in this system are 2.32 GHz, 2.38 GHz, 2.44 GHz and 2.5 GHz respectively, the method of lumped parameter has better performance in low frequency band, and the theory of lumped parameter is used to design the bandpass filter.

However, converting from lumped bandpass filter to microstrip bandpass filter, it is necessary to make use of the resistive inverter. As shown in Eq. (1), the series resonator is converted into a parallel resonator. Each series resonator is replaced by two inverters and one parallel resonator (see Fig. 2)

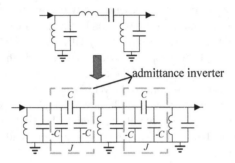

Fig. 2. Conversion diagram of series resonator

$$Z_{eq} = K^2 \Big/ Z \quad Y_{eq} = J^2 \Big/ Y \tag{1}$$

The design adopts the structure of bandpass filter consisting of cascaded coupled microstrip line nodes is shown (see Fig. 3).

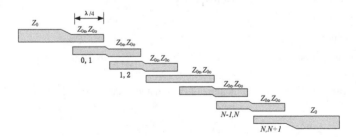

Fig. 3. Structure of fourth-order coupled microstrip bandpass filter

The length of each coupling unit in the filter is 1/4 of the wavelength corresponding to the center frequency and it is shown (see Fig. 4).

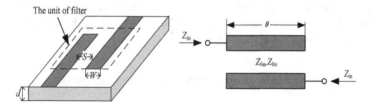

Fig. 4. The unit of coupled microstrip

The coupled microstrip line can be equivalent to the model (see Fig. 5).

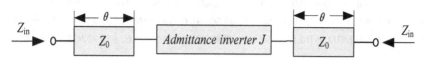

Fig. 5. Equivalent model of coupled microstrip

The plate of tunable wideband bandpass filter is selected by rogers_4350B, the dielectric constant is 3.66 (this value is selected according to the frequency of plate and the corresponding dielectric constant in the Rogers_4350B manual), the tangent loss is 0.0031, the thickness of the dielectric substrate is 0.762 mm and the copper thickness is 0.035 mm. The specific steps for designing a microstrip edge-coupled bandpass filter are as follows [11, 12]:

1. According to stopband suppression, ripple parameters, passband range and Tables 5.2 to 5.6 in Ref. [10], the normalized parameters of the low-pass prototype devices are $g_0 = 1, g_1 = 1.6703, g_2 = 1.1926, g_3 = 2.3661, g_4 = 0.8419, g_5 = 1.9841$ respectively.

2. According to the requirement of bandwidth in the design, the bandwidth of every bandpass filter is 60 MHz, and the center frequency is calculated by $\omega_0 = (\omega_L + \omega_U)/2$. According to the normalized bandwidth formula $BW = (\omega_U - \omega_L)/\omega_0$ of filter, the normalized bandwidth is determined. The following parameters are recalculated by the bandwidth, as shown in the Eq. (2). These parameters can be used to calculate the odd model impedance of the transmission line by Eq. (3) and the characteristic impedance of the even mode is as Eq. (4).

$$J_{0,1} = \frac{1}{Z_0}\sqrt{\frac{\pi BW}{2g_0g_1}} \quad J_{i,i+1} = \frac{1}{Z_0}\frac{\pi BW}{2\sqrt{g_ig_{i+1}}} \quad J_{N,N+1} = \frac{1}{Z_0}\sqrt{\frac{\pi BW}{2g_Ng_{N+1}}} \quad (2)$$

$$Z_{0o}|_{i,i+1} = Z_0\left[1 - Z_0J_{i,i+1} + \left(Z_0J_{i,i+1}\right)^2\right] \quad (3)$$

$$Z_{0e}|_{i,i+1} = Z_0\left[1 + Z_0J_{i,i+1} + \left(Z_0J_{i,i+1}\right)^2\right] \quad (4)$$

Where, the subscript (i, i + 1) represent the coupled microstrip line elements. Z_0 is the characteristic impedance of the microstrip line bandpass filter at the input and output ports. In this design, Z_0 is 50 Ω.

Therefore, the relevant parameter $Z_0 J_{i,i+1}$ is calculated according to Eq. (2) and the characteristic impedances of odd and even modes are calculated by using Eqs. (3) and (4). The calculated values are shown in Table 3.

Table 3. Parameter values of tunable wideband bandpass filter

The center frequency are 2.32/2.38/2.44/2.5 GHz

$i, i + 1$	$Z_0 J_{i,i+1}$	$Z_0(Ω)$	$Z_{0o}(Ω)$	$Z_{0e}(Ω)$
0, 1	0.155/0.153/0.151/0.150	50	43.43/43.489/43.57/43.62	58.997/58.88/58.74/58.64
1, 2	0.028/0.028/0.027/0.026	50	48.606/48.639/48.68/48.7	51.47/51.44/51.396/51.37
2, 3	0.024/0.023/0.022/0.022	50	48.824/48.85/48.88/48.91	51.234/51.20/51.17/51.15
3, 4	0.028/0.028/0.027/0.026	50	48.606/48.639/48.68/48.7	51.47/51.44/51.396/51.37
4, 5	0.155/0.153/0.151/0.150	50	43.43/43.489/43.57/43.62	58.997/58.88/58.74/58.64

3. Considering the edge effect of the microstrip line, the size of each microstrip line needs to be corrected. The size of the microstrip line calculated by the previous step may not meet the requirements and it need to be optimized by using the optimization tools in ADS. The optimized size of the microstrip line is shown in Table 4.

Table 4. Optimized size of tunable wideband bandpass filter

The center frequency are 2.32/2.38/2.44/2.5 GHz

Line description	Width (mm)	Gap (mm)	Length (mm)
50 ohm-line	1.627/1.627/1.627/1.627	–	19.20/18.72/18.25/17.82
Coupled lines 1 and 5	1.530/1.602/1.765/1.982	0.67/0.51/0.307/0.407	21.673/16.36/13.718/17.234
Coupled lines 2 and 4	2.046/2.314/4.019/2.667	1.949/2.615/2.8/2.48	15.366/20.483/23.553/17.00
Coupled lines 3	3.392/1.652/1.956/2.678	2.25/2.38/2.35/2.95	22.453/16.40/13.688/17.068

4   Test Results

In this design, the PLL generates local oscillation frequencies are 2195 MHz, 2255 MHz, 2315 MHz, and 2375 MHz, respectively. DDS output IF signal from 115 MHz to 135 MHz. The structure diagram is shown in Fig. 6. Physical picture of tunable wideband bandpass filter is shown in Fig. 7. The size of tunable wideband bandpass filter is 288.18 * 140.84 * 0.762 mm^3.

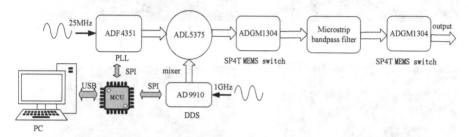

Fig. 6. The structure diagram of each module in the system.

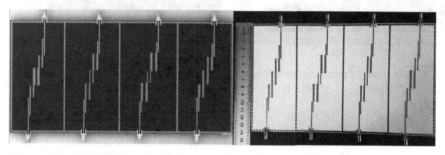

Fig. 7. Physical picture of tunable wideband bandpass filter

The tunable wideband bandpass filter are tested by an Agilent E5062A vector network analyzer. The test results are shown in Fig. 8.

The center frequency of filter is 2.32 GHz, 2.38 GHz and 2.5 GHz and it can completely realize the preset target and filter the spurious spectrum effectively. The test results show the filter with center frequency of 2.44 GHz is slightly deviated, but other spurious spectrum is also filtered out. The reason is the tunable wideband bandpass filter is composed of four filters with different central frequencies. And in order to connect the SMA connector to the real edge, it is necessary to add a different length of microstrip line on the layout, and results in a great edge effect at the open end of the coupling element microstrip line.

In order to verify the performace of the tunable wideband bandpass, the output spectrum of the hybrid frequency synthesizer is tested by spectrum analyzer ADVANTEST R3131A. The result of the test is shown in Fig. 9. The PLL generates local oscillator frequencies of 2195 MHz, 2255 MHz, 2315 MHz, and 2375 MHz respectively, the intermediate frequency signal of 125 MHz is output by DDS.

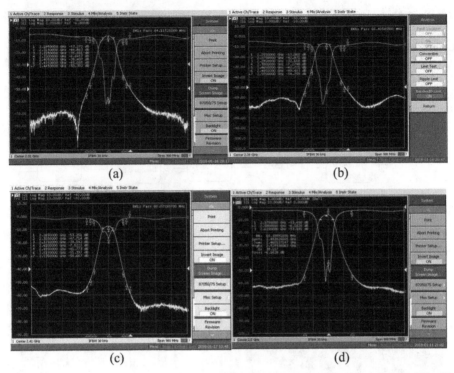

(a)   (b)

(c)   (d)

Fig. 8. Test results of tunable wideband bandpass filter. (a) The center frequency is 2.32 GHz. (b) The center frequency is 2.38 GHz. (c) The center frequency is 2.41 GHz. (d) The center frequency is 2.5 GHz.

When the tunable wideband bandpass filter is unconnected, the test results shown the output spectrums of hybrid frequency synthesizer are special complicated and include a number of spur. After the spectrum of DDS and PLL are mixed, the new spurs are generated and the near end spurs are relatively large. When the tunable wideband bandpass filter is connected, the test results shown the spurious components and unwanted frequency components are removed. It meets the design requirements of index and the expected design goal is realized.

The power values of the near-end spurs and the main frequency spectrum are tested. The range of tests from 2.29 GHz to 2.53 GHz and the interval of main frequency spectrum is 10 MHz. The power of main frequency fluctuates slightly at 2.45 GHz (see Fig. 10). The reason is that tunable wideband bandpass filter is shifted 30 MHz to the left at the frequency of 2.44 GHz and tunable wideband bandpass filter is a passive microstrip line edge coupled bandpass filter, which has a certain attenuation in the band. The frequency points of near-end spurs are concentrated near 2.41 GHz. The reason is that the influence of DDS on near-end spurs is greater than that of PLL. However, DDS is fixed to 125 MHz, and PLL's step is 10 MHz in this test, so when testing the spurious values at different frequencies, the frequency conversion of the PLL is the main influence on spurs. Therefore, the frequency values of near-end spurs is basically unchanged.

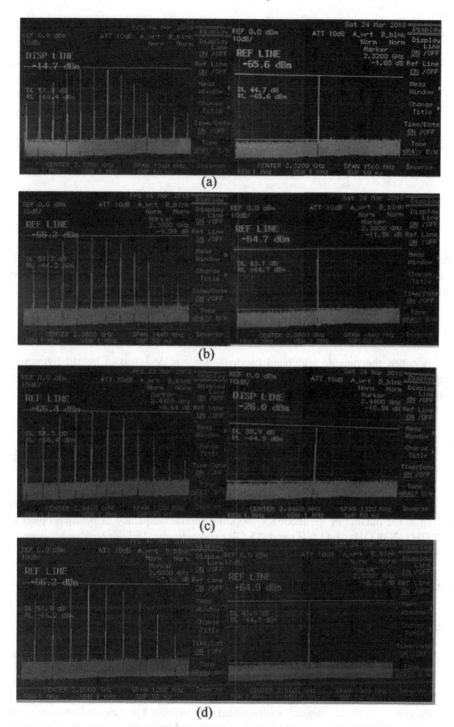

Fig. 9. The output spectrum distribution graph of the system. a) Central frequency is 2.32 GHz; b) Central frequency is 2.38 GHz; c) Central frequency is 2.44 GHz; d) Central frequency is 2.5 GHz.

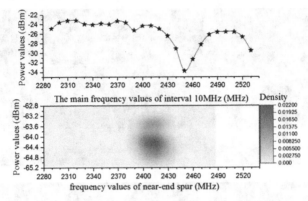

Fig. 10. Test power of the near-end spurs and main frequency

The power difference between the main frequency and the near-end spurs is about 40 dB. The spurs suppression is effective by tunable wideband bandpass filter. It is demonstrated that the tunable wideband bandpass filter achieves the best filtering effect.

5   Conclusion

In this paper, the tunable wideband bandpass filter is designed in hybrid frequency synthesizer of PLL+DDS mixing in the outside of the feedback loop. The major design difficulties of the tunable wideband bandpass filter is shown in the following:

I.   It is difficult to filter the spurs, which is brought about by the DDS spur;
II. It is difficult to keep the band of output signals and suppress the near-end spur, which it is necessary that the tunable wideband bandpass filter must have a steep transitional zone.

In order to meet the demand of the hybrid frequency synthesizer of PLL+DDS mixing in the outside of the feedback loop, the central frequency of bandpass filter is 2.32 GHz, 2.38 GHz, 2.44 GHz and 2.5 GHz respectively. And the bandwidth is up to 240 MHz. Finally, physical tests show the spurious components and unwanted spectral components, especially near-end spurs at the center frequency are suppressed effectively compression by the tunable wideband bandpass filter.

References

1. Yang, G.M., et al.: Miniaturized Antennas and planar bandpass filters with self-biased NiCo-Ferrite films. IEEE Trans. Magn. **45**(10), 4191–4194 (2009)
2. Yang, S., et al.: Design and simulation of a parallel coupled microstrip bandpa-ss filter. In: Southeastcon IEEE, p. 1 (2014). https://doi.org/10.1109/secon.2014.695069-5)
3. Marimuthu, J., et al.: Compact bandpass filter with multiple harmonics supper-ssion using folded parallel coupled microstrip lines. In: Microwave Conference IEEE, p. 1 (2016) https://doi.org/10.1109/apmc.2015.7413198)

4. Choudhury, S.R., Sengupta, A., Das, S.: Bandpass filters using multilayered microstrip structures. In: 2018 Emerging Trends in Electronic Devices and Computational Techniques (EDCT), Kolkata, pp. 1–3 (2018). https://doi.org/10.1109/edct.2018.8405065

5. Munir, A.: Development of dual-band microstrip bandpass filter based on split ring resonator. In: 2016 International Conference on Electromagnetics in Advanced Applications (ICEAA), Cairns, QLD, pp. 712–715 (2016). https://doi.org/10.1109/iceaa.2016.7731498

6. Sahin, E.G., Gorur, A.K., Karpuz, C., Gorur, A.: Design of wideband bandpass filters using parallel-coupled asymmetric three line structures with adjustment elements. In: 2019 49th European Microwave Conference (EuMC), Paris, France, pp. 464–467 (2019). https://doi.org/10.23919/eumc.2019.8910941

7. Zhang, M., et al.: The simulation of microstrip band pass filters based on AD-S. In: ISAPE. International Conference on IEEE, p. 909 (2012). https://doi.org/10.1109/isape.2012.640 892-0

8. Tang, C., Hsu, Y.: A microstrip bandpass filter with ultra-wide stopband. IEEE Trans. Microwave Theory Tech. **56**(6), 1468–1472 (2008). https://doi.org/10.1109/TMTT.2008. 923900

9. YongKe, L.: The design of wide BW frequency synthesizer based on the DDS&PLL hybrid method. In: 2009 9th International Conference on Electronic Measurement & Instruments, Beijing, pp. 2-689–2-692 (2009). https://doi.org/10.1109/icemi.2009.5274484

10. Gatti, R., et al.: Design of frequency synthesizer for wireless communication. In: 2017 2nd IEEE International Conference on Recent Trends in Electronics, Information & Communication Technology (RTEICT), Bangalore, pp. 1794–1798 (2017). https://doi.org/10.1109/rte ict.2017.8256908

11. Ludwig, R., Bogdanov, G.: RF Circuit Design: Theory and Applications. 2nd edn., p. 172. Upper Saddle River (2000)

12. Ferh, A.E., Jleed, H.: Design, simulate and approximate parallel coupled microstrip band-pass filter at 2.4 GHz. In: 2014 World Congress on Computer Applications and Information Systems (WCCAIS), Hammamet, pp. 1–5 (2014). https://doi.org/10.1109/wccais.2014.691 6620

Enhanced WPA2/PSK for Preventing Authentication Cracking

Chin-Ling Chen[1($\boxtimes$)] and Supaporn Punya[2]

[1] Department of Information Management, National Pingtung University,
Pingtung, Taiwan
clchen@mail.nptu.edu.tw
[2] Department of Computer Science, RMUTT, Klong Luang, Thailand

Abstract. With the popularization of mobile phones and Wi-Fi
hotspots, the diversification of wireless communication applications has
rapidly growing. Wi-Fi Protected Access (WPA), offered by network
user authentication and communication encryption, is the most generally used mechanism to protect users in wireless networks. This paper
has discussed the weakness of 4-way handshake procedure in Wi-Fi Protected Access 2/Pre-Shared Key (WPA2/PSK) and proposed an enhance
WPA2/PSK by adding timestamp parameter to prevent authentication
cracking. The experiments have compared WPA2/PSK with Enhanced
WPA2/PSK cracking using Kali Linux tool and the result is given.

Keywords: WPA2/PSK · Authentication cracking · Kali Linux tool

1 Introduction

Recently, mobile APPs are developing at a rapid pace. The security measures taken in detecting and preventing for attack cannot be ignored. Several
researches have introduce the various threats and vulnerabilities related to 802.11
wireless networks. How to conduct ethical hacking and make wireless network
more secure is a matter of the concern to management.

Reddy et al. (2010) have discusses the entire process of cracking WEP encryption on Wi-Fi networks, focusing on manipulating some scanning tools, such as:
Cain, NetStumbler, Kismet, and MiniStumbler, to assist ethical hackers or security
management in understanding the investigation of wireless security and testing to
strengthen security [1]. Wi-Fi Protected Access (WPA) is the evolved version of
WEP. Some studies have discussed the security issues of WPA/WPA2 encryption
methods for wireless networks and have analyzed how to crack them. WPA2 now is
widely deployed in Wi-Fi communication to combat wireless attacks due to its efficiency and security. WPA2 is considered a Robust Security Network (RSN) capable protocol because of supporting the process of authentication and exchange of
cryptographic keys between station (STA) and Access Point (AP).

There are two modes for WPA2 targeting the different users: WPA-Personal
and WPA-Enterprise. WPA-Personal is for home and small office use, requiring

© ICST Institute for Computer Sciences, Social Informatics and Telecommunications Engineering 2020
Published by Springer Nature Switzerland AG 2020. All Rights Reserved
W. Li and D. Tang (Eds.): MOBILWARE 2020, LNICST 331, pp. 156–164, 2020.
https://doi.org/10.1007/978-3-030-62205-3_15

no authentication server. All wireless devices, such as mobile phones and laptop computers, in the same hotspot use the same 256-bit pre-shared key (PSK), called as WPA2/PSK. On the other hand, WPA-Enterprise is designed for large businesses and requires a RADIUS authentication server that provides automatic key generation and authentication throughout the entire enterprise. However, advanced versions of new wireless attacks have been developed, which is capable of exploiting the vulnerabilities of WPA2-Enterprise.

Cui and Yin (2011) have conducted some experiments on WEP and WPA/WPA2 encryption modes [2]. Some effectual findings have been proposed based on these results. WPA uses a pre-shared key (PSK) for authentication and encryption, causing limited degree of protection. If hackers hold a PSK, they can eavesdrop on other authorized users. Alqahtani and Aloraini have proposed an improved version of Wi-Fi encryption, called Wi-Fi Secure Access (WSA), reducing limitations of WPA protection and offering more confidentiality [3].

In Linux-like systems, BackTrack5 has been used to capture WPA/WPA2 4-way handshake encrypted packets. Zhang et al. (2012) have proposed a new cracking method, in which the captured handshake packets are copied to window system and then cracked with EWSA-GPU [4]. Using a more capable GPU makes it easier to crack the password. Analysis result has proved that the proposed method can greatly improve the cracking speed by comparing BackTrack5.

Pandurang and Karia (2015) have used OpenVPN, located at the entrance of the wireless local area network (WLAN), to set up a tunnel within public network. Performance metrics of WLAN WEP and WPA2, such as throughput, delay, and frame loss rate are measured [5]. Penetration tests have been performed via Backtrack5 R3 and Fern Wi-Fi Cracker. Yacchirena et al. have used Snort and Kismet as Wi-Fi intrusion detection systems (IDS) and used Ettercap monitored IDS response [6]. Subsequent evaluations after the attack have been given. This study has analyzed the captured traffic with Wireshark to determine the response characteristics of Snort and Kismet. Radivilova and Hassan have analyzed wireless network security algorithms WPA and WPA2, whose weaknesses are described [7]. The ways of how to attack WPA and WPA2 Enterprise Wireless Networks and the results are also given. Abo-Soliman and Azer have clarified emerging attack methods and have implemented WPA2/EAP-TTLS prototypes for testing and evaluation [8]. Chang et al. have proposed an Intelligent Deauthentication Method (IDM) to capture the encrypted packets for analysis [9]. The proposed method has the capability of determining the length and strength of de-authentication decisively.

Authentication is one of the major security objectives for any wireless protocol. It ensures that associated STAs are really those who they claim. Both Dictionary attacks and Brute force are the most common methods that target authentication by stealing access pin, key, password or passphrase. To obtain a password is the best way to control the AP. The first step in authentication cracking is to obtain an encrypted packet, held by the four parties. However, there is no detailed description on how to obtain it. In this article, we have analyzed WPA2-personal supporting 4-way handshake, and described the basic

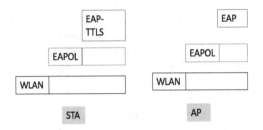

Fig. 1. Layer structure of EAP-TTLS/EAP/EAPOL/WLAN

principles, weaknesses, and launch the techniques of how to attack WPA2-personal in WLAN. The attack process and results are described. Finally, enhanced encryption is presented to counter cracking methods.

The rest of the paper is organized as follows. Section 2 describes fundamental principle of WPA2 and enhanced WPA2. Experiment and results are given in Sect. 3. Section 4 concludes this paper.

2   Fundamental Principle

2.1   Enhanced WPA2/PSK 4-Way Handshake

In WPA2/PSK, generation of the keys for authentication and data encryption during 4-way handshake comes from one shared passphrase agreed on both STAs and AP, which is carried by Extended Authentication Protocol (EAP). All the transmitted EAP messages between STA and AP are encapsulated in EAP over LAN (EAPOL) frames, which are further encapsulated in 802.11 WLAN format. EAP/EAPOL/WLAN messages allow handshaking between STA and AP without the need for IP layer. EAP-TTLS is one of Tunneled EAP method, which is usually a combination of two EAP methods: outer and inner authentication technique. The former creates a secure tunnel, while the latter performs user/device authentication. The layer structure is depicted at Fig. 1.

Enhanced WPA2/PSK 4-way handshake exchanges 4 messages between AP and STA. Let ANonce and SNonce be the randomly generated number at the AP and STA, respectively. AP sends the first message carrying ANonce to STA. STA generates PMK and PTK accordingly. Pairwise Master Key (PMK) is produced by Password based Key Derivation Function 2 (PBKDF2), in which passphrase combines timestamp, Service Set ID (SSID) and SSID length through 4096-time repeating hashing to generate a set of 256-bit key. In this regard, we call it as Enhanced-PMK (or Enhanced-PSK). A 384-bit Enhanced Pairwise Temporary Key (PTK) is generated by Pseudo Random Function (PRF), in which Enhanced-PMK associate with AP MAC address, STA MAC address, ANonce and SNonce. The Enhanced-PTK can be categorized into 3 sets of 128-bit keys. They are Key Confirmation Key (KCK), Key Encryption Key (KEK) and Temporal Key (TK). STA uses KCK as a key to calculate Message Integrity Code (MIC).

STA responds the second message carrying SNonce and MIC to AP. Consequently, AP generates its own MIC and then checks the integrity by comparing the received MIC. AP sends the third message, carrying Group Transient Key (GTK) protected by KEK, and MIC to STA. Since our objective is to authentication cracking for unicast transmission, GTK and TK can be ignored for the latter discussion and analysis. STA installs PTK and responds the fourth message back to AP to acknowledge the handshake completion.

2.2 Passphrase Cracking Procedure

We first search and display a list of detected APs and connected STAs in the surrounding. We obtain the frames from the selected channel and replay periodically in order to crack the traffic. In cracking WPA2/PSK encrypted packets, the key point is not to see how many packets are captured, but to capture the 4-way handshake packets. The 4-way handshake packets can be retrieved only when a new connection between AP and STA has established. If the handshake packet has not been captured successfully, we need to force to disconnected the exist and reestablish new one. Password/passphrase cracking can be attempted during association or periodic re-authentication. All STAs in the same WLAN use one shared passphrase to access the AP. It implies that successful passphrase cracking leads to providential access to all the keys during WPA2/PSK handshake. To prevent hacker to retrieve and crack other people's packets at will, we have proposed an Enhanced WPA2/PSK, in which time-stamp is added to generate a new PMK, called Enhanced-PMK. The time unit of time-stamp parameter in 802.11 is defined to be micro-second. AP and STA need to use its own time-stamp for making Enhanced-PMK to generate the individual MIC. The granularity of time-stamp for making an Enhanced-PMK could be tuned to be mini-second to make sure the integrity of MIC between AP and STA. However, coarse granularity of time-stamp may incur higher possibility of hacking by generating the same Enhanced-PMK, which will be $10^{-3} \times 10^{-3} = 10^{-6}$.

In next section, we try to crack both WPA2/PSK and enhanced WPA2/PSK encrypted packets.

3 Experiment and Results

An experiment is given to performance measurement of cracking technology for WPA2/PSK authentication. We have used the device like DIR-615 access points and DWL-G122 adapters from D-Link. The penetration procedures can be listed as below.

1. Install VirtualBox into your laptop.
2. Install Kali Linux Image on VirtualBox.
3. Plugin USB Wi-Fi external adapter to your laptop.
4. Use aircrack-ng tool to crack WPA2/PSK packets. Open Kali terminal and find out the name of the wireless adapter connected to the laptop by using command "iwconfig" (Fig. 2).

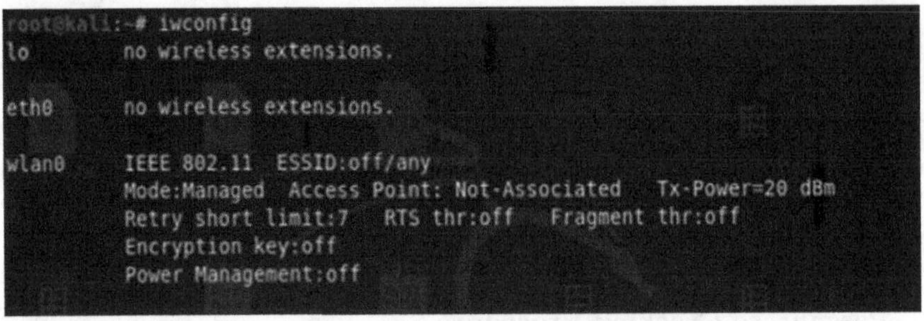

Fig. 2. Find out the name and related parameters of wireless adapter

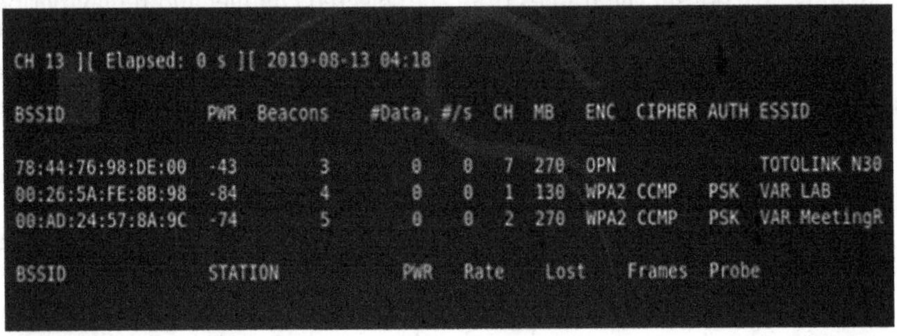

Fig. 3. Search APs in the surroundings and the STAs connected to that AP

5. Set the wireless adaptor in monitor mode by using command "airmon-ng".
6. Search the access points (APs) in the surroundings and also the clients connected to that AP by using command "airodump-ng" (Fig. 3).
7. Capture more packets for a specified channel by adding some parameters in the command "airodump-ng". In this case, the command will be "airodump-ng -c [channel] -b [bssid of wifi] -w [path to write the data of packets] [interface]"
8. The 4-way handshake packets can be retrieved only when a new client establishes a connection. If the handshake packet has not been captured successfully, we need to use airreplay-ng deauth command to force the disconnection and reestablish new one.
9. Force clients to reauthenticate to capture WPA2/PSK handshakes, which will appear on the "airodump" terminal. Leave "airodump-ng" running and open a second terminal. In this terminal, type the command "aireplay-ng [attack option] [n] -a [AP bssid] -c [client bssid] [interface]". In this case, [attack option] is "deauth" and [n] is the number of attacking (Fig. 4).
10. Obtain WPA2/PSK handshake packets and write into Packet Capture file (ar1-01.cap, in this case) in using the command "airodump-ng" (Fig. 5). The first line shows the current channel, elapsed time, current date/time, "WPA handshake: 00:26:5A:FE:8B:98". That means a WPA2/PSK handshake is successfully captured for the BSSID 00:26:5A:FE:8B:98.

Fig. 4. Force clients to reauthenticate to capture WPA2 handshake messages

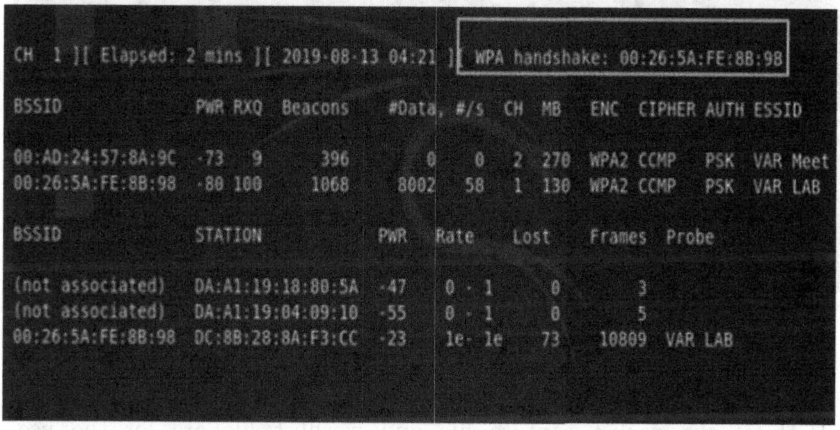

Fig. 5. Obtain WPA/WPA2 handshake message

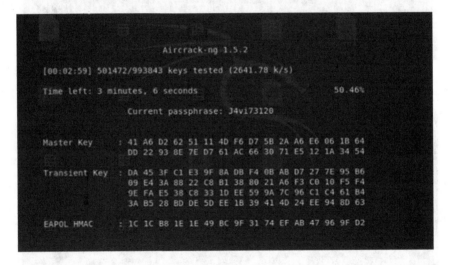

```
root@kali:~# aircrack-ng -w /root/Desktop/darkc0de.txt /root/ar1-01.cap
Opening /root/ar1-01.capwait...
Read 12370 packets.

  #  BSSID              ESSID              Encryption

  1  00:26:5A:FE:8B:98  VAR LAB            WPA (1 handshake)
  2  00:AD:24:57:8A:9C  VAR MeetingRoom    No data - WEP or WPA

Index number of target network ? 1

Opening /root/ar1-01.capwait...
Read 12990 packets.

1 potential targets
```

Fig. 6. Use Wordlist (.txt) and Packet Capture file (.cap) for authentication cracking

```
                        Aircrack-ng 1.5.2

      [00:02:59] 501472/993843 keys tested (2641.78 k/s)

      Time left: 3 minutes, 6 seconds                    50.46%

                   Current passphrase: J4vi73120

      Master Key     : 41 A6 D2 62 51 11 4D F6 D7 5B 2A A6 E6 06 1B 64
                       DD 22 93 8E 7E D7 61 AC 66 30 71 E5 12 1A 34 54

      Transient Key  : DA 45 3F C1 E3 9F 8A DB F4 0B AB D7 27 7E 95 B6
                       09 E4 3A 88 22 C8 B1 38 80 21 A6 F3 C0 10 F5 F4
                       9E FA E5 38 C8 33 1D EE 59 9A 7C 96 C1 C4 61 B4
                       3A B5 28 BD DE 5D EE 1B 39 41 4D 24 EE 94 8D 63

      EAPOL HMAC      : 1C 1C B8 1E 1E 49 BC 9F 31 74 EF AB 47 96 9F D2
```

Fig. 7. Successful cracking passphrase for the wordlist

11. Both of the packet capture file and wordlist file are for the use in
    "aircrack-ng" for cracking the WPA2/PSK authentication. Type the com-
    mand "aircrack-ng -w [path to wordlist] [path to packet capture file]".
    [path to wordlist] and [path to packet capture file] mean the path to
    a wordlist and a packet capture file that have located, respectively. In
    this case, we have a wordlist called "darkc0de.txt" in the root/Desktop/
    folder. [path to wordlist] [path to packet capture file] should be replaced by
    "/root/Desktop/darkc0de.txt" and "/root/Desktop/ar1-01.cap", individu-
    ally (Fig. 6).

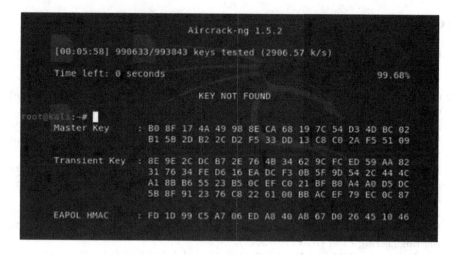

Fig. 8. Failure of cracking passphrase in Enhanced WPA2/PSK

12. Cracking the passphrase might take a long time depending on the size of the wordlist. It takes 5 min here. If the passphrase is in the wordlist, the terminal of aircrack-ng will show as Fig. 7.
13. Fail to crack in Enhanced WPA2/PSK, even the passphrase is in the wordlist. The result of "key not found" is shown in Fig. 8.

4   Conclusions

In this regard, we have study some fundamental principle and weaknesses of WPA2/PSK. The 4-way handshake of EAPOL exchanges 4 messages between AP and STA to generate encryption keys which can be used to protect handshake and encrypt actual data. The existing rainbow tables have the top 1000 SSIDs and a large number of passwords/passphrase for general use. The hackers can speed up cracking by quick querying the rainbow tables. If WPA2/PSK wireless network is provided for free use in public places, the password/passphrase is shared with for all users in the hotspot. One password/passphrase generates one PSK. WPA2 does not have forward secrecy. Once a hacker obtains a set of PSK, they can decrypt all past and future packets encrypted with this set of PSK. Enhanced WPA2/PSK can effectively protect from the hackers who get passwords/passphrases, with time-stamp parameter added to produce a different PSK. Enhanced WPA2/PSK could be vulnerable to cracking only if hacker has used the same timestamp. However, the smaller the time granularity in timestamp, the lower the possibility for hacker to crack.

References

1. Reddy, S.V., Rijutha, K., SaiRamani, K., Ali, S.M, Reddy, C.P.: Wireless hacking - a WiFi hack by cracking WEP. In: 2nd International Conference on Education Technology and Computer (2010)
2. Cui, K., Yin, D.: Research on the security of the encrypted WLAN. In: International Conference on Computer Science and Service System (CSSS) (2011)
3. Alqahtani, S.A., Aloraini, M.: Resolving wireless security limitations using a new Wi-Fi secure access. In: IEEE 12th International Conference on Computer and Information Technology (2012)
4. Zhang, L., Yu, J., Deng, Z., Zhang, R.: The security analysis of WPA encryption in wireless network. In: 2nd International Conference on Consumer Electronics, Communications and Networks (CECNet) (2012)
5. Pandurang, R.M., Karia, D.C.: Performance measurement of WEP and WPA2 on WLAN using OpenVPN. In: International Conference on Nascent Technologies in the Engineering Field (ICNTE) (2015)
6. Yacchirena, A., Alulema, D., Aguilar, D. Morocho, D., Encalada, F, Granizo, E.: Analysis of attack and protection systems in Wi-Fi wireless networks under the Linux operating system. In: IEEE International Conference on Automatica (ICA-ACCA) (2016)
7. Radivilova, T., Hassan, H.A.: Test for penetration in Wi-Fi network: attacks on WPA2-PSK and WPA2-enterprise. In: International Conference on Information and Telecommunication Technologies and Radio Electronics (UkrMiCo) (2017)
8. Abo-Soliman, M.A., Azer, M.A.: A study in WPA2 enterprise recent attacks. In: 13th International Computer Engineering Conference (ICENCO) (2017)
9. Chang, T.-H., Lin, J.-W., Lai, G.H.: The method of capturing the encrypted password packets of WPA and WPA2, automatic, semi-automatic or manual? In: IEEE Conference on Dependable and Secure Computing (DSC) (2018)

Big Data, Data Mining and Artificial Intelligence

Reinforcement Learning for Rack-Level Cooling

Yanduo Duan[1], Jianxiong Wan[1,2(✉)], Jie Zhou[1], Gaoxiang Cong[1],
Zeeshan Rasheed[1], and Tianyang Hua[1]

[1] Inner Mongolia University of Technology,
Inner Mongolia, People's Republic of China
jxwan@imut.edu.cn

[2] Inner Mongolia Autonomous Region Engineering and Technology Research Center
of Big Data Based Software Service, Hohhot, China

Abstract. In recent years, we have seen a rapid growth in big data and
cloud computing industry, because of the rapid development in Internet technology. That's why the number and scale of data center have
increased rapidly. A data center is a warehouse-level IT facility that hosts
many servers. Because of the uneven heat production and heat dissipation of the servers in a rack, the hot spots emerges. In order to maintain
the CPU temperature hence the computing performance, the server cooling is very critical. A common solution is to increase the speed of the
Computer Room Air Handler (CRAH) blower and increase the flow of
cold air. Nevertheless, this solution can only partially address the issue
and raise the cooling energy consumption.

In this paper, we study how to mitigate rack hot spots without significantly increasing the power of air conditioning system. We propose
the Active Ventilation Tiles (AVTs), i.e., ordinary ventilation tiles with
attached fans, to enhance the local cold air delivery and improve the
cooling performance. In particular, we propose an AVT control algorithm adapted from the Reinforcement Learning techniques to tackle
the complex data center environment and thermo dynamic process. The
reinforcement learning algorithm adjusts the temperature distribution of
the rack by controlling the fan speed installed on the ventilation tile, and
guides the fan speed according to the feedback temperature to mitigate
hot spots. Due to the slow learning speed of the traditional Tabular-Q-
Learning algorithm, we integrate the Tabular-Q-Learning algorithm with
the Dyna architecture to accelerate the learning speed and improve the
algorithm performance in the early stage. Experimental results reveal
that Tabular-Q-learning based on Dyna has better performance.

Keywords: Reinforcement learning · Data center · Hotspot

1 Introduction

A data center is a server hosting facility that provides users with more storage
and computing resources. In recent years we has seen the rapid development in

© ICST Institute for Computer Sciences, Social Informatics and Telecommunications Engineering 2020
Published by Springer Nature Switzerland AG 2020. All Rights Reserved
W. Li and D. Tang (Eds.): MOBILWARE 2020, LNICST 331, pp. 167–173, 2020.
https://doi.org/10.1007/978-3-030-62205-3_16

Internet technology and 5G communication technology. That's why number and scale of data center has increased rapidly.

However, a reality often faced by the data center operators is that the local server overheating, or hot spot, is commonplace in practice. Usually the main causes of hot spots are server load fluctuations and cold air supply imbalance[2]. To solve this problem, someone used AVT. Ventilation tiles in the raised-floor data centers can be classified as Passive Ventilation Tiles (PVTs) and Active Ventilation Tiles (AVTs), AVTs have attached fans and PVTs where the tile flow completely determine by the pressure differential between above- and underfloor spaces [1]. AVTs are more flexible since fans can draw the cold air actively to cold aisles even if the under-floor pressure is ill-distributed [7]. In previous paper, researcher focused on measurement or simulation based performance modeling and evaluation. The impact of various factor, such as airflow angle, tile position, containment structure CRAC blower speed, on the tile flow was investigated in [3–5]. The general conclusion of these articles is that AVTs can improve local cooling delivery. No one has proposed a relevant study on the control problem of AVTs under actual working conditions.

In this paper, we propose an AVTs control algorithm based on reinforcement learning. The difficulty with AVTs control is the diversity of different data center environments. Due to the diversity of the environment and the lack of a complete grasp of the environment, reinforcement learning is more appropriate solution to solve such problems. We use Tabular-Q-Learning and Tabular-Q-Learning Based On Dyna algorithms to solve the control problem of AVTs. Because the algorithm is completely online learning. It can learn the external environment through limited environmental exploration, without considering the establishment of complex airflow and heat exchange model, thus improving the universality of AVTs and control algorithm.

2   Markov Decision Process Formulation

Reinforcement learning is a computational approach to understanding and automating goal-directed learning and decision making. It is distinguished from other computational approaches by its emphasis on learning by an agent from direct interaction with its environment, without requiring exemplary supervision or complete models of the environment. Reinforcement learning uses the formal framework of Markov decision processes to define the interaction between a learning agent and its environment in terms of states, actions, and rewards [6]. Our main target is control the fan speed of AVT and provide the average temperature distribution to the rack. Tabular based approach requires that the state and behavior of the MDP model should have discrete value and space of the state and behavior should be small. Because all values in this method are stored in the tabular (Q tabular), Q tabular is the result of the algorithm update and learning. The advantage of this method is that the optimal solution of the problem learned by agent. Following is the tabular approach of MDP modeling:

- System states. We discretize the duty cycle of PWM and divide it by 25% equidistance, that is, the single state dimension of the system is one, the system state space $\mathcal{S} = \{0\%, 25\%, 50\%, 75\%, 100\%\}$.
- Actions. Action behavior defined the different condition of fan speed, which is increase, decrease and static state of fan speed. The behavior space of the system $\mathcal{A} = \{inc, dec, nop\}$, for ease of calculation $\mathcal{A} = \{1, -1, 0\}$.
- Reward. The main purpose of this paper is provide the average temperature to the rack and reduced the fan energy consumption. Therefore, the immediate reward is divided into two parts:1) The temperature part of the reward:

$R_{t,T} = \frac{\sum_{i \in t}(T_{t,i} - \overline{T_t})^2}{|\mathcal{I}|}$ Where, $T_{t,i}$ is the temperature of the ith sensor on the front panel of the rack at time t, $\mathcal{I}$ is the temperature and humidity sensor set, and $|\mathcal{I}|$ is the total number of sensors. $\overline{T_t}$ is the frame reference temperature at time t. It is obvious that the smaller $R_{t,T}$ is when the sensor temperature is closer to the reference temperature. That is, the more uniform the temperature distribution of the rack. On the premise of 1), reduce fan energy consumption. Energy consumption and fan speed is 3 power relationship, so energy consumption part of the reward $R_{t,E} = \left(\frac{s_t}{S_{ref}}\right)^3$,among them $s_t \in \mathcal{S}$,S_{ref} is the reference value that keeps $R_{t,T}$ and $R_{t,E}$ of the same order. Obviously, the smaller the fan speed, the lower the energy consumption. Therefore, the immediate reward of the system is set as:

$$R_t = -(1-\omega)R_{t,T} - \omega R_{t,E}. \tag{1}$$

Where ω is to determine which part of $R_{t,E}$ or $R_{t,T}$ contributes more weight to R_t. Therefore, all of them have negative values, and maximizing R_t (tending to 0) is the optimization direction of this topic. Finally, the AVT control problem can be defined as the following decision problem:

$$\max_{a_t} \sum_{t=0}^{\infty} \gamma^k R_t, a_t \in \mathcal{A}, \forall t \in \{0, 1, ..., \infty\}. \tag{2}$$

3 Algorithm Design

3.1 Tabular-Q-learning

In order to solve the problem of Eq. (2), in this paper we used the Q function to quantify the advantages of behavior at under state s_t:

$$Q(s, a) = E\left[\sum_{k=0}^{\infty} \gamma^k R_{t+k+1} \Big| s = s_t, a = a_t\right]. \tag{3}$$

There is a unique optimal Q function satisfying Bellman equation:

$$Q^*(s_t, a_t) = \max_{s_{t+k}, \mathcal{A}} E\left[\sum_{k=0}^{\infty} \gamma^k R_{t+k+1} \Big| s_t, a_t\right] = E\left[R_{t+1} + \gamma \times \max_{a_{t+1} \in \mathcal{A}} Q^*(s_t, a)\right]. \tag{4}$$

According to formula (4), the optimal behavior can be selected as follows:

$$a_t = \arg\max Q^*(s_t, a) \tag{5}$$

In Q-learning, the update of Q function is as follows:

$$\begin{cases} Q_{t+1,target} = R_{t+1} + \gamma \max_{a \in \mathcal{A}} Q(s_{t+1}, a). \\ Q(s_{t+1}, a) = Q(s_{t+1}, a) + \alpha \times (Q_{t+1,target} - Q(s_t, a_t)). \end{cases} \tag{6}$$

where, $Q_{t+1,target}$ is the Q sample received at time t+1, s_{t+1} is the system state at time t+1, and $\alpha \in [0, 1]$ is the learning rate. Tabular q-learning algorithm, after the initialization of the Q tabular, carries out Tabular update learning according to the above formula.

Algorithm 1. A basic Tabular-Q-learning algorithm for solving the AVT control problem.

1: Define
    t = Time index;
    s_t = State at time t;
    a_t = Action at time t;
    q_table = Matrix with size:$|S| * |A|$;
    ε = Exploration factor;
    ω = Reward the weight;
2: t=0,$\varepsilon = [0, 0.99]$,$\omega = 0.3$;
3: Randomly initialize q_table with 0 except that q_table [0, -1] = min and q_table [4, 1] = min(min is a very small number);
4: Initialize S;
5: **loop**

$$a_t = \begin{cases} \arg\max Q(s_t, a), with\ probability\ \varepsilon. \\ a\ random\ action\ from\ \mathcal{A},\ with\ probability\ 1 - \varepsilon. \end{cases} \tag{7}$$

6: Observe the next state s_{t+1} and the temperature distribution of the rack inlet,compute reward R_{t+1}(see Eq.(1));
7: Update the $q\_table[s_t, a_t]$(see Eq.(6));
8: **end loop**

Q-Learning requires a Q tabular. If Q tabular has to many states, then required large amount of space for storage and need large amount of time to search data. Q-Learning has the problem of overestimation, because Q-Learning uses the action corresponding to the optimal value at the next moment when updating Q function, which cause to the "overestimation". In order to solve the slow convergence rate of Q-Learning, we proposed Q-Learning integrated with Dyna framework.

3.2   Tabular-Q-learning Based on Dyna

Dyna is a generic term for a class of algorithmic frameworks that integrate model-based reinforcement learning with non-model-based reinforcement learning. Dyna can learn both from models and from the experience of environmental interactions.

Compared with Q-Learning alone, Tabular-Q-learning Based On Dyna adds an L-size experience replay buffer B to store the learning samples as the model of interaction with the environment. In addition, a thread was opened in the program. After one step of algorithm training, M samples were randomly selected from the experience replay buffer for model training.

Tabular-Q-learning Based On Dyna Algorithm adds the experience replay buffer storage transition (s, a, r_{t+1}, s_{t+1}) between 5–6 lines of the above algorithm, and selects M-size samples for model training.

4   Result Analysis

This experiment we did in a real data center. We collect the temperature by installing sensors on the rack and air conditioning, and then transferred the data to the computer for intensive learning algorithm training. In algorithm Tabular-Q-learning, $\varepsilon = [0, 0.99]$, $\omega = 0.3$, $\alpha = 0.01$; In algorithm Tabular-Q-learning Based On Dyna, $L = 5000$, $M = 100$.

The total reward based on Q-Leaning with Dyna is closer to 0 than the total reward based on Q-Leaning. As can be seen from the figure. The average of algorithm Tabular-Q-learning Based On Dyna total rewards is higher than algorithm Tabular-Q-learning, (see Fig. 1).

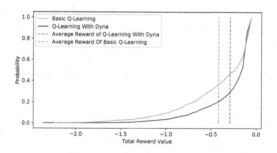

Fig. 1. Total reward (CDF)

The average Q value of algorithm Tabular-Q-learning Based On Dyna tends to converge in 40 steps, and fluctuates slowly in 400–500 steps. After 500 steps, the average value of Q Tabular becomes stable, and the average value of Q Tabular converges in the range of $[-0.2, -0.3]$. However, in Tabular-Q-learning the time steps of the average Q Tabular value from 0 to 1750 was continuously declined. The average value of Q Tabular is down from –1.1, and there is no convergence. The convergence speed of Tabular-Q-learning Based On Dyna is much faster than tabular Q learning, and the average value of Tabular-Q-learning Based On Dyna is larger, which proves that the algorithm learns a great reward and its performance is better, (see Fig. 2).

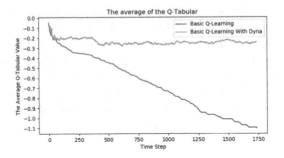

Fig. 2. The average of the Q-tabular

5   Conclusion

In this paper, we describe the rack hot spot issues facing today's data centers, as well as the shortcomings of solving these problems in the past. Due to the complexity of the data center environment, we propose a solution based on the reinforcement learning algorithm AVT control. We introduce the establishment of Markov decision process, and introduce reinforcement learning algorithm Tabular-Q-Learning and Tabular-Q-Learning Based on Dyna. By comparison, For algorithm Tabular-Q-learning Based On Dyna, it can accelerate the convergence of Q tabular. It is found that algorithm Tabular-Q-learning Based On Dyna has better performance in dealing with Tabular problems. Algorithm Tabular-Q-Learning converges at least four times faster than algorithm Tabular-Q-Learnig Based on Dyna.

Acknowledgements. This work was funded in part by the National Natural Science Foundation of China (NSFC) under Grants. 61862048, 61762070, and 61962045, Inner Mongolia Key Technological Development Program (2019ZD015), Key Scientific and Technological Research Program of Inner Mongolia Autonomous Region (2019GG273), and Inner Mongolia Autonomous Region Special Program for Engineering Application of Scientific and Technical Payoffs (2020CG0073).

References

1. Khalili, S., Tradat, M.I., Nemati, K., Seymour, M., Sammakia, B.: Impact of tile design on the thermal performance of open and enclosed aisles. J. Electron. Packag. **140**(1), 010907 (2018)
2. Patankar, S.V.: Airflow and cooling in a data center. J. Heat Transf. **132**(7), 073001 (2010)
3. Song, Z.: Numerical cooling performance evaluation of fan-assisted perforations in a raised-floor data center. Int. J. Heat Mass Transf. **95**, 833–842 (2016)
4. Song, Z.: Thermal performance of a contained data center with fan-assisted perforations. Appl. Thermal Eng. **102**, 1175–1184 (2016)
5. Song, Z.: Studying the fan-assisted cooling using the Taguchi approach in open and closed data centers. Int. J. Heat Mass Transf. **111**, 593–601 (2017)
6. Sutton, R.S., Barto, A.G., et al.: Introduction to Reinforcement Learning, vol. 2. MIT press, Cambridge (1998)
7. Wan, J., Gui, X., Kasahara, S., Zhang, Y., Zhang, R.: Air flow measurement and management for improving cooling and energy efficiency in raised-floor data centers: a survey. IEEE Access **6**, 48867–48901 (2018)

Traffic Sign Recognition Algorithm Model Based on Machine Learning

Hui Li[✉], Jun Feng, Jialing Liu, and Yanli Gong

School of Electronics and Automation, Inner Mongolia Electronic Information
Vocational Technical College, Hohhot, Inner Mongolia 010070, China
278540115@qq.com

Abstract. At present, the development of our country is getting better
and better, the vehicles running on the road are also increasing, so the
traffic problems are becoming more and more obvious. This kind of problem will also set up the development of the modern city. At this time, the
intelligent transportation technology has also developed, and the above
problems are gradually treated by new methods. It has become one of
the hot topics in the field of an intelligent transportation system to use
the advantages of machine learning technology to deal with traffic congestion and improve the traffic efficiency of the road network. It has high
theoretical and practical significance to detect road traffic signs in the
actual scene. A method based on directional gradient histogram features
combined with a support vector machine classifier is proposed. Each type
of traffic sign has its own characteristics. By classifying its appearance
and color, many recognition methods are produced, and the target area
is retained by a unique method, thus the feature can be extracted and
identified. Make the paving. The main work is to obtain a training sample, and then add the direction gradient histogram of the sample library
into the SVM for training, to get a one to many classifiers to be tuned
continuously, it can realize the rapid and accurate judgment of multiple
traffic signs.

Keywords: Gradient histogram · SVM · Traffic detection

1 Introduction

With the continuous progress of the global economy, transportation, which is an
important channel for global liaison, has also developed at a high speed, and it
has also brought some transportation difficulties. To cope with these difficulties,
related researchers have become extremely interested in solving transportation
problems through machine learning methods. After years of continuous research
and development, many vehicles have added new functions that assist vehicle
owners to better understand traffic conditions [1], of which intelligent transportation systems [2] have a good effect on many difficulties in this field, So more
and more people are researching it. Intelligent transportation systems generally
consist of only three parts: intelligent roads, intelligent vehicles, and intelligent

© ICST Institute for Computer Sciences, Social Informatics and Telecommunications Engineering 2020
Published by Springer Nature Switzerland AG 2020. All Rights Reserved
W. Li and D. Tang (Eds.): MOBILWARE 2020, LNICST 331, pp. 174–186, 2020.
https://doi.org/10.1007/978-3-030-62205-3_17

auxiliary facilities [3]. If you want to improve the safety and reliability of vehicles, you need to combine related applications with machine learning technology. This can solve a series of hidden safety problems such as traffic jams caused by unknown road conditions. In recent years, many researchers feel that the use of machine learning methods in the following areas can better improve traffic performance: they are interactions between drivers and vehicles, interactions between different individuals, and access to traffic data Networks, and performance modification of the car itself [4]. Among them, the researchers found that combining the driver's state, the specific conditions of nearby roads, and the recognition of traffic sign information can better improve traffic performance. In terms of providing traffic information to drivers, traffic signs can be described as the top priority. Better recognition of traffic signs is also an issue that requires further research. The detection and recognition system of traffic signs is to extract the information of traffic signs through related technologies, and then feed it back to the driver. The driver can obtain the required traffic information through the recognition system. More advanced traffic assistance systems can even help the driver directly Vehicles, which can better control the vehicle to improve the safety of drivers and passengers. Research in this area is not only one of the hot topics today, but also one of the difficulties to be overcome in the field of machine learning.

Automatically providing road information to drivers and alerting drivers in specific situations can help drivers deal with problems in a timely and correct manner, and also have a positive impact on the entire road network that includes other driving vehicles. This is a new concept in the field of machine learning [5]. There are many problems to be solved in this field, and the detection of traffic signs is one of them. Many current researchers have used machine learning to extract and identify some signs in traffic, but it will take a long time to apply them. These methods should also incorporate more knowledge, such as data extraction, image processing, big data technology, etc., continuously improve the accuracy of recognition, and shorten the recognition time to achieve high efficiency and speed.

2   Related Work

Some countries have greatly improved their economic levels compared to their relatively backward economic levels, and some of their related technologies have also developed very high. This has laid a good foundation for the research and development of transportation-related technologies. For example, some countries have researched related fields 30 years ago [6], Europe and the United States have in the past few years made AI vehicle road systems and "Prometheus" related topics; German warning pattern extraction and recognition technologies have achieved With very effective progress, the logo can be determined within 0.2s, and the timeliness is very high. With the continuous development of the times, everyone's enthusiasm for this technology is continuously increasing, attracting more and more people to study in this field, so its related technology has also continued to become proficient and has made rapid progress. At the beginning of this century, researchers at the University of Wisconsin completed a model for detecting traffic signs. The sample they have is 540 collected images, and the recognition accuracy rate is 95%. [7]; A multi-traffic sign recognition system was developed together. Its accuracy rate is 95%, but its real-time performance is not up to standard. [8]: In 2009, Australia's National Information and Communication Technology Laboratory also achieved many improvements. Traffic sign shapes are detected and identified, but they are susceptible to light and weather conditions [9]. Although our country started a bit late in this direction, as the economy and overall national strength recovered and improved, research and development in this area have become faster and faster, and Baidu has also developed its undeveloped unmanned car. Our researchers are also investing more and more energy in this field. As more and more high-level technical personnel join the research of this technology and carry out continuous innovative applications, many institutes now apply machine learning. Technology makes a great product. Many of these projects have provided new ideas for researchers, such as the unmanned driving system developed by Baidu. Baidu has incorporated many new technologies into it through its resource advantages, reflecting the innovativeness of the era [8], and in 2016 Baidu's self-driving car products were exhibited at the World Intel Conference in 2015, and received a lot of praise from experts at home and abroad. Recently, related research institutions in China also released some of their achievements-accurate identification of some speed signs [10].

3   Preliminaries

3.1   Common Traffic Sign Detection Methods

In recent times, scholars at home and abroad have continuously improved the technology, achieved a lot of output of traffic recognition products, each has its characteristics in the use of the product, and has achieved the establishment of many algorithm models. For example, the area to be detected in the instruction information in a traffic sign. You can extract information from it, and then you can identify why it is a type of sign and what it means. These processes can be handled step by step, but all need to provide some useful information [9]. The detection part mainly starts from two aspects: one is to classify the colors and classify the markers to be detected by a certain method; on the other hand, to extract the features of the shape. Because it is not under external pressure, its shape Generally, it does not change, so you can classify the detection results, but we need to get the target area where the detected object is located so that it will not be affected by other areas to have a better recognition effect. From the above, this paper proposes a scheme that combines color and shape features to complete the detection process.

Detection Method Based on Color Features

Humans have a unique ability to classify and distinguish colors. According to many theories and experiments, people's ability to transform colors into various spaces is getting better and better [10]. Besides, with the continuous development of science and technology, the quality of image acquisition equipment often used in research has also been improved, and it can better meet the needs of today. Therefore, image processing gradually changes from gray to color. After the color space conversion of the image in daily life, the corresponding feature extraction method should be used first, and then the corresponding color information unique to the traffic sign should be changed in the corresponding transformation mode to make the recognition difficult. During the color conversion, some features are made more obvious through different methods, and their information can be better explained [11]. Generally, the color is composed of 3 pixels. We call it 3 primary colors, and get more effective feature information after conversion, which is convenient for us to identify.

Detection Method Based on Shape Features

Recognition of shape information is an important link in the detection process, but a large part is identified by the shape of the grayscale image, regardless of its color attributes. By performing edge detection on it, the amount of calculation can be greatly reduced. This method can remove some irrelevant information, thereby retaining those content that is important to the image. The canny operator is currently a popular method for shape detection. He can outline the edge area of the target so that it can accurately determine its shape. There are currently other detection algorithms.

3.2   Common Algorithms for Traffic Recognition

SVM

SVM was proposed by Vapnik et al. Based on many years of statistical theory. Its advantage is that it can perform supervised learning on labeled data, and find the optimal hyperplane among different types of data sets, and has good speed performance [12].

In SVM, the most important thing is to first calibrate the labeled training samples. The features of the samples can be obtained according to the feature extractor, and the obtained features and labels are sent to the training model. Finally, the appropriate segmentation is found by the machine itself. line. If the input data is linear, then we can easily find a straight line to divide it. If the input data is non-linear, then the feature vector must be mapped to a high dimension for classification.

Adaboost Weak Classifier

Adaboost is an iterative classifier. Its main working principle is to make multiple types of classifiers for a sample database so that it can be combined into a better classifier after being carefully divided. His implementation is to change the distribution of samples, get the correct rate of the results after this training, and then assign weights to them according to the correct rate. This can determine its weight and send samples that have changed weight A similar operation is performed here for the next classifier, and then the obtained classifiers are combined to obtain a final classification model. Through this algorithm, some features with little correlation can be discarded, and important features can be left, so that better results can be obtained.

Its essential feature is that it constantly changes the weights and continuously strengthens the weak classification. It can continuously improve its ability to classify through continuous training. This step of it is as follows:

1. Training the obtained data to obtain a weak classification model;
2. Combine the data that has been identified incorrectly with the data that has not yet been identified and then train to obtain a new classifier;
3. Reorganize the data that was identified incorrectly twice and other data for new training, so that you can get another weak classifier;
4. In the end, you will get a strong classifier. Which classifier each sample is assigned to is determined by the weight of each model.

KNN

The main principle of KNN is that distance calculation is performed between the sample and the training sample, and the obtained distances are arranged. Within k ranks, which category has the largest number determines which category this sample belongs to. This algorithm only relies on the nearest few sample points for category judgment when identifying. Therefore, it has a relationship with a small number of samples when discriminating. Because this algorithm relies on its recent data, and is not distinguished by class domain, this method is very useful for samples with many categories.

3.3   Transportation Sample Library

The establishment of a traffic sign sample database is related to the final recognition result. A good database should contain many different categories, each of which has a large amount of data, and samples under various conditions and environments are included. Try to ensure the diversity of the samples, to provide effective training samples for identification. Rich data is extremely important for the robustness of the training model so that the model is more universal. Since our country started late in this regard, there is no systematic database yet, but other countries have accumulated several relatively large data sets that can be used publicly. The following categories are listed:

(1) Sample of German road signs;
(2) A sample of Belgian road signs;
(3) Samples of Swedish road signs;
(4) Sample of RUG road signs;

Each of the above datasets has spent a lot of time and experience of the researchers. They constantly collect data to build and update the database. The amount of data in the RUG dataset is a little less than the others. However, these data sets still occupy a small part of actual use. The library used in this design is GTSBR. Samples from the library are as Fig. 1:

This paper is the feature extraction of the graphs in this sample library.

Fig. 1. Samples

4   Traffic Sign Recognition

4.1   Traffic Sign Recognition Algorithm Framework

The concept of image recognition is the basic concept of road sign detection, and it is the actual detected object. These samples also have many characteristics such as their color, structure, and so on. Therefore, when performing marker detection, it can make better use of its characteristics. This simplifies the design of the additional measurement model, and can greatly improve the detection efficiency and accuracy. As can be known from the concept of image recognition, the basic image recognition structure is shown in Fig. 2 below, which mainly includes the following main parts [13].

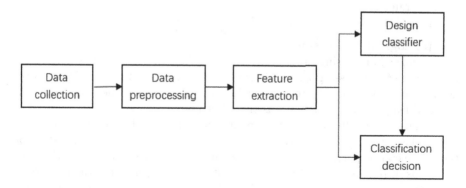

Fig. 2. Identification process

At the beginning of recognition, the ROI area where traffic signs may exist can be detected by distinguishing their colors. After the traffic signs are detected, they need to be classified and understood. Each type of traffic sign has a specific shape, so it can make full use of the shape feature information to train the classifier, and finally use the trained classifier to classify and understand the traffic sign. If these points are fully considered in the design of the traffic sign recognition system, the design of the additional test model can be simplified, and the detection efficiency and accuracy can be greatly improved. The detection system process studied in this paper is shown in Fig. 3.

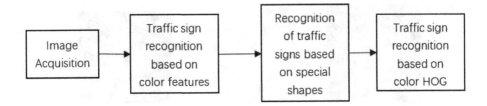

Fig. 3. Detection system process

4.2 Traffic Sign Recognition Based on Color Features

Image Segmentation Based on Local Color Features

The colors of the indicator signs are as follows: they consist of two bright colors, red or blue, which are relatively rare in the natural environment. Each type of sign has a unique background color. We choose the color segmentation technology to achieve the preliminary positioning of the possible areas of traffic signs. To ensure the real-time nature of the algorithm. The original design is to convert the RGB color space to the HSV color space [14]. It is easier to represent a specific color in the HSV color space than in the BGR space. If we want to extract a blue object. Here are the steps we need to take: first get a frame of the image from the video, convert the image to HSV space, then set the HSV threshold to the blue range.

Figure 4, Fig. 5 and Fig. 6 is the detection effect.

Morphological Processing

Morphological processing can remove the interference in the image by performing morphological processing on the image. To process the above Fig. 5, we only need to open the image, corroding the interference part, and then expanding the required features. Figure 7 below is the effect map.

It can be seen from the above figure that the interference factors in the picture have been completely dealt with, and only the expansion operation on the image can be performed to display the features we need. Through the above two steps of processing, a binary image obtained by segmenting the real traffic scene image for red and blue is obtained. It can be seen from the above results that although some parts are not taken out perfectly, the overall effect is still good. This method lays a good foundation for subsequent traffic detection.

Recognition Area Extraction

The area to be identified can be extracted in the form of a multi-directional moving window. The sliding window detection scheme can use a fixed window to extract the feature of the detection position of the image to be detected [15] so that a matching sample can be obtained. It can be seen that only samples of the same size can be obtained in this way. To be able to detect more target areas, a multi-scale detection scheme is used, that is, the image to be detected is scaled. Usually, a multi-scale Sliding window strategy to ensure that the target to be inspected at a certain size is similar to the window size.

Fig. 4. original image

Fig. 5. Mask map

4.3   SVM

Classification Process

The Fig. 8 below is the overall flowchart of traffic sign recognition.

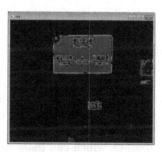

Fig. 6. Extracted feature map

The most important process of traffic sign detection is to classify it as a whole, extract the features of the obtained recognition area, and then send it to the classification module. The traffic sign classification module determines the types of signs contained in the area, and then the Provide auxiliary information for the

Fig. 7. Morphological processing

driving environment [16]. Exploring a robust and reliable traffic sign classification algorithm has great application significance for promoting a machine vision-based traffic sign recognition assisted driving system. However, there are dozens or even hundreds of types of traffic signs, and the process of classifying and identifying them is cumbersome. In this way, it is a difficult task to effectively extract them. The entire classification process is divided into two processes: first, the coarse-grained feature vector of the region of interest is extracted and sent to the first-class classifier of the SVM to distinguish large categories; then, the image of the region of interest of each large category is extracted The color HOG feature is input to the corresponding SVM fine classifier, and the fine classification of traffic sign subclasses is performed to obtain the final classification result.

HOG Feature Extraction

The sample image obtained is subjected to HOG feature extraction, and then the extracted information is sent to the SVM classification training model, and then the sample to be detected is identified using the trained model. The specific operation method of how to obtain its hog feature is shown below:

1) Grayscale, regard RGB of the image as equal value;
2) The Gamma correction method is used to normalize the incoming sample image so that its contrast can be changed, which can reduce the negative effects caused by small areas of shadow and light, and also protect against noise.
3) Gradient calculation is performed on each adjacent pixel of the image, to obtain the characteristic data of its outline, and it can also reduce the interference of light again.
4) Split the image into small units, which can make an 8×8 pixel area;
5) After performing statistics on the histogram data of different units, the characteristic data of each unit can be obtained;
6) Make several units into one block, and combine the features of all the units in a single block to get the hog features of this sample;
7) Combine the features of all the units in all blocks in the sample to obtain the hog feature data of this sample.

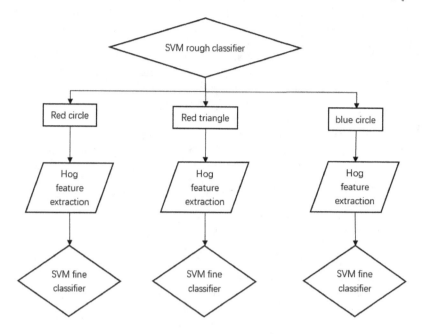

Fig. 8. Classification flowchart

SVM Classification

1) Based on color and basic shape, extract HOG features for coarse classification and send them to SVM for training model.
2) According to the detailed HOG features of each category, the details are classified and sent to the SVM to train the model.
3) According to the obtained model, the region of interest can be identified.

5   Experiment

The sample selected this time was downloaded on the GTSRP platform, and the HOG features it has already modeled were used to select the eight categories in the sample for classification testing, the result of test are as Fig. 9.

Because the sample data of category 0 is too small, the established model has poor recognition ability, but the recognition effect of other categories belongs to the normal range, and even some sample recognition rates can reach 100%. It reached 100%, and the recognition rate of the third and seventh samples was also 99%. The lowest recognition rate was also 67% for the fifth sample, and the average recognition rate was 83%. With more and more classifiers, the actual effect will be closer to the real situation.

The following figure Fig. 10 is the classification result obtained by the KNN algorithm.

0	0.00	0.00	0.00	210
1	0.79	0.81	0.80	2220
2	0.72	0.92	0.81	2250
3	0.99	0.75	0.85	1410
4	0.97	0.93	0.95	1980
5	0.67	0.73	0.70	1860
6	1.00	1.00	1.00	420
7	0.99	0.85	0.91	1440
avg / total		0.83	0.83	0.82	11790

```
[[  0  166   25    2   14    3    0    0]
 [  0 1798  245    1    4  169    0    3]
 [  0   23 2079    0    4  144    0    0]
 [  0   28  127 1053   11  189    1    1]
 [  0   17   83    0 1839   36    0    5]
 [  0  253  235    4   13 1350    1    4]
 [  0    0    1    0    0    1  418    0]
 [  0    1   92    0    8  116    0 1223]]
```

Process finished with exit code 0

Fig. 9. Result of SVM

By comparison, it can be seen that the classification result of SVM is better than that of knn. Among the categories identified by the knn algorithm, there is no 100% recognition sample data. The highest sample recognition categories are category 6 and category 7. The sample recognition rate reached 99%, but in practical applications, knn calculation takes a lot of time, need to use test samples to compare the information of each sample, the real-time performance is not good, and SVM can establish the model directly next time Use, the time required is very short at the level of 10ms, and the real-time performance is very strong, so SVM has a huge advantage in this regard. The experimental results show that the SVM plus hog traffic sign detection and classification method can obtain higher recognition accuracy than the knn algorithm, and can also meet the real-time requirements in actual work.

	precision	recall	f1-score	support
0	0.00	0.00	0.00	35
1	0.80	0.81	0.80	445
2	0.71	0.90	0.79	451
3	1.00	0.66	0.79	304
4	0.96	0.92	0.94	395
5	0.57	0.72	0.64	340
6	0.99	0.99	0.99	89
7	0.99	0.77	0.87	299
avg / total	0.82	0.80	0.80	2358

```
[[  0  27   4   0   4   0   0   0]
 [  0 360  52   0   2  30   0   1]
 [  0   5 405   0   1  40   0   0]
 [  0   5  29 200   3  66   1   0]
 [  0   3  16   0 364  12   0   0]
 [  0  51  40   1   1 246   0   1]
 [  0   0   0   0   0   1  88   0]
 [  0   0  26   0   3  39   0 231]]
```

Fig. 10. Result of KNN

6   Conclusion

This paper conducts research on traffic sign recognition technology. Compared with other people's use of image matching technology, it is proposed to use the distinctive color characteristics of traffic signs to distinguish them from other objects in the traffic scene at the stage of traffic sign detection, to extract potentially interesting areas of traffic signs in the image; At the stage of traffic sign classification, the local shape features of traffic signs were further used, and the long time-consuming Knn algorithm commonly used in general research was abandoned, and the SVM classifier was used to classify traffic signs. The experimental results show that the above-mentioned traffic sign detection and classification method can obtain higher recognition accuracy and higher real-time performance (re-use time is about 10 ms), so it can be basically in terms of real-time performance and accuracy. Meet the requirements of practical applications.

Acknowledgment. The authors wish to thank Inner Mongolia Higher Education Research Project under Grant NJZY17474.

References

1. Ling, Z., Yajie, Y., et al.: Comparison and analysis of traffic signs recognition algorithm. Softw. Eng. **019**(001), 28–31 (2016)
2. Yuan, X., Xiaoliang, X., et al.: Pedestrian detection combining with SVM classifier and hog feature extraction. Comput. Eng. **42**(1), 56–60 (2016)
3. Di, W., Xiaodong, C., et al.: A level-adaptive algorithm for vehicle types recognition based on HOG and SVM. J. Guilin Univ. Electron. Technol. **36**(1), 23–28 (2016)
4. Yixin, C., Feng, Y., et al.: Detection and recognition of traffic signs based on HSV vision model and shape features. J. Jianghan Univ. (Nat. Sci. Ed.) **44**(2), 119 (2016)
5. Radman, A., Zainal, N., Suandi, S.A.: Automated segmentation of iris images acquired in an unconstrained environment using HOG-SVM and growcut. Dig. Sig. Process. **64**, 60–70 (2017)
6. Zhi-guo, J., Xiao-lin, C.: Traffic sign recognition algorithm based on feature matching. J. Jishou Univ. (Nat. Sci. Ed.) **34**(1), 28–32 + 41 (2013)
7. Ying, C., Qi-Guang, M., et al.: Advance and prospects of adaboost algorithm. Ph.D. thesis, Acta Automatica Sinica (2013)
8. Xuefeng, W., Fei, Y.: Microbus identifying of surveillance video based on HOG and SVM. Microcomput. Appl. **32**(17), 34–37 (2013)
9. Cai, L., Zhu, J., Zeng, H., Chen, J., Cai, C., Ma, K.K.: HOG-assisted deep feature learning for pedestrian gender recognition. J. Franklin Inst. **355**(4), 1991–2008 (2018)
10. Zhen-long, L., Jian-long, H., et al.: Comparison of drunk driving recognizing methods based on KNN and SVM. J. Transp. Syst. Eng. Inf. Technol. **15**(5), 246–251 (2015)
11. Liu, L., Zhu, S.: Comparative research of two intelligent traffic sign classifiers. Comput. Eng. Sci. **29**(2), 62–65 (2007)
12. Lai-rong, C., Rong-hua, J., et al.: Research on SVM-based license plate recognition. J. Highway Transp. Res. Dev. **23**(5), 126–129 (2006)
13. Shuangdong, Z., Lanlan, L.: The traffic sign detection based on color information and SVM network. Process Autom. Instrum. **30**(3), 72–75 (2009)
14. Zhiming, Z., Jie, Q.: Research of preceding vehicle identification based on HAAR-like features and adaboost algorithm. Electron. Measur. Technol. **40**(5), 180–184 (2017)
15. Zhi-jie, L., Jian, W.: A study on license plate recognition algorithm based on multi-classification SVM. Logist. Eng. Manage. **38**(5), 260–263 (2016)
16. Chujin, Z., Yaonan, W., et al.: Front-vehicle detection algorithm based on hypothesis and verification of improved hog feature. J. Electron. Measur. Instrum. **29**(2), 165G171 (2015)

Remote Sensing Image Recognition Using Deep Belief Network

Min Li[✉]

School of Computer Engineering, Jingchu University of Technology, Jingmen 448000, Hubei, China
49035084@qq.com

Abstract. How to acquire high-dimensional data such as remote sensing image efficiently and accurately has become a research hotpot recent years. Deep learning is a kind of learning method which uses many kinds of simple layers to learn the mapping relation of complex layers. The authors will attempt to apply the deep belief network model (DBN), which is important in deep learning, to remote sensing image recognition. Using the new large-scale remote sensing image data set with abundant changes as the research object, the hierarchical training mechanism of DBNs is studied and compared with CNNS, the results show that the accuracy and speed of DBNs is better than that of CNNS, and more effective information can be obtained.

Keywords: Remote sensing image recognition · DBNs · CNNs

1 Introduction

With the development of remote sensing technology, remote sensing image processing has become the focus of research in many fields such as security, aerospace, medical, scientific research and so on. In 2016, Deng et al. [1] applied a method of remote sensing image classification based on Fisher-BP to improve the efficiency and accuracy of remote sensing image classification. In 2015, Li et al. [2] used SVM, K-means and limit learning to identify and classify the bad geological objects in remote sensing images. In foreign countries, Mantero et al. [3] have put forward a classification method based on the minimum error decision in the literature, which can well deal with the recognition and classification of remote sensing ground reference data. In the early 1970s, many image analysis methods using remote sensing images were developed to analyze each pixel. With the development of remote sensing technology, the spatial resolution becomes more and more fine, the pixels are not isolated, but filled into the image which is full of spatial pattern. For some typical ground use recognition tasks, pixel or even super-pixel, all existing data sets have some limitations, which severely restrict the development of new data-driven Algorithms. With this in mind, Cheng et al. [4] in 2016 presented a large-scale benchmark data set named "nwpu-resc45". This data set overcomes the limitations of the existing data set, such as the small scale of the number of class images and the

© ICST Institute for Computer Sciences, Social Informatics and Telecommunications Engineering 2020
Published by Springer Nature Switzerland AG 2020. All Rights Reserved
W. Li and D. Tang (Eds.): MOBILWARE 2020, LNICST 331, pp. 187–194, 2020.
https://doi.org/10.1007/978-3-030-62205-3_18

total number of images, the lack of scene changes and diversity, and the saturation of classification accuracy, so this paper chooses this data set as the research object of the deep belief network model. Remote sensing image recognition and classification Image recognition is based on the existing information in memory to judge the information into the sensory organs at this time, so as to achieve the re-recognition of the image. The recognition of remote sensing image is related to the recognition of common images. In urban planning and management, the impact of remote sensing image classification is very important [5].

In recent years, deep learning has become a new direction in the field of machine learning. By simulating the multi-level structure of human brain, feature data are extracted from the bottom layer to the top layer in order to find the regularity of data in time and space and improve the accuracy of classification. The classification of remote sensing image is mainly based on the characteristics of remote sensing image of electromagnetic radiation. The classification map can be used as an intermediate result of other applications, such as target detection and recognition, to provide auxiliary information, and as the final result of basic geographic information in other fields such as resource management, disaster relief, urban planning, etc. According to whether the prior knowledge of the data is needed, the remote sensing classification method is divided into two kinds, one is parameterized and the other is non-parameterized. The first method consists of a maximum likelihood classifier (MLC) [6], a minimum distance classifier (MDC) [7], and an Expectation-Maximization (EM) algorithm [8], all of which presupposes the distribution of data. However, there are also data distribution laws are often difficult to predict the situation, such as multi-time and multi-source remote sensing data. Therefore, the second method is more widely used in remote sensing image classification, including decision tree [9], artificial neural network (ANN) [10], Support vector machine (SVM) and so on [11–13]. The classification of commonly used remote sensing images mainly embodies in two aspects. One is unsupervised classification. It is a clustering analysis method, no training samples in advance, no label information, the data needs to be directly modeled. There are EM algorithm, K-MEANS clustering algorithm, self-coding Algorithm and so on. The other is the supervision of classification. It predicts the class attributes of unknown data instances based on the association pattern between the known data attributes and the class attributes. Common Algorithms include Support vector machine, linear regression, neural network, decision tree, and KNN. Deep belief network model.

At present, general machine learning belongs to the category of shallow learning, which is relatively weak in characterizing complex data or features. In this paper, we introduce the Deep Belief Network (DBN), which uses the layered mechanism to improve the training speed and the ability to deal with complex classification problems. The most common network models used in deep learning include SAE, DBN, and CNN. DBN is the most common and classic model.

2 Premilaries

DBN is a probability generation model consisting of a series of RBM units. RBM is a two-layer undirected graph with no connected models between each layer of nodes.

Where the input visible layer v, h, h'. It is a hidden layer that represents feature extraction. Visible layer v Visible unit m Hidden layer h Hidden unit n. The unit, and all visible hidden units are usually random two value variable nodes (only values of 0 and 1) whose distribution satisfies the Bernoulli distribution.

RBM is a typical energy-based model consisting of a visible layer and a hidden layer. The joint configuration energy of these two layers is expressed as:

$$E(v, h; \theta) = -\sum_{i}\sum_{j} w_{ij}v_{i}h_{j} - \sum_{i} a_{i}v_{i} - \sum_{j} b_{j}h_{j} \qquad (1)$$

In the formula: $\theta = (W, a, b)$, 3 RBM is a very important parameter; visible layer junction i And hidden layer nodes j The weight value of the connection between w_{ij} Visible layer i The offset value of each node a_{i}, the hidden layer j The offset value of each node is b_{j}; visible layer i The status value of each node is v_{i}, And hidden layer j The status value of each node is h_{j}.

As shown in Fig. 1, v Indicates the visible layer, h Indicates a hidden layer, W Represents the connection weight between two layers. Among them, the visible layer and the hidden layer, the inter-layer neurons are fully connected, and the intra-layer neurons are not connected.

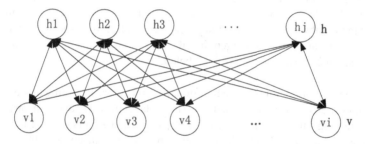

Fig. 1. Schematic diagram of the restricted Boltzmann machine

As a DL model, DBNs have been successfully applied in many fields such as object recognition and speech recognition. For remote sensing images, the pixel layer corresponds to the visible layer, and the feature description factor corresponds to the hidden layer as show in Fig. 2.

The BP algorithm is the most classical algorithm for training neural networks. The Convolutional Neural Network (CNN) used in deep learning algorithms is also trained by similar algorithms. The training methods used by DBNs are quite different from those of traditional neural networks: BP network algorithm for multiple hidden layer networks, the first is that the training time is too long; secondly, the weight adjustment process is from the output layer, the input layer is reversed. To the transmission, when the residual propagates to the first layer, there are many errors, so the weight adjustment is not accurate enough, the algorithm is not efficient, and the training method is not ideal. There are several main problems with the BP training method:

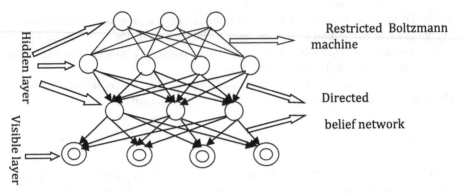

Fig. 2. Deep belief network (DBNs) structure model

(1) BP is the process from the output layer to the input layer. After several hidden layers, the gradient becomes more and more sparse, the error correction signal becomes smaller and smaller, and the weight change is very small.

(2) The weight of the neural network is randomly assigned to the initial value of the backpropagation algorithm. This algorithm may cause the algorithm to converge locally to a minimum.

(3) The marked data can be used for BP algorithm training, because the weight adjustment in the subsequent propagation process must adjust the expected value through the tag value and error, which requires the back-propagation of the neural network in the sample, the actual data is not labeled.

Due to many shortcomings of the traditional neural network training model, DL uses a new training method, which is to establish a multi-layer neural network in unsupervised data. The training time is divided into two steps: the first step is divided into training networks, each training a level. The second step is the parameter adjustment process, which is to monitor the fine adjustment.

The training process of DBN adopts layer-by-layer training. The training only has one layer of RBM at a time. The process of RBM is exactly the same as this training, and the parameters are adjusted separately. After one layer of training, the result is input as the next layer of RBM; so until each layer RBM is trained and this process is called pre-training. After the RBM training is completed, the BP algorithm is used to fine tune according to the tag value of the sample.

3   Remote Sensing Image Recognition Using Deep Belief Network

3.1   Experimental Object and Pretreatment

The experiment selected in this paper is based on the MNIST dataset and the NWPU-RESISC45 dataset is selected [4]. Some remote sensing image is made into subjects. The NWPU-RESISC45 dataset is a publicly available benchmark for Resensing Image Scene Classification (RESISC) created by Northwestern Polytechnical University (NWPU).

In order to get the closest to the standard experiment, the color image was processed, and a batch of remote sensing images similar to figure a were preprocessed and turned into gray image b, and the experimental training set and test set were constructed, As shown in Fig. 3:

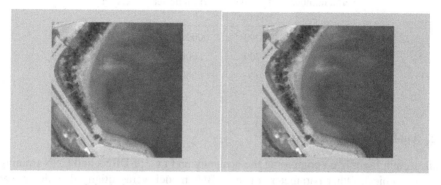

a original picture   b gray image

Fig. 3. Preprocessing of remote sensing maps

This experiment still uses a double-layer DBNs structure, similar to the MNIST data set, and the two hidden layer units are set to 1000 and 200 respectively, because this paper selects five categories of beaches, clouds, deserts, islands, and lakes. Remote sensing image, so the output layer is 5 units. In the DBNs training phase, set the number of iterations of the two layers of RBM to 200, And the learning rate is set to 0.1. After completing the training of the DBNs, the NN is initialized with the weights learned by the system, and the network parameters are fine-tuned; the iteration number of the NN is 100, the learning rate is 0.1, and the NN partial activation function is set to "Sigmoid". Draw the weight map according to the learned weight as shown in Fig. 4.

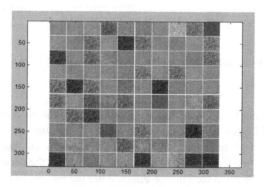

Fig. 4. DBN weight map

The training set and test set are shown in Table 1:

Table 1. Test training data set

Serial number	Total data volume	Training set	Test set
1	70000	60000	10000
2	700	600	100
3	7000	6000	1000

3.2 Analysis of Experiments

This section focuses on comparing the accuracy and rate of DBNs and CNN training the same object. Other parameters of the DBNs model were initialized in this paper as follows: the learning rate of pre-training and fine-tuning was set to 0.05, and the mini-batch size was set to 100.

When training models with the MNIST dataset, compare DBNs with CNN. The influence of iteration times on the recognition and classification accuracy of CNN is shown in Fig. 5.

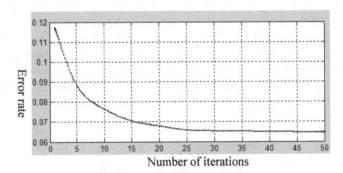

Fig. 5. CNN change with changes in the number of iterations to identify the classification accuracy curve

It can be seen from Fig. 5 that when the number of iterations reaches 50, the recognition error rate of CNN reaches a minimum value. At this time, the recognition classification accuracy in the network is the largest, and the network classification effect is the best. However, when the number of iterations reaches 25, the network has reached a relatively good classification recognition effect. After the number of iterations continues to increase, the curve still has a downward trend, which means that the classification accuracy will still be improved. Improve, but not much improvement. Therefore, in some cases, the number of iterations can be reasonably selected within a certain range

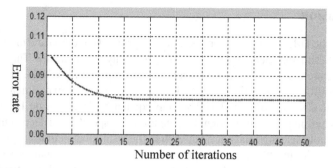

Fig. 6. DBN identifies the accuracy curve of the classification as the number of iterations changes

of variation according to the specific requirements of training time and recognition accuracy.

It can be clearly seen from the trend of the curve in Fig. 6 that when the number of iterations reaches 15, even if the number of iterations continues to increase, the classification accuracy of the DBN network does not increase, and basically goes to a stable value. It is 0.078, that is, the accuracy is as high as 92.2%. This is because the weight of the DBN backward trimming stage is pre-adjusted in the process of forward propagation, avoiding random initialization, and adopting this divergence algorithm to train each layer of RBM, so after dozens of times After the number of iterations, the network can get a good result.

Because DBN is a layered training, and CNN is a training method from the next iteration; A training process of CNN requires alternating convolution and sampling, both of which are time-consuming. Therefore, the forward propagation velocity is relatively low. The backward propagation of CNN includes two processes, deconvolution and ascending sampling, both of which are rather complicated. With multiple levels of CNN, the time of gradient descent is naturally longer. In contrast, DBNs have obvious advantages. As shown in Table 2.

Table 2. DBN and CNN time-consuming comparison

Network model	Total time (seconds)	Error rate
DBN	0.15	0.08
CNN	1.79	0.07

In this experiment, it can be clearly seen that when the DBNs model and the CNN model are training the same object, the training time is shorter, that is, the DBNs have a higher rate in remote sensing image recognition.

4 Conclusion

In this paper, the DBNs model is deeply studied, its principle, method and model structure are analyzed, and the idea structure of RBM is analyzed in detail. The mechanism of DBNs hierarchical training is discussed and compared with CNNS, which greatly reduces the difficulty and training time of model training. The experiment shows that compared with CNNS, DBNs model is basically equal in recognition rate, but has obvious advantage in training rate. The recognition accuracy and speed of the deep belief network model for remote sensing image are better than the traditional neural network learning method. It is also an attempt and improvement to select a new and superior remote sensing scene image data set as the research object of DBNs model in extracting image features.

Acknowledgment. This work was supported by the Education and teaching research project of Jingchu university of technology (No. JX2019-032).

References

1. Deng, J., Zhao, L.C.: Classification of remote sensing images based on Fisher and neural network fusion. Inner Mongolia Norm. Univ. News (Chin. Version Nat. Sci.) **45**(1), 46–49 (2016)
2. Li, X., Zhang, H.: Identification of remote sensing image of adverse geological body based on classification. In: Gong, M., Pan, L., Song, T., Tang, K., Zhang, X. (eds.) BIC-TA 2015. CCIS, vol. 562, pp. 232–241. Springer, Heidelberg (2015). https://doi.org/10.1007/978-3-662-49014-3_21
3. Mantero, P., Moser, G., Serpico, S.B.: Partially supervised classification of remote sensing images through SVM-based probability density estimation. IEEE Trans. Geosci. Remote Sens. **43**(3), 559–570 (2005)
4. Cheng, G., Han, J., Lu, X.: Remote Sensing Image Scene Classification. Benchmark and State of the Art. Proc. IEEE **105**(10), 1865–1883 (2017)
5. Qi, L., Yong, D., Xin, N.: Remote sensing image classification based on DBN model. Comput. Res. Dev. **51**(9), 1911–1918 (2014)
6. Hagner, O., Reese, H.: A method for calibrated maximum likelihood classification of forest types. Remote Sens. Environ. **110**(4), 438–444 (2007)
7. Alberga, V.: A study of land cover classification using polarimetric SAR parameters. Int. J. Remote Sens. **28**(17), 3851–3870 (2007)
8. Kban, K.U., Yang, J., Zhang, W.: Unsupervised classification of polarimetric SAR images by EM algorithm. IEICE Trans. Commun. **E90-B**(12), 3632–3642 (2007)
9. Pal, M., Mather, P.M.: An assessment of the effectiveness of decision tree methods for land cover classification. Remote Sens. Environ. **86**(4), 1145–1161 (2003)
10. Heermann, P., Khazenic, N.: Classification of multispectral remote sensing data using a back-propagation neural network. IEEE Trans. Geosci. Remote Sens. **30**(1), 81–88 (1992)
11. Lardeux, C., Frison, P., Tison, C., et al.: Support vector machine for multifrequency SAR polarimetric data classification. IEEE Trans. Geosci. Remote Sens. **47**(12), 4143–4152 (2009)
12. Nin, X., Ban, Y.F.: Multi-temporal RADARSAT-2 polarimetric SAR data for urban land-cover classification using an object-based support vector machine and a rule based approach. Int. J. Remote Sens. **34**(1), 1–26 (2013)
13. Niu, X., Ban, Y.F.: A novel contextual classification algorithm for multitmporal polarimetric SAR data. IEEE Geosci. Remote Sens. Lett. **11**(3), 681–685 (2014)

Blockchain and Internet of Things

A Review of Routing Protocols in Energy Harvesting Wireless Sensor Networks

Genxiong Zhang[✉]

Inner Mongolia Electronic Information Vocational Technical College, Hohhot, China
33384146@qq.com

Abstract. With the development of wireless networks in recent years, battery-powered wireless sensor networks are gradually moving towards energy harvesting wireless sensor networks. Energy harvesting technology overcomes the problems of limited energy and difficulty in replacing batteries in traditional wireless sensor networks, and is therefore widely used in various fields. In an energy harvesting wireless sensor network, due to time, space, location, placement angle, energy source, technology, etc., the energy that each sensor node can collect is also different. And nodes with different energy will affect the network life, or data loss occurs on some nodes. Therefore, for this type of network, it is very important to improve and optimize energy usage across the entire network. This article mainly introduces the existing routing protocol optimization algorithms in this type of network. It summarizes studies, analyzes, finds the advantages and disadvantages, and further optimizes ideas for this type of research.

Keywords: Wireless sensor network · Energy harvesting · Routing protocol

1 Introduction

The development of energy harvesting technology has promoted the development of EH-WSN [1]. In our living environment, there are many scattered energy, such as solar energy, wind energy, vibration energy, thermal energy and radio frequency energy [2], etc. A lot of research has been done on how to collect and use the environmental energy. The node in EH-WSN is an energy harvesting system added to the node of traditional WSN. EH-WSN can collect energy from the environment and convert it into electrical energy and store it in the energy storage device of the node. At present, the research on energy harvesting nodes mainly focuses on the environmental energy collection technology and energy storage technology. Literature [3] used hot-spot generator technology to convert the temperature difference into usable electrical energy. Literature [4] uses wind energy sensors to collect wind energy in the surrounding environment to power its own nodes. Literature [5] proposed a method of optimizing solar collectors to maximize the energy transferred from solar panels to energy storage devices. Literature [6] designed a new type of energy harvesting device to enable nodes to collect RF energy in the environment (Fig. 1).

W. Li and D. Tang (Eds.): MOBILWARE 2020, LNICST 331, pp. 197–203, 2020.
https://doi.org/10.1007/978-3-030-62205-3_19

Fig. 1. Energy harvesting wireless sensor networks

The sensor node collects energy from the environment and converts it into electrical energy and stores it in a capacitor to provide energy to the sensor node. The research and development of energy harvesting technology has avoided the process of manually replacing the battery of the node. Theoretically, when the harvesting energy is sufficient, the permanent operation of EH-WSN can be realized. However, in practical applications, it is still challenging to use energy harvesting technology for sensor nodes, because of 1) the size of the sensor nodes and related technologies, energy harvesting equipment still cannot provide enough energy to maintain the node's continuous work. Energy harvesting technical issues also need to consider how to collect, store and effectively use this natural energy in a small scale, and power small wireless sensor nodes. 2) Due to the ever-changing nature of nature, the energy collected from nature is also unstable. 3) Due to the gap between the development of supercapacitors and lithium batteries and theoretical research, there are many problems in the process of energy harvesting, conversion and storage, such as low conversion rates and energy loss. In view of the above problems, EH-WSN needs further research and optimization (Fig. 2).

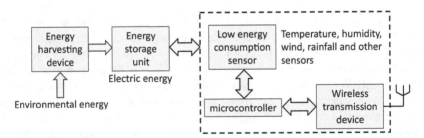

Fig. 2. The structure of energy harvesting wireless sensor

2 Related Work

EH-WSNs technology was proposed by Raghunathan [7] and others as early as 2005, using MicaZ wireless sensor nodes and Solar Inc's solar panels to realize self-powered wireless sensor networks. In 2011, Alippi [8] et al. proposed an energy-based TDMA protocol based on the MicaZ wireless sensor node, and implemented an underwater illumination environment monitoring system for near- and long-range wireless communication [8, 9]. In recent years, in addition to solar-powered WSNs, vibration energy WSNs, wind energy WSNs, etc. have also received extensive attention and active research. EH-WSNs can be divided into battery-operated Energy Harvesting Wireless Sensor Networks (B-EHWSNs) and pure energy harvesting (without batteries) wireless sensor networks (Energy Harvesting Wireless Sensor Networks) from the power supply mode., EH-WSNs). Earlier studies were conducted on the first model. A typical example is the Heliomote Energy Harvesting System designed by a Srivastava team led by UCLA (UCLA) in 2005. Through the prediction of the energy collected by the sensor nodes within a certain period of time [10–12], they achieved the optimal work cycle and the optimal task scheduling [13, 14] to optimize the system performance.

Because the collectible energy in the environment changes in real time, the node energy collection rate also changes over time. Therefore, an effective energy prediction algorithm is very useful for EH-WSN's task scheduling, MAC protocol and routing protocol, etc. [15]. For a variety of collectible energy sources, solar energy is diurnal and periodic to a certain degree [16], so most of the existing energy prediction algorithms are designed for solar energy. Weather Conditioned Moving Average (WCMA) [17] considers the effect of weather conditions on harvestable energy. In energy-efficient Routing Protocol [18], the author first divides each node between the source node and the destination node into multiple levels. Then use the method of Dynamic programming to get the path with the smallest number of hops in the network. Among multiple paths with the smallest number, select the optimal path.

In Adaptive Energy-Harvesting Aware Clustering routing protocol (AEHAC) [19], at first, they takes node energy state into cluster head election algorithm. and can adjust its parameter according to the network deploying environment. We analyze and evaluate the routing performance in terms of two metrics available node number and network throughput.

This article mainly introduces the existing routing protocols in EH-WSN, and summarizes and analyzes the advantages and disadvantages and possible challenges of each routing protocol. The structure of this paper is as follows: Sect. 2 introduces several groups of existing routing protocols. The third chapter analyzes and summarizes current routing protocols and points out future challenges. The fourth chapter is the summary of this work.

3   Typical Routing Protocols

In this section we introduce several typical routing protocols of EP-LEACH, AODV-EHA, Opportunistic routing protocol of EH-WSN and an Energy Neutral Routing (ENR) Protocol.

3.1 An Effective Routing Protocol for Energy Harvesting Wireless Sensor Networks

Meng [20] et al. introduces Energy Potential Function which is utilized to measure the node's capability of energy harvesting and extend the traditional LEACH to Energy Potential LEACH (EP-LEACH). EP-LEACH uses a new energy potential function to measure the node's energy acquisition capability. In LEACH, the original cluster head selecting function was extended to an energy potential function to measure the ability of a node to collect energy, as well as the ability of a node to run continuously. The algorithm works as follows: at first, the LEACH protocol is carried out according to a "round" cycle, and each round is divided into two phases. In each round, each cluster remains the same. However, the cluster head is re-selected each round. At the beginning of each round, the LEACH protocol randomly selects sensor nodes as cluster heads. Then an energy potential function (EP-Function) is introduced to measure node capability of energy harvesting. Therefore, each round of cluster head selection, nodes with potential energy should have a greater chance of being elected as cluster heads. There is no limit to the number of times each node can be elected as the cluster head. Compared with LEACH, it improves the throughput, reduces the data error rate, and reduces the possibility of node death. The evaluation results show that the proposed EP-LEACH exhibits a better performance than previous work in terms of lifetimes and throughput.

3.2 Energy Harvesting Aware AODV (AODV-EHA)

The Energy Harvesting Aware AODV (AODV-EHA) [21] protocol combines the traditional AODV protocol with energy harvesting, which is not only suitable for changing network topology structures, but also achieves energy efficiency for a longer network life cycle. All these functions utilize the existing mechanisms of the AODV protocol without additional complexity and routing overhead. The AODV-EHA protocol tries to find the least transmission cost on the route instead of the minimum number of hops. In actual operation, the AODV-EHA protocol is similar to the traditional AODV protocol, and there are some changes in the composition of communication messages: routing requests, routing responses. Relative to the traditional AODV protocol's routing request and routing response message format, in the AODV-EHA protocol, the "hop count" is replaced by the "energy count". The energy count here means the predicted average transmission cost of a data packet was successfully provided from the initiator node to the destination node. The experimental results show that with the increase of nodes, the average point-to-point transmission cost of AODV-EHA is decreasing, and the cost of AODV-EHA is always lower than the AODV protocol. Compared with the AODV protocol, AODV-EHA can usually find the path with the lowest transmission cost, but it is the longest path.

3.3 Opportunistic Routing in Wireless Sensor Networks Powered by Ambient Energy Harvesting

In literature [22], for accurate evaluation, the authors define and present a realistic outdoor solar energy harvesting model. On the basis of the real model, they proposed an opportunistic routing protocol EHOR. The main idea is as follows: 1) EHOR divides the possible set of forwarding neighbors into several regions for determining the best forwarding candidates and gives different IDs to the regions according to the distance of a sender and the sink node. For a transmission, the further a region from the sender, the lower probability of receiving the data packet it has, nodes further away from the sender; on the contrary, the nearer a region from the sender, the lower probability of sending the data packet it has. 2) After deciding the forwarding region, the EHOR considers the priority of a forwarding node according to the remaining energy of the node and quality of the link in the selected forward region. Here, they refers the weight of the forwarding priority in terms of β and the simulation results show that proposed EHOR achieves high goodput, efficiency, data delivery ratio and fairness.

3.4   Energy Neutral Routing (ENR) Protocol

The Energy Neutral Routing [23] protocol can keep sensor network in a state which energy consumption of the sensor is smaller than to the energy or equal to the energy that could be collected within a certain amount of time. The ENR protocol is implemented in three phases. In the first phase, the network sets the minimum hop count from all nodes to the sink node named gradients to 0 to initialize the network. Sink generates data packets to obtain data information, after that, nodes updates their gradients according to ENR algorithm and select nodes that have smaller gradients to form network. After receiving the data packet, the receiver will generate a reinforcement interest (RI) packet to extract the data. In the second phase, The node that received the reinforcement interest from the sink node hopes to look for the next-hop neighbor and transmit on the RI to the data source. The node will forward the RI message to the optative neighbor node, if the RI message will destroy the neutrality of the optative neighbor node, the optative neighbor node will broadcast refusion information. The node will successively send the RI message to the optative neighbor nodes among the remaining nodes until all neighbor nodes send RM messages, and the node will broadcast the RM message related to the RI message. In the third phase, The node receiving the RI will enter the data transmission stage by forwarding a packet about data in the light of the higher data rate designated in the reinforcement interest. After entering the data transmission phase, relay node checks interest cache. If the relay node does not find a matching entry in the data packet in the data cache, then the data packet is sent to the next hop node. Empirical research shows that ENR can usefully supply energy-neutral operations within the network, and can significantly increase the rate of packet distribution.

3.5   Open Problems and Challenges

Although the proposed routing protocol improves the performance of energy harvesting wireless sensor networks, there are still some problems not considered and solved.

In EH-WSN, the ability of node acquisition is asymmetric, which is ignored by most routing protocols, which limits the performance of practical application networks. At the same time, due to the different energy states of nodes, it is difficult for each node to keep the energy neutral state for routing data transmission and keep the network running continuously in theory. In addition, due to the unbalanced energy consumption of network nodes, multi hop transmission produces energy hole problem, which greatly reduces the throughput and energy consumption efficiency of the network. The existing routing protocol research on this problem needs to be further explored.

4 Conclusions

Wireless sensor networks are widely used in various fields, such as environmental monitoring, security monitoring, industrial control, and military. The biggest challenge of traditional wireless sensor networks is to use non-rechargeable batteries as the energy supply. The sensor network will die. Energy harvesting wireless sensors successfully solve this problem. This paper introduces seven routing protocols for energy harvesting wireless sensor networks. When choosing an energy harvesting sensor network routing protocol, according to the different deployment environments and requirements of the sensors, the energy harvesting wireless sensor network has the following characteristics: The performance of different performances, such as rates, is different, so choosing the right routing protocol can make the network show better performance and achieve the expected goal.

Subject category: Regional planning project support
Subject approval number: 2018MGH061.

References

1. Tan, Y.K., Panda, S.K., Tan, Y.K.: Review of energy harvesting technologies for sustainable WSN. Sustain. Wirel. Sens. Netw. (2010)
2. Wan, Z.G., Tan, Y.K., Yuen, C.: Review on energy harvesting and energy management for sustainable wireless sensor networks. In: IEEE International Conference on Communication Technology. IEEE (2011)
3. Kim, R.Y., Lai, J.S., York, B., et al.: Analysis and design of maximum power point tracking scheme for thermoelectric battery energy storage system. IEEE Trans. Industr. Electron. 56(9), 3709–3716 (2009)
4. Ang, R.J., Tan, Y.K., Panda, S.K.: Energy harvesting for autonomous wind sensor in remote area (2007)
5. Dondi, D., Bertacchini, A., Brunelli, D., et al.: Modeling and optimization of a solar energy harvester system for self-powered wireless sensor networks. IEEE Trans. Industr. Electron. 55(7), 2759–2766 (2008)
6. Nintanavongsa, P., Muncuk, U., Lewis, D.R., et al.: Design optimization and implementation for RF energy harvesting circuits. IEEE J. Emerg. Sel. Top. Circ. Syst. 2(1), 24–33 (2012)
7. Raghunathan, V., Kansal, A., Hsu, J., Friedman, J., Srivastava, M.: Design considerations for solar energy harvesting wireless embedded systems. In: IPSN 2005 Proceedings of the 4th International Symposium on Information Processing in Sensor Networks, Article No. 64 (2005)
8. Alippi, C., Camplani, R., Galperti, C.: A robust, adaptive, solar-powered WSN framework for aquatic environmental monitoring. IEEE Sens. J. 11(1), 45–55 (2011)
9. Alippi, C., Galperti, C.: Energy storage mechanisms in low power embedded systems: twin batteries and supercapacitors. In: 1st International Conference on Wireless Communication, Vehicular Technology, Information Theory and Aerospace & Electronic Systems Technology, 17–20 May 2009 (2009)

10. Raghunathan, V., Kansal, A., Hsu, J., Friedman, J., Srivastava, M.B.: Design considerations for solar energy harvesting wireless embedded systems. In: Proceedings of the IEEE IPSN, pp. 457–462, April 2005
11. Kansal, A., Hsu, J., Zahedi, S., Srivastava, M.B.: Power management in energy harvesting sensor networks. ACM Trans. Embed. Comput. Syst. 6(4), 651–656 (2007)
12. Kansal, A., Hsu, J., Srivastava, M.B., Raghunathan, V.: Harvesting aware power management for sensor networks. In: Proceedings of the ACM/IEEE DAC, pp. 651–656, July 2006
13. Hsu, J., Zahedi, S., Kansal, A., Srivastava, M.B., Raghunathan, V.: Adaptive duty cycling for energy harvesting systems. In: Proceedings of the ISLPED, pp. 180–185, October 2006
14. Vigorito, C.M., Ganesan, D., Barto, A.G.: Adaptive control of duty cycling in energy harvesting wireless sensor networks. In: Proceedings of the IEEE SECON, pp. 21–30, June 2007
15. Bergonzini, C., Brunelli, D., Benini, L.: Algorithms for harvested energy prediction in batteryless wireless sensor networks. In: International Workshop on Advances in Sensors & Interfaces. IEEE (2009)
16. Folcarelli, I., Susu, A., Kluter, T., et al.: An opportunistic reconfiguration strategy for environmentally powered devices. In: Conference on Computing Frontiers. ACM (2006)
17. Nangare, R.: Prediction of solar energy harvesting with optimal battery management system of a wireless sensor node. Int. J. Electron. Commun. Technol. 8 (2017)
18. Cui, R., Qu, Z., Yin, S.: Energy-efficient routing protocol for energy harvesting wireless sensor network. In: IEEE International Conference on Communication Technology. IEEE (2013)
19. Meng, J., Zhang, X., Dong,Y., Lin, X.: Adaptive energy-harvesting aware clustering routing protocol for wireless sensor networks. In: 7th International Conference on Communications and Networking in China, Kun Ming, pp. 742–747 (2012)
20. Meng, X., Xuedan, Z., Yuhan, D.: An effective routing protocol for energy harvesting wireless sensor networks. In: IEEE Wireless Communications and Networking Conference (WCNC), pp. 2080–2084 (2013)
21. Gong, P., Xu, Q., Chen, T.M.: Energy harvesting aware routing protocol for wireless sensor networks. In: 2014 9th International Symposium on Communication Systems, Networks & Digital Sign (CSNDSP) (2014)
22. Eu, Z.A., Tan, H.: Adaptive opportunistic routing protocol for energy harvesting wireless sensor networks. In: 2012 IEEE International Conference on Communications (ICC), Ottawa, ON, pp. 318–322 (2012)
23. Peng, S., Low, C.P.: Energy neutral routing for energy harvesting wireless sensor networks. In: 2013 IEEE Wireless Communications and Networking Conference (WCNC), Shanghai, pp. 2063–2067 (2013)

IoT-Oriented Designated Verifier Signature Scheme

Min Li[✉]

School of Computer Engineering, Jingchu University of Technology, Jingmen 448000, Hubei,
China
49035084@qq.com

Abstract. In order to reduce the computational cost of digital signature scheme
in internet of things and improve the security of signature, based on analyzing the
security requirement of Internet of things and SM2 Algorithm, a secure digital
signature scheme in internet of things is proposed. The elliptic curve is used to
construct the scheme, which improves the computing efficiency and meets the
lightweight requirement in IoT environment. Specifies the verifier feature that
meets the security requirements of a particular environment. The analysis shows
that the scheme has the characteristics of message integrity, anti-repudiation,
designated verification and anti-forgery.

Keywords: Internet of things · SM2 · Digital signature · Privacy protection

1 Introduction

IoT is a collection of interconnected objects, services, people, and devices that enable
information exchange and data sharing in different domains. The Internet of things is
used in many fields, such as transportation, agriculture, medicine, electricity, logistics,
etc. The goal of building the Internet of things is to change the way people live their lives
by enabling the smart devices around us to do the daily chores, such as smart homes,
smart city, smart transportation. The Internet of things has many applications, from the
personal environment to the Enterprise Environment [1]. In personal and social IoT
applications, IoT users can interact with their environment and other users to build and
maintain social relationships. In the transportation applications of the Internet of things,
various smart cars, smart roads and smart traffic lights can improve traffic efficiency and
safety. In the business and industry applications of the Internet of things, such as finance,
banking, marketing, and so on, interactivity within and between organizations can be
achieved. In recent years, due to the radio frequency identification (RFID) and wireless
sensor network (WSN) technology progress, the rapid development of the Internet of
things. Each device can be tagged with RFID, thus having a unique identity and being
uniquely identified. With WSN, every "thing", that is, people, devices, etc., can be
recognized wirelessly and communicate in the physical, network, and digital world.
Although the Internet of things has brought convenience to people's life, similar to the

W. Li and D. Tang (Eds.): MOBILWARE 2020, LNICST 331, pp. 204–210, 2020.
https://doi.org/10.1007/978-3-030-62205-3_20

traditional Internet system, all kinds of security attacks come along, which seriously affect the development of the Internet of things and People's privacy security.

This paper first analyzes the security requirements of the Internet of things, then introduces the construction of SM2 digital signature scheme, then gives the concrete construction of the security digital signature scheme, and finally analyzes the security of the proposed scheme.

2 Premilaries

2.1 Security Requirements of IoT

The basic security goals of the Internet of things include confidentiality, integrity, and integrity in general network systems. However, due to the Heterogeneity of devices and the limitation of computing and communication resources, IoT has different security problems. The security challenges facing the Internet of things can be broadly divided into two categories: structural challenges and security challenges [2]. Structural challenges stem from the heterogeneity and ubiquity of the Internet of things itself, and security challenges are related to the principles and functions of the system, its basic goal is to construct the security network by the enforcement mechanism. Resolving structural challenges usually requires consideration of wireless communications, scalability, power and distribution, while resolving security challenges requires consideration of authentication, confidentiality, end-to-end security, integrity, etc., security mechanisms must be enforced throughout the life cycle of system development and operations [3]. Common security requirements include that all software running on IoT devices must be licensed, and that the network must authenticate IoT devices before they can be turned on to collect and send data; Due to the limited computing and storage resources of IoT devices, it is necessary to use a firewall network to filter packets directed to the device; updates and patches to IoT devices should be installed in a manner that does not increase the additional bandwidth consumption.

Overall, the security needs of the Internet of things include the following:

(1) confidentiality ensures that data is secure and available only to authorized users. In the Internet of things, users can be people, machines, services, internal objects (devices in the network) and external objects (devices outside the network). For example, you must ensure that the sensor does not disclose the data it collects to a nearby node [4]. Another confidentiality consideration is how to manage data, and it is important for IoT users to be aware that data management mechanisms are applied to process or people management to ensure that data is protected throughout the process [5].

(2) Integrity. Since the Internet of things is based on the exchange of data between many different devices, it is important to ensure that the data is accurate; that it comes from the right sender and that it is not tampered with or intentionally or unintentionally interfered with during transmission. Although data traffic can be managed by using firewalls and protocols, due to the limited computing and communication resources of IoT nodes, the security of endpoints cannot be guaranteed, so other mechanisms must be considered to achieve the integrity.

(3) Usability. The IoT vision is to connect as many smart devices as possible to make all the data available to IoT users at any time. However, data is not the only part of the Internet of things, and devices and related services must be and can be accessed whenever they are needed. Approaches that support usability may require both generic approaches such as fault tolerance and cryptology-based mechanisms.

(4) Authentication. Every object in IoT should be able to be recognized and identified by other objects, but the nature of IoT makes it challenging to identify and identify, which involves multiple types of entities such as devices, people, service providers, and so on. The design of the authentication mechanism needs to be compatible with all types of entities in heterogeneous systems. There is also a need to consider special scenarios where objects may need to interact with other entities that have not previously shared information [6].

(5) Lightweight. In addition to the usual security goals, considering that IoT nodes are usually resource constrained devices, lightweight is also a factor to consider when designing security mechanisms. Therefore, in the design and implementation of the corresponding encryption, authentication, integrity verification protocols or algorithms, it is not advisable to directly apply the traditional security schemes to the Internet of things.

2.2 SM2 Algorithm

SM2 [7] consists of three stages, including generation of keys, generation of signature, verification of signature:

Generation of keys:

(1) randomly selects d, $d \in [1, q-1]$;
(2) computes $P = dG$, set P as the public key, and d as the private key.

Generation of signature:

(3) the signer selects a random number $k \in [1, q-1]$, computes $kG = (x1, y1)$;
(4) computes $r = Hash(m) + x1 \bmod q$, where m is the message to be signed, Hash is a one-way function; if r = 0 or r + k = q, select another k.
(5) computes $s = (1+d)^{-1}(k - rd) \bmod q$; if s = 0, select another k; otherwise, take r, s as the signature.

Verification of signature:

(6) when the verifier receives m, r, s, checks $r, s \in [1, q-1]$, $r+s \neq q$; then computes

$$(x_1^1, y_1^1) = sG + (r+s)P$$

(7) computes $r^1 = Hash(m) + x_1^1 \bmod q$; checks r and r^1 is equal or not, if yes, accepts the signature; otherwise, reject the signature.

2.3 SM2 Based Signature for IoT

Suppose a node A in the Internet of things needs to sign message M and send it to another node B to verify. At the same time, the content of message M is sensitive information, so m cannot be disclosed to third parties. The transmission network is a non-secure network, so there may be various types of attackers in the transmission process. The system model of the scheme is shown in Fig. 1.

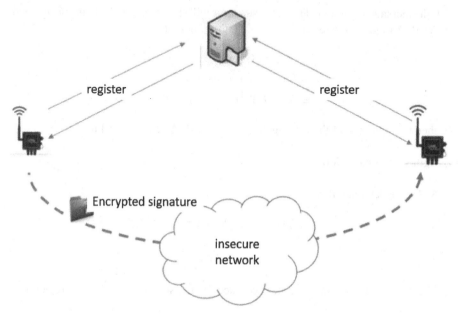

Fig. 1. The architecture of the scheme

In order to realize the signature that can protect the message content, this paper designs a digital signature scheme based on SM2. In the scheme, in addition to the IoT nodes, there is a trusted third party called as a key generation center KGC, which is responsible for registering and maintaining the public keys of each node, all nodes in the IoT join the system by first submitting the public key and other necessary information to the KGC for registration. The algorithm is constructed based on SM2 digital signature algorithm, so it is similar to SM2 digital signature algorithm, including system initialization, key generation, signature generation and signature verification, as follows:

(1) System initialization

Selects a big primer number p which is larger than 160 bits, then select a secure elliptic curve
$y = x^3 + ax + b(4a^3 + 27b^2 \neq 0 mod p)$, chooses the basis G with the degree n. chooses a secure hash function H.

(2) Key generation

A randomly chooses $dA \in [1, q-1]$ as the private key then computes the public key $P_A = d_A G$; B randomly chooses $dB \in [1, q-1]$ as the private key then computes the public key $P_B = d_B G$. A afterwards and B register themselves in KGC.

(3) Signature generation

If the message to be signed is M, the sender A will sign it and send it to the designated verifier B. A randomly select $k \in [1, q-1]$,then compute

$$V = kP_B = (x_1, y_1)$$
$$r = H(m\|V) + x_1 \bmod q$$
$$s = (1 + d_A)^{-1}(k - rd_A) \bmod q$$

and then the signature of the message m is $\sigma = \{r, s\}$, A sends $\{m, \sigma\}$ to B.

(4) Signature verification

As B receives $\{m, \sigma\}$, computes

$$V' = sd_B G + (r + s)d_B P_A = (x_1', y_1').$$

$$r' = H(m\|V') + x_1'$$

Checks r and r' are equal or not. If yes, accepts the signature; otherwise, reject it.

3 Analysis

3.1 Correctness

Theorem 1. If the signature is not damaged during transmission, the verifier can accept the signature according the equation in the stage Signature verification.

Proof: Actually, the verifier can computes V' as follows,

$$\begin{aligned}
V' &= sd_B G + (r + s)d_B P_A \\
&= sP_B + sd_A P_B + rd_A P_B \\
&= (1 + d_A)sP_B + rd_A P_B \\
&= (1 + d_A)(1 + d_A)^{-1}(k - rd_A)P_B + rd_A P_B \\
&= (k - rd_A)P_B + rd_A P_B \\
&= KP_B
\end{aligned}$$

That is to say $V = V'$, then there exists $x_1' = x_1$, thus r and r 'are equal, and the signature is valid.

3.2 Security

(1) Integrity

Because of the use of a secure hash function H in this scheme, if the message M is corrupted during encryption or during signature transfer, then verifier B does not compute the same as R, according to the Hash function, the resulting hash value must be different and the signature verification cannot pass. Therefore, the integrity of the scheme is guaranteed.

(2) Designated verifiability

According to the signature verification equation, no one other than designated verifier B can verify the validity of the signature because they do not have the private key of B. If the attacker attempts to push his private key through B's public key to complete the verification, he will face the problem of discrete logarithm. Therefore, the designated verifiability of this scheme is established.

(3) Non-repudiation

If A tries to deny its signature on M, because the scheme is constructed based on SM2 signature scheme, the scheme can satisfy the existence-unforgeable property, it is impossible for anyone but a to forge another message that is different from M and that is signed as. Therefore, A cannot disavow the signature it generated for M. Based on this, the scheme realizes the non-repudiation.

(4) Lightweight

The proposed signature scheme is constructed based on SM2 digital signature scheme, and SM2 digital signature scheme is implemented based on secure elliptic curve. As we all know, elliptic curve cryptography (ECC) has high computing efficiency. Using 160-bit key in ECC Algorithm, the security strength of 1024-bit key in RSA can be obtained. Therefore, the scheme is lightweight and suitable for the Internet of things environment.

4 Conclusion

Based on the analysis of the security requirements of Internet of things (IoT), this paper proposes a secure digital signature scheme based on SM2 algorithm considering the limited computing and communication resources and dynamic changes of nodes in IoT environment. The scheme uses a symmetric encryption algorithm with high efficiency and security to guarantee the confidentiality of the signature content. The signature based on SM2 ensures the scheme's high efficiency, this scheme is suitable for the security requirement of digital signature of sensitive content in internet of things.

Acknowledgment. This work was supported by the Research Fund Project of Jingchu university of technology (No. YB201808), the Special Funds of Jingchu University of Technology (No. QD201801), and the Outstanding Youth Science and Technology Innovation Team Project of Colleges and Universities in Hubei Province (No. T201923).

References

1. Samie, F., Bauer, L., Henkel, J.: IoT technologies for embedded computing: a survey. In: Proceedings of the Eleventh IEEE/ACM/IFIP International Conference on Hardware/Software Codesign and System Synthesis, p. 8. ACM (2016)
2. Mahalle, P.N., Anggorojati, B., Prasad, N.R., Prasad, R.: Identity authentication and capability based access control (iacac) for the internet of things. J. Cyber Secur. Mob. **1**, 309–348 (2013)
3. Leo, M., Battisti, F., Carli, M., Neri, A.: A federated architecture approach for Internet of Things security. In: Euro Med Telco Conference (EMTC), pp. 1–5 (2014)
4. Farooq, M., Waseem, M., Khairi, A., Mazhar, S.: A critical analysis on the security concerns of internet of things (IoT). **111**(7), 1–6 (2015)
5. Khan, M.A., Salah, K., Salah, K.: IoT security: review, blockchain solutions, and open challenges. Future Gener. Comput. Syst. **82**, 395–411 (2018)
6. Roman, R., Zhou, J., Lopez, J.: On the features and challenges of security and privacy in distributed internet of things. Comput. Netw. **57**, 2266–2279 (2013)
7. Ming, S., Ma, Y., Lin, J., et al.: SM2 elliptic curve threshold cryptographic algorithms. Chin. J. Cryptogr. **1**(2), 155–166 (2014)

A Group Signature-Based Anonymous Authentication Scheme with Controllable Linkability for VANTEs

Yousheng Zhou[1,2(✉)] and Xiaofeng Zhao[2]

[1] School of Cyber Security and Information Law, Chongqing University of Posts
and Telecommunications, Chongqing 400065, China
zhouys@cqupt.edu.cn
[2] School of Computer Science and Technology, Chongqing University of Posts
and Telecommunications, Chongqing 400065, China

Abstract. Vehicle sensor networks (VSN) play an increasingly important part in smart city, due to the interconnectivity of the infrastructure.
However similar to other wireless communications, vehicle sensor networks are susceptible to a broad range of attacks. In addition to ensuring security for both data-at-rest and data-in-transit, it is essential to
preserve the privacy of data and users in vehicle sensor networks. Many
existing authentication schemes for vehicle sensor networks are generally
not designed to also preserve the privacy between the user and service
provider (e.g., mining user data to provide personalized services without
infringing on user privacy). Controllable linkability can be used to facilitate an involved entity with the right linking key to determine whether
two messages were generated by the same sender, while preserving the
anonymity of the signer. Such a functionality is very useful to provide
personalized services. Thus, in this paper, a threshold authentication
scheme with anonymity and controllable linkability for vehicle sensor
networks is constructed, and its security is analyzed under the random
oracle model.

Keywords: Threshold authentication · Controllable linkabilty · Group
signature · Vehicle sensor networks

1 Introduction

While vehicle sensor networks research is fairly mature [1], there is plenty of
research opportunities in this space due to continuing and rapid advances in

Our work was jointly supported by the National Natural Science Foundation of China
(No. 61872051, No. 61702067), the Chongqing Natural Science Foundation of China
(No. cstc2020jcyj-msxmX0343) and the Venture & Innovation Support Program for
Chongqing Overseas Returnees (No. CX2018122).

W. Li and D. Tang (Eds.): MOBILWARE 2020, LNICST 331, pp. 211–221, 2020.
https://doi.org/10.1007/978-3-030-62205-3_21

vehicular communication technology and other underpinning technologies (e.g., smart/driverless vehicles and other Internet-connected technologies in a smart city). In vehicle sensor networks, there are two key types of entities – see Fig. 1, namely: wireless on-board units (OBUs) on vehicles to supply wireless communication ability, and roadside unit (RSU) located on the road or buildings within a certain coverage. Normally, a remote central authority (CA) is also deployed to assist OBUs or RSU to perform a given task, such as authentication. These parties can support two types of communications, namely: vehicle-to-infrastructure (V2I) communication and vehicle-to-vehicle (V2V) communication [2]. Such communications can be used to support activities such as reporting of traffic congestion and accidents/incidents. However, due to characteristics such as self-organizing, rapid-changing and open channel, vehicle sensor networks are susceptible to a broad range of attacks. Achieving secure and efficient authentication services is a basic and critical component [3,4], but increasingly there are other properties/features that should be considered. Examples include privacy preservation [6,7,9], and the related notions such as anonymity and unlinkability [5,10].

In general, striking a balance between preserving user privacy and maximizing the utility of user data (e.g., to offer better and customized services, based on mining and analysis of user data) is tricky [8]. For example, a key characteristic required to provide personalized services is linkability, which contradicts the privacy requirement. Controllable linkability, first proposed by Hwang et al. [18], is one potential solution. In such a concept, an entity who owns a linking key can dervie whether two authentication messages were generated by the same user (or not). Doing so does not infringe the user's anonymity since the identity of the message signer cannot be obtained. Since the seminal work of Hwang et al. [18], a great many group signature schemes with controllable linkability have been investigated in the literature [18–20]. However, the verifier can only check the valid signature message generated by a group member but cannot decide whether the message has been fabricated. Threshold authentication can, however, mitigate such a limitation. Specifically, the receiver accepts a message only after it has been confirmed by the specified threshold number of user.

In this work, we present a group signature-based anonymous authentication scheme for vehicle sensor networks, which is designed to achieve threshold authentication, anonymity, non-repudiation, and controllable linkability. In addition, we will demonstrate that it is more efficient than similar existing schemes in regard to both communicational and computational costs, based on the findings from our evaluations using the widely accepted OpenSSL library. We also demonstrate the security of the scheme under the random oracle model, as well as explaining how it achieves the other desirable security properties.

2   Related Work

In recent years, authentication schemes with different properties have been investigated in the literature. For instance, Raya and Hubaux [14] introduced an anonymous authentication scheme for vehicle sensor networks by employing anonymous certificates. In such a scheme, a vehicle is preloaded with large anonymous certificates such that the vehicle can employ different public/private key pairs during each authentication process to avoid being traced. However, the public/private key pairs must have a short lifetime so as to achieve privacy preservation; otherwise, there will be significant storage and management costs. Lu et al. [15] presented a new method to deal with the challenge of preloading a mass of anonymous certificates, by leveraging RSUs. To update the anonymous certificate in order to keep linkability of the message, each vehicle would request the RSU to issue a short-time anonymous certificate when the vehicle passes by the RSU. Consequently, frequent interaction between vehicle and RSU may influence the performance of the entire vehicle sensor networks. Huang et al. [16] proposed two certificateless signatures scheme; however, anonymity is not achieved because the public key of the user is needed during verification.

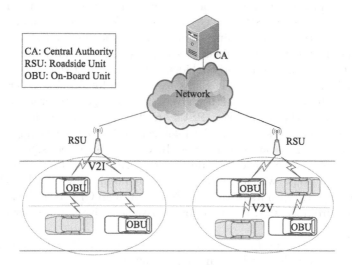

Fig. 1. Simulation results for the network.

Group signature schemes can also be used to achieve privacy preservation [12,13,17]. For example, Hwang et al. [18–20] introduced three group signature schemes with controllability linkability, for purpose of preserving the privacy between the users and service providers. However, these schemes do not support threshold authentication and require significant computing cost due to the number of exponentiation operations and bilinear pairings operations.

Threshold authentication is a common approach to assure the authenticity of the received (traffic) information [21–23]. For example, Shao et al. [24,25] introduced two threshold anonymous authentication schemes for vehicle sensor networks, designed to resist an attack on a single malicious message. However, the cost of computation of these schemes is significantly high on account of the employment of exponentiation and bilinear pairing.

Therefore, in this work, we construct a group signature-based anonymous authentication scheme with controllable linkability, based on Shao et al.'s [24,25] scheme. However, our proposed scheme is more efficient because we utilize the point multiplication operation instead of the exponentiation operations.

3   Preliminaries

Before the construction of our scheme, preliminaries including the system and security models and the Bilinear groups are introduced in this section.

3.1   System and Security Models

Our proposed protocol comprises four entities, namely: central authority (CA), service providers (SP), RSUs and OBUs (see also Fig. 2). CA is mainly tasked with issuing of the corresponding public key certificates for both RSUs and OBUs after their respective public keys have been successfully authenticated. Moreover, CA can uncover the original identity of the sender who is found to send a fabricated message in VANET. SP is responsible for providing personalized services, first by examining whether given two messages are produced by the same sender with the linking key. RSUs are densely deployed along the road, and each of them is assumed as the manager of a group consisting of OBUs within its communication area. Besides, RSUs are also responsible for issuing group certificates for vehicles equipped with OBUs when they enter into its communication range, which can be used to communicate with other OBUs by signing the message with its private key. Note that if an OBU is in the revocation list obtained from the CA, it would not be assigned with a group certificate by its RSU.

CA is assumed to be fully honest, whereas SPs and RSUs are presumed to be semi-honest (i.e., honest but curious), in the sense that they would honestly follow the proposed protocol and would not conspire with other RSUs. However, they are curious about the user's identity information and trace information, and hence may passively seek to collect group signatures and gather other information. Honest OBUs can accept a message only when they have received the number of valid signatures whose number is greater than the threshold value on the same message. However, OBUs could also be malicious, in the sense of attempting to obtain the user's identity information and trace information by launching either passive or active attack. For instance, they may attempt to broadcast many fabricated message signatures without being perceived or conspire with each other.

3.2 Bilinear Groups

Let G_1, G_2 and G_3 denote three different additive groups over elliptic curve with the same order q, where q is a prime number, and they all satisfy non-degenerated properties and are used to construct a bilinear map $e : G_1 \times G_2 \to G_3$, such that $e(aP_1, b\tilde{P}_1) = e(P_1, \tilde{P}_1)^{ab}$ for all $a, b \in Z_q^*$, any $P_1 \in G_1$ and $\tilde{P}_1 \in G_2$. For convenience, the symbol "$\sim$" is used to label the elements in G_2.

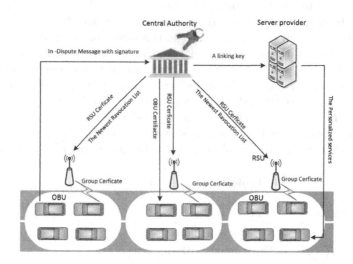

Fig. 2. System model.

We analyze the security of the proposed threshold anonymous authentication scheme based on the eCDH assumption and the eDDH assumption, which are defined as follows [25],

Definition 1 (eCDH Assumption): Given $P, aP, bP \in G_1$ and $\tilde{P}, a\tilde{P} \in G_2$, where $a, b \in Z_q^*$, to output abP. The (t, ε) eCDH assumption states that there is no t-time algorithm that can break the eCDH assumption with a non-negligible advantage of at least ε.

Definition 2 (eDDH Assumption): Given $P, aP, bP, cP \in G_1$ and $\tilde{P}, a\tilde{P}, b\tilde{P} \in G_2$, where $a, b, c \in Z_q^*$, to decide whether $abP = cP$ holds or not. The (t, ε) eDDH assumption states that there is no t-time algorithm can break the eDDH assumption with non-negligible advantage of at least ε.

4 Proposed Authentication Protocol

The construction of our proposed group signature-based anonymous authentication scheme with controllable linkability is illustrated here, and the scheme includes initialization, registration, joining, signing, verifying, linking, and tracing stage.

First, the CA follows the initialization process to produce public/private key pairs for itself and the public parameters for the entire system. Before each RSU and OBU join the network, they need to follow the registration process to produce the pairs of the public key and private key for itself and obtain corresponding public certificates from the CA. RSUs are deployed on critical points along the road (e.g., roadsides or building and other installations). When a vehicle employed with an OBU enters into a new range covered by a certain RSU, it has to follow the joining process to obtain the corresponding group certificate from the RSU. Then, the vehicle can sign and broadcast messages. After that, the receiver can perform the threshold authentication process to verify any received messages and signatures. In order to identify the malicious signer, the CA can perform identity tracing process to uncover the identity of the singer corresponding to the suspicious signature. To provide personalized service, one can perform linking process to check whether two given pairs of signatures and messages are from the same sender.

The definition of used notations is shown as Table 1, and details of our proposed authentication scheme is illustrated in the remaining of this section.

Table 1. Summary of notations

Notation	Definitions
q	A secure large prime
G_1, G_2, G_3	Three groups with the same order q
P_1, P_2	The primitive generator of G_1
$\tilde{P}_1$	The primitive generator of G_2
x_{ca}	The private key of CA to issue certificates
x_{tm}	The private key of CA to trace
x_{rsu}	The private key of RSU
x_{obu}	The private key of OBU
P_{link}	The linking key of SPs
$(P_{ca}, \tilde{P}_{ca}, \tilde{P}_{tm})$	The public key of CA
$\tilde{P}_{rsu}$	The public key of RSU
$\tilde{P}_{obu}$	The public key of OBU
Z_q^*	The collection including all primes in $\{0, 1, ..., q-1\}$
H_1	A hash function mapping to G_1
H_2	A hash function mapping to Z_q^*
τ	A signature of message

4.1 Initialization

In this stage, CA produces the key pairs for itself and the public parameters for the entire system. The detailed description is as follows.

- First, CA produces the public parameter $q, P_1, P_2 \in G_1, \tilde{P}_1 \in G_2, e : G_1 \times G_2 \to G_3, H_1(\cdot) : \{0,1\}^* \to G_1, H_2(\cdot) : \{0,1\}^* \to Z_q^*$.
- Then, CA randomly chooses $x_{ca}, x_{tm} \in Z_q^*$, and computes $P_{ca} = x_{ca}P_1, \tilde{P}_{ca} = x_{ca}\tilde{P}_1$ and $\tilde{P}_{tm} = x_{tm}\tilde{P}_1, P_{link} = -x_{tm}P_1$. Finally, CA sets P_{link} as the linking key, $(P_{ca}, \tilde{P}_{ca}, \tilde{P}_{tm})$ as its public key and keeps (x_{ca}, x_{tm}) as its private key.

4.2   Registration

The registration stage consists of two parts, namely: RSU registration and OBU registration. CA assign RSUs and OBUs with the corresponding public certificates by performing this process.

RSU Registration. Each RSU registers itself as follows,

- RSU selects $x_{rsu} \in Z_q^*$ randomly as its private key, and evaluates $\tilde{P}_{rsu} = x_{rsu}\tilde{P}_1$ as its public key.
- RSU sends $\tilde{P}_{rsu}$ to CA through a secure channel. After receiving the message, CA produces a public certificate $cert_{rsu}$ on $\tilde{P}_{rsu}$, and sends $cert_{rsu}$ and the current revocation list CRL to RSU, where CRL is defined as

$$CRL = ((cert_{obu\_1}, \tilde{P}'_{obu\_1}), (cert_{obu\_2}, \tilde{P}'_{obu\_2}), \cdots ,$$
$$(cert_{obu\_n}, \tilde{P}'_{obu\_n}))$$

Vehicle OBU Registration

- Each OBU selects $x_{obu} \in Z_q^*$ randomly as its private key and evaluates $P_{obu} = x_{obu}P_1$ as its public key.
- Then, OBU sends P_{obu} and $\tilde{P}_{obu} = x_{obu}\tilde{P}_1$ to CA through a secure channel. After receiving the message, if $e(P_{obu}, \tilde{P}_1) = e(P_1, \tilde{P}_{obu})$ holds, then CA produces corresponding public certificate $cert_{obu}$ on P_{obu}, and sends $cert_{obu}$ to the OBU. Finally, CA records $(cert_{obu}, \tilde{P}_{obu})$ in the user list.

4.3   Joining

In this stage, RSUs will issue corresponding group certificate for the OBUs within their radio coverage. When OBU_i gets into the communication area covered by a new RSU, the joining stage is activated between OBU_i and the particular RSU. The detailed steps are as follows.

- To begin with, OBU_i sends a request message to RSU for obtaining its public key,
- Upon receiving the request from OBU_i, RSU returns its certificate and public key $(cert_{rsu}, \tilde{P}_{rsu})$ to OBU_i.

- Upon receiving $(cert_{rsu}, \tilde{P}_{rsu})$, OBU_i checks $(cert_{rsu}, \tilde{P}_{rsu})$. If it is not valid, OBU_i would be required to send another request message again; otherwise, OBU_i selects $k, n \in Z_q^*$ randomly and computes $P'_{obu} = x_{obu}P_{ca}$. Then, it uses the public key of RSU $\tilde{P}_{rsu}$ to encrypt P'_{obu}, where the encrypting process is found by computing $k\tilde{P}_{rsu} = (x_1, y_1)$ and $C_{obu} = (k\tilde{P}_1, P'_{obu} + x_1P_1)$. Finally, OBU_i sends $(cert_{obu}, P_{obu}, C_{obu}, n)$ to RSU, where n is a random number chosen from Z_q^*.
- Upon receiving $(cert_{obu}, P_{obu}, C_{obu}, n)$, RSU uses its private key x_{rsu} to decrypt C_{obu} and obtains P'_{obu}, and checks whether $cert_{obu}$ exists in the revocation list CRL. Then it checks whether $e(P_{obu}, \tilde{P}_{ca}) = e(P'_{obu}, \tilde{P}_1)$. If it does not holds, then it terminates at this stage; otherwise, RSU chooses two random numbers $r, t \in Z_q^*$ and computes group certificate $cert_g = (c_1, c_2)$, where $c_1 = x_{rsu}P_2 - r(P'_{obu}), c_2 = rP_1$. Finally, RSU adds OBU_i's certificate $cert_{obu}$ to member list(ML) and uses OBU_i's public key P_{obu} to encrypt $cert_g$, where the encrypting process is found by computing $tP_{obu} = (x_2, y_2)$ and $C_{rsu} = (tP_1, c_2 + x_2P_1, c_1 + x_2P_1)$. It then broadcasts (C_{rsu}, n, CRL_{rsu}) within its communication range, where CRL_{rsu} is the latest and is obtained from CRL and $cert_{obu}$ exists in ML of this RSU.
- When OBU_i receives (C_{rsu}, n, CRL_{rsu}), OBU_i first determines whether this message is sent to itself by using the value n. If it holds, then OBU_i uses its private key x_{obu} to decrypt C_{rsu} and obtains $cert_g$, prior to checking whether $e(c_1, \tilde{P}_1) \cdot e(x_{obu}c_2, \tilde{P}_{ca}) = e(P_2, \tilde{P}_{rsu})$. If it holds, then OBU_i accepts this group certificate $cert_g = (c_1, c_2)$; otherwise, OBU_i sends the request message to RSU again.

4.4   Signing

When an OBU intends to broadcast a message m, it performs the following steps to sign the message.

- OBU_i chooses $r', \alpha, s \in Z_q^*$ randomly.
- Randomizes the group certificate as $\tau_1 = c_1 - r'(x_{obu}P_{ca})$ and $\tau_2 = c_2 + r'P_1$.
- Encrypts $\tilde{P}_{obu}$ for tracing as $\tilde{\tau}_3 = \alpha \cdot \tilde{P}_1$, $\tilde{\tau}_4 = x_{obu} \cdot \tilde{P}_1 + \alpha \cdot \tilde{P}_{tm}$.
- Binds (τ_1, τ_2) and $\tilde{\tau}_3, \tilde{\tau}_4$ together by $\tau_5 = x_{obu} \cdot \tau_2$ and $\tau_6 = \alpha \cdot \tau_2$.
- Computes $\tau_7 = x_{obu}H_1(m)$, which would be employed to determine whether two given signatures for a certain message are produced by a same OBU or not. However, the characteristic of threshold authentication is enabled by τ_7.
- A bundle of the above evaluated values is made by $S_1 = s \cdot \tau_2$, $S_2 = s \cdot H_1(m)$, $\sigma_8 = H_2(m||\tau_1||\cdots||\tau_7||S_1||S_2)$, $\tau_9 = s - \tau_8 x_{obu}$.
- Set $\tau = \{\tau_1, \tau_2, \tilde{\tau}_3, \tilde{\tau}_4, \tau_5, \tau_6, \tau_7, \tau_8, \tau_9\}$ and broadcast (m, τ).

4.5   Verifying

Upon receiving a message m and its signature τ, OBU_j uses CA's public key $(\tilde{P}_{ca}, \tilde{P}_{tm})$, RSU's public key $\tilde{P}_{rsu}$, and the revocation list CRL_{rsu} to verify this signature as follows:

- Signature verification: Initially check if the signature $\{\tau_1, \tau_2, \tilde{\tau}_3, \tilde{\tau}_4, \tau_5, \tau_6, \tau_7, \tau_8, \tau_9\}$ is valid by checking the following equations.
  - $e(\tau_1, \tilde{P}_1) \cdot e(\tau_5, \tilde{P}_{ca}) = e(P_2, \tilde{P}_{rsu})$
  - $e(\tau_2, \tilde{\tau}_3 + \tilde{\tau}_4) = e(\tau_5, \tilde{P}_1) \cdot e(\tau_6, \tilde{P}_{tm} + \tilde{P}_1)$
  - $S_1 = \tau_9 \tau_2 + \tau_8 \tau_5$
  - $S_2 = \tau_9 H_1(m) + \tau_8 \cdot \tau_7$
  - check $\tau_8 = H_2(m||\tau_1|| \cdots ||\tau_7||S_1||S_2)$
- Revocation check: Check whether the signer within this RSU range is not revoked, by checking the equation $e(\tau_1, \tilde{P}_1) \cdot e(\tau_2, \tilde{P}'_{obu\_i}) \neq e(P_2, \tilde{P}_{rsu})$, for all $\tilde{P}'_{obu\_i} \in CRL_{rsu}$.

If all equations hold, then OBU_j believes the validity of the signature, i.e., the sender of the signature has not been revoked. Once OBU_j had received exceeding threshold number of valid signatures about the same message from distinctive OBUs, it would accept and believe the message.

In addition, the OBU can also use batch verification to speed up the verification on $\{m_1, \tau^1\}, \{m_2, \tau^2\}, \cdots, \{m_n, \tau^n\}$, as follows,

$$- e(\sum_{i=1}^{n} \tau_1^i, \tilde{P}_1) \cdot e(\sum_{i=1}^{n} \tau_5^i, \tilde{P}_{ca}) = e(P_2, \tilde{P}_{rsu})$$

$$- \prod_{i=1}^{n} e(\tau_2^i, \tilde{\tau}_3^i + \tilde{\tau}_4^i) = e(\sum_{i=1}^{n} \tau_5^i, \tilde{P}_1) \cdot e(\sum_{i=1}^{n} \tau_6^i, \tilde{P}_{tm} + \tilde{P}_1)$$

4.6 Linking

With the linking key P_{link}, SP can check whether two given pairs (m', τ') and (m, τ) are generated by a same user, as follows:

- First, it performs the verification process to check the validity of two given signatures.
- If the pairs are not valid, $\perp$ would be returned; otherwise, it examines whether the equation $e(P_{link}, \tilde{\tau}'_3) \cdot e(P_1, \tilde{\tau}'_4) = e(P_{link}, \tilde{\tau}''_3) \cdot e(P_1, \tilde{\tau}''_4)$ holds or not. If yes, 1 would be returned, i.e., the pairs are linked; otherwise, 0 would be returned, i.e., the pairs are unlinked.

4.7 Tracing

In this stage, CA can recover the real identity of the sender corresponding to a valid pair (m, τ), then it updates the CRL and sends CRL to each RSU. The detailed process is as follows.

- First, CA reveals the identity of signer corresponding to the signature message (m, τ) by computing $\tilde{P}_{obu} = \tilde{\tau}_4 - x_{tm} \tilde{\tau}_3$.
- Then, CA finds signer's certificate $cert_{obu}$ in user list and computes $\tilde{P}'_{obu} = x_{ca} \tilde{P}_{obu}$.
- Finally, CA records $(cert_{obu}, \tilde{P}'_{obu})$ in CRL and sends CRL to each RSU.

5   Conclusion

In this paper, a group signature-based anonymous authentication scheme with controllable linkabilty was proposed. The scheme is designed to enable providers who have an linking key to determine whether two messages were produced by the same signer, while preserving the user's anonymity. Threshold authentication enables the receiver to figure out whether the received signature is produced by the same sender to prevent the replay attack. In addition, the function of verifier-local revocation is supported (i.e., a verifier is able to check whether a received signature is generated by a revoked user). Security and performance evaluations demonstrated the utility of our presented scheme.

References

1. Hubaux, J.P., Capkun, S., Luo, J.: The security and privacy of smart vehicles. IEEE Secur. Priv. **3**(2), 49–55 (2004)
2. Chuang, M.C., Lee, J.F.: TEAM: trust-extended authentication mechanism for vehicular ad hoc networks. IEEE Syst. J. **8**(3), 749–758 (2014)
3. Zhou, Y., Zhao, X., Jiang, Y., Shang, F., Deng, S., Wang, X.: An enhanced privacy-preserving authentication scheme for vehicle sensor networks. Sensors **17**(12), 2854 (2017)
4. Huang, X., Xiang, Y., Chonka, A., Deng, R.H.: A generic framework for three-factor authentication: preserving security and privacy in distributed systems. IEEE Trans. Parall. Distr. **22**(8), 1390–1397 (2011)
5. Bohli, J.M., Pashalidis, A.: Relations among privacy notions. ACM **14**(1), 362–380 (2011)
6. Li, J., Lu, H., Guizani, M.: ACPN: a novel authentication framework with conditional privacy-preservation and non-repudiation for VANETs. IEEE Trans. Parall. Distr. **26**(4), 938–948 (2015)
7. Hao, H., Lu, R., Cheng, H.: TripSense: a trust-based vehicular platoon crowdsensing scheme with privacy preservation in VANETs. Sensors **16**(6), 803 (2016)
8. Fayyad, U.M., PiatetskyShapiro, G., Smyth, P.: From data mining to knowledge discovery: an overview. Adv. Knowl. Disc. Data Min. **17**(3), 1–34 (1996)
9. Wang, H., Qin, B., Wu, Q., Domingo-Ferrer, J.: TPP: traceable privacy-preserving communication and precise reward for vehicle-to-grid networks in smart grids. IEEE Trans. Inf. Forensics Secur. **10**(11), 2340–2351 (2017)
10. Zhao, D., Peng, H., Li, L., Yang, Y.: A secure and effective anonymous authentication scheme for roaming service in global mobility networks. Wirel. Pers. Commun. **78**(1), 247–269 (2014). https://doi.org/10.1007/s11277-014-1750-y
11. Chaum, D., van Heyst, E.: Group signatures. In: Davies, D.W. (ed.) EUROCRYPT 1991. LNCS, vol. 547, pp. 257–265. Springer, Heidelberg (1991). https://doi.org/10.1007/3-540-46416-6_22
12. Boneh, D., Boyen, X., Shacham, H.: Short group signatures. In: Franklin, M. (ed.) CRYPTO 2004. LNCS, vol. 3152, pp. 41–55. Springer, Heidelberg (2004). https://doi.org/10.1007/978-3-540-28628-8_3
13. Chaurasia, B.K., Verma, S., Bhasker, S.M.: Message broadcast in VANETs using group signature. In: IEEE Fourth International Conference on Wireless Communication Sensor Networks (WCSN 2009), pp. 131–136, December 2008

14. Raya, M., Hubaux, J.P.: Securing vehicular ad hoc networks. J. Comput. Secur. **15**(1), 39–68 (2007)
15. Lu, R., Lin, X., Zhu, H., Ho, P.H., Shen, X.: ECPP: efficient conditional privacy preservation protocol for secure vehicular communications. In: Proceedings of IEEE Infocom, pp. 1229–1237, 14–18 April 2008
16. Huang, X., Mu, Y., Susilo, W., Wong, D.S., Wu, W.: Certificateless signatures. Comput. J. **55**(4), 457–474 (2012)
17. Lin, X., Sun, X., Ho, P.H., Shen, X.: GSIS: a secure and privacy-preserving protocol for vehicular communications. IEEE Trans. Veh. Technol. **56**(6), 3442–3456 (2007)
18. Hwang, J.Y., Lee, S., Chung, B.H., Cho, H.S., Nyang, D.H.: Short group signatures with controllable linkability. In: Proceedings of LightSec, pp. 44–52, March 2011
19. Hwang, J.Y., Lee, S., Chuang, B.H., Cho, H.S., Nyang, D.H.: Group signatures with controllable linkability for dynamic membership. Inform. Sci. **222**(3), 761–778 (2013)
20. Hwang, J.Y., Chen, L., Cho, H.S., Nyang, D.H.: Short dynamic group signature scheme supporting controllable linkability. IEEE Trans. Iin. Foren. Sec. **10**(6), 1109–1124 (2015)
21. Harn, L.: Group authentication. IEEE Trans. Comput. **62**(9), 1893–1898 (2013)
22. Zhang, L., Wu, Q., Solanas, A., Domingo-Ferrer, J.: A scalable robust authentication protocol for secure vehicular communications. IEEE Trans. Veh. Technol. **59**(4), 1606–1617 (2010)
23. Morshed, M.M., Atkins, A., Yu, H.: Efficient mutual authentication protocol for radiofrequency identification systems. IET Commun. **6**(16), 2715–2724 (2012)
24. Shao, J., Lu, R., Lin X., Zou, C.: New threshold anonymous authentication for VANETs. In: IEEE ICC, pp. 1–6, November 2015
25. Shao, J., Lin, X., Lu, R., Zou, C.: A threshold anonymous authentication protocol for VANETs. EEE Trans. Veh. Technol. **65**(3), 1711–1720 (2016)

Author Index

Printed in the United States
By Bookmasters